OCKHAM'S THEORY OF TERMS

Ockham's Theory of Terms

PART I OF THE SUMMA LOGICAE

Translated and Introduced
by
Michael J. Loux

UNIVERSITY OF NOTRE DAME PRESS

NOTRE DAME   LONDON

Copyright © 1974

University of Notre Dame Press

Notre Dame, Indiana 46556

Library of Congress Cataloging in Publication Data

Ockham, William, d. ca. 1349.
  Ockham's theory of terms, part I of the Summa logicae.

  1. Logic—Early works to 1800. 2. Philosophy—Terminology. I. Title.
BC60.0252   160   74-12565
ISBN 0-268-00550-8
ISBN 0-268-00551-6 pbk.

Manufactured in the United States of America

To Frederic Bieter

Contents

Preface

Despite the historical importance and contemporary relevance of Ockham's philosophy, little that he wrote has been translated into English. Hoping in a modest way to fill this vacuum I have translated a text (Part I of the *Summa Logicae*) which provides a comprehensive introduction to the key themes of Ockham's ontology and philosophy of language.

In preparing the translation I have employed the Boehner edition of the *Summa*. While it is unfortunate that my translation was completed before the publication of the proposed critical edition, the Boehner edition has proved more than adequate for my purposes. As Boehner himself claims, his edition is very nearly a critical edition; and since it will provide the basis for the proposed critical edition, variations between the two texts are likely to be minimal.

Although on a few occasions I chose one of the variant readings, I have almost always followed Boehner's reading of the text. Like Boehner I do not find chapter 51 authentic. As he suggests, the style of chapter 51 deviates markedly from the style of the rest of the *Summa*; furthermore, although the general tone of the chapter is Ockhamistic, there are a number of points made there that are explicitly repudiated in other chapters. The most glaring case is the account of the contrariety of relatives found in chapter 51. In chapter 53, a clearly authentic section of the *Summa*, that account is presented only to be rejected. But while chapter 51 is not authentic, textual tradition incorporates it into the *Summa*. In my translation I have honored that tradition.

The major difficulty confronting the translation of Ockham is presented by the structural complexity and redundancy of his style, and early in the project I realized that a *literal* translation in readable English would be difficult if not impossible. I opted for readability, but while the translation sometimes departs from the peculiarities of Ockham's style, I have endeavored throughout to make it an *accurate* translation.

The examples Ockham employs also provide some difficulty. Upon occasion, these examples depend upon grammatical features of Latin that have no parallel in English, so that it is impossible to translate these examples into English while retaining their point in the text. Where such examples were essential I retained the Latin, where non-essential I eliminated them.

The only other point that should be noted is my set of conventions for distinguishing between material, simple, and personal supposition. Material supposition is marked by single quotes ('x'); terms exhibiting simple supposition are italicized (x); and terms which have personal supposition are not marked at all (x). Two remarks about these conventions are necessary. First, if we are to be faithful to Ockham's account of supposition we must construe x, 'x', and x not as three different terms, but as three styles or modes in which one and the same term can appear. Second, the marker for simple supposition must be construed as neutral between simple and personal supposition. In the same way the marker for material supposition is meant to indicate that the marked term is exhibiting either material or personal supposition. Ockham holds that any categorematic form in any context can exhibit personal supposition, but he claims that a term can exhibit material or simple supposition only in certain clearly defined contexts. It is such contexts that my single quotes and italics are meant to mark.

In some cases it was difficult to determine whether Ockham is using a term in material or simple supposition. In those cases I opted for single quotes. In a few places, especially the section on the predicables, this convention forced arbitrary choices upon me; but alternative conventions would have involved considerable semantical and syntactical awkwardness.

Preceding the translation are two essays, one dealing with Ockham's ontology and the other focusing on Ockham's theory of supposition. Since there are already a number of useful introductions to Ockham's life and overall philosophy,[1] I have limited my introductory essays to a consideration of the central themes of Part I of the *Summa.*

After a blanket expression of appreciation to all those colleagues who so patiently listened as I droned on about Ockham, I would like to thank Professors Guido Kung, Earl Ludman, and Ralph McInerny, all of whom read the introductory papers and offered helpful comments. I would also like to thank Mr. Alfred Freddoso and Mr. Michael Baumer, who used the translation in a reading course in Late Medieval Philosophy. They both provided suggestions that improved the translation in many ways. Doubtless, the greatest debt of

---

[1] See the introduction to Philotheus Boehner's *Ockham: Philosophical Writings* (London: Thomas Nelson and Sons, 1957); see also chapter 1 of Ernest Moody's *The Logic of William of Ockham* (New York: Russell and Russell, 1965); and Moody's contribution to the *Encyclopedia of Philosophy* 8: 306-317.

thanks is owed Professor Mary Sirridge who worked through the translation line by line. She furnished me with a list of corrections that was many times longer than I would like to admit.

More general thanks are due Rev. Ernan McMullin. He established the junior sabbatical program in the department of Philosophy at the University of Notre Dame. Without the leave of absence provided by that program this translation would never have been completed. I would also like to thank Professor Manley Thompson who introduced me to the *Summa*. Finally I want to express my appreciation to Rev. Frederic Bieter who taught me classics as an undergraduate. To him this book is dedicated.

May, 1974
University of Notre Dame
Notre Dame, Indiana

The Ontology of William of Ockham

Michael J. Loux

The distinctions between singular and general terms, on the one hand, and abstract and concrete terms, on the other, play crucial roles in discussions of ontological issues. Although these dichotomies can be expressed in purely grammatical terms, they have traditionally been thought to point to two over-arching distinctions among things. Philosophers have frequently claimed that the singular-general term distinction is rooted in a distinction between objects that are particulars and objects that are universals; whereas, the distinction between concrete and abstract terms forces us to confront the distinction between substances (minimally interpreted to include material bodies and persons) and the various characteristics they possess or exhibit.

But because they appear to carry these far-reaching metaphysical implications, these grammatical dichotomies receive detailed treatment at the hands of the nominalist. If his theory is to be at all plausible, the nominalist must have the resources for providing a metaphysically neutral account of the singular-general and concrete-abstract dichotomies. In this essay I want to examine William of Ockham's ontology by focusing on his treatment of these distinctions. My aim here is twofold. By examining Ockham's analysis I hope to provide an introduction to the central themes of Part I of the *Summa Logicae* and to clarify the concept of a nominalistic ontology in general.

I

Like most philosophers in the Aristotelian tradition, Ockham distinguishes between propositions and the terms out of which they are composed. Central to Ockham's analysis of the concept of a term is his distinction between *categorematic* and *syncategorematic* terms. We can get at this dichotomy if we distinguish between expressions that do and expressions that do not yield a meaningful proposition when substituted for '*x*' in 'This *x*-es' or 'This is (a/an) *x*'. The former (including predicate-expressions, proper names, demonstratives, and pronouns) Ockham calls categorematic terms; the latter (including articles,

1

particles, interjections, quantifiers, and truth-functional connectives) he calls syncategorematic terms.[1]

It is among categorematic terms that Ockham locates the distincion between singular and general, or employing Ockham's own terminology, the distinction between *discrete* and *common* terms. Very roughly, this is the distinction between categorematic terms that can and categorematic terms that cannot function as predicate in subject-predicate propositions, or that at least is the way a contemporary Ockhamist would express the dichotomy. Ockham himself construes the subject-predicate nexus more broadly to include identity-statements, existential propositions, and propositions incorporating either the universal or particular quantifier. Against this broad interpretation of subject-predicate discourse, Ockham tells us that while the discrete term is predicable of just one thing, the common term is predicable of many.

I have indicated that this distinction has traditionally been associated with the distinction between universals and particulars. For the medieval, the view that these two distinctions are related was legitimized by Aristotle's claim that the universal is that which is predicable of many. In a number of medieval philosophers this relation was explicated in terms of the notion of *signification*. The claim was that while discrete or singular terms signify particulars, common or general terms signify universals.

In medieval semantics, 'signify' was used as a transitive verb linking categorematic terms with their non-linguistic counterparts. Underlying this usage was the notion that categorematic terms are signs of objects, and the concept of a sign at work here was interpreted in psychological terms. A categorematic term is the sign of an object in the sense that the utterance of the expression has the effect of "bringing that object before the mind" of anyone familiar with the conventions governing the language in which the expression is embedded. The fact that signification involves a word-thing relationship suggests that the medieval notion of signification corresponds to the contemporary notion of reference; but in fact, the two concepts are quite different. The contemporary view tends to be that terms refer (or are used to refer) to objects only within the context of a proposition. The medievals, however, held that the signification of a term is a property which it exhibits quite independently of its role in any particular proposition; and they claimed that, at least in the case of univocal terms, the significatum of a categorematic expression is invariant over the various referential uses to which the term is put. Although it is explicitly relational, the medieval notion of signification is probably closer to the contemporary notion of meaning. In contemporary terms, the medievals were claiming that to know the meaning of a categorematic term is to know which object is its significatum.

At any rate, medieval philosophers frequently held that while discrete terms signify particulars, general terms take universals as their significata. This view is attacked throughout the *Summa.* Ockham wants to claim that a general term like 'man' does not have just one significatum—a universal; on the contrary, 'man' signifies indifferently each of the many individuals of which it can be truly predicated. Thus, knowing what that term signifies does not involve any cognitive relationship with a Platonic entity; it merely involves the ability to distinguish between objects that are and objects that are not men.

Nor do general terms introduce universals when they function as the predicates of subject-predicate propositions. In predicating a general term of an object, Ockham insists, we are not saying that the object exemplifies a universal; we are merely ascribing to the object a name which is common to several things. Thus, in the simplest kind of case (the affirmative, present-tensed proposition where the referent of the subject-term actually exists) a subject-predicate proposition is true if the subject is numbered among the things signified by the predicate term; otherwise, it is false.[2] The account may become more complex as we introduce into subject-predicate discourse negation, the various modalities, and past and future tenses; but in no case will our account require the existence of any objects other than those that can serve as logical subjects in predication.[3]

While he insists that general terms do not signify universals and that universals construed as extra-linguistic objects are irrelevant to the analysis of predication, Ockham grants that the distinctions between singular and general terms and particulars and universals, are intimately related. What he wants to deny and what he takes Aristotle to be denying is that the latter distinction lies hidden somewhere beneath the former. Ockham contends that Aristotle's point is that the two distinctions are identical: the only universals are elements in language—terms predicable of many. The mistake is to construe 'universal' as an expression marking out a kind of object in the real order; the term points to a distinction in the logical order, a distinction among linguistic elements.[4]

Ockham does not, however, mean to claim that universals are mere *flatus vocis*, that they are simply noises or marks on a page. He interprets language more broadly to include, besides spoken and written language, human thinking. The view is that human thinking proceeds by way of a mental language. This language incorporates terms, and like the terms of spoken language they are either categorematic or syncategorematic. These mental terms play different roles, but unlike the terms of spoken language they play these roles naturally. They are not items that are conventionally assigned certain linguistic roles. It is rather that mental words—in their intrinsic nature—just are the sorts of things that can play the roles they play.

Ockham describes the mental language, which is the vehicle of thinking, in terms of concepts appropriate to spoken language. Mental language incorporates different parts of speech: names, verbs, adverbs, etc., and the mental terms belonging to these grammatical categories exhibit many of the

grammatical features of spoken terms. Thus, mental names exhibit both case
and number; whereas, mental verbs exhibit mood, voice, number, etc. Although he wants to describe mental language by employing concepts pertaining to spoken language, Ockham insists on the ontological priority of mental
language. For one thing speech is a mere extension of thinking. In this connection Ockham tells us that speech is related to thinking in much the way
that writing is related to speech. Written language is an extension of spoken
language in contexts where speech is impossible. It involves a complex set of
conventions according to which marks on a page perform the same functions
as spoken words. In the same way, we want to think out loud, so to speak,
and since the elements of mental language cannot be used in this way, we
must employ new materials. Unlike the original linguistic elements, these new
materials are not in their intrinsic nature suited to play the variety of linguistic roles. We need conventions, then, assigning this or that role to this or
that phoneme or string of phonemes. Thus, speech is an outgrowth of thinking: the terms of spoken language are signs that conventionally play the roles
naturally played by mental terms. But the ontological priority of mental
language comes out in another way. Ockham tells us that preceding every tokening of a linguistic unit in speech there is a mental tokening of the natural
sign to which the relevant spoken sign is subordinated. It is plausible to interpret this remark in terms of causation. Mental tokenings, one wants to say,
cause the relevant spoken tokenings.

Mental language like spoken language exhibits the distinction between discrete and common terms. Some elements in mental language are appropriate
to just one object; whereas, other mental words signify many and, consequently, can function as predicates in mental propositions. Thus, mental words like
spoken words conform to Aristotle's characterization of the universal. In fact,
the concept of universality applies most properly to mental terms. The common terms of mental language are universals by nature. They are not items
to which mere convention attributes universality; of and by themselves, they
are just the sorts of things that are predicable of many. Further, it is here
that we find the roots of all universality. On the one hand, the common
terms of conventional language represent a mere extension of the common
terms of mental language: they are mental words thought out loud. On the
other hand, the tokenings of mental universals are causally responsible for the
physical tokenings of spoken universals: occurrences of mental universals
cause occurrences of conventional universals.

But with what objects are we to identify the natural universals of
mental language? Here Ockham provides us with a bit of leeway. While pointing to three different accounts he suggests that only one is correct. The first
two accounts are not clearly distinguished in Ockham. They agree, however,
in exhibiting an act-object analysis of human thinking. On these views, al-

though universals have a merely mental existence, they are numerically distinct from acts of thinking and are construed as the objects of those acts. On the third view, universals are identified with the different acts of thinking themselves. Here, we are to distinguish for example, thinkings-of-a-man from thinkings-of-a-dog. The two are construed as acts intrinsically different from each other, and the universals *man* and *dog* are identified respectively with these different mental acts. Ockham expresses a guarded preference for this view:

> But all the theoretical advantages that derive from postulating entities distinct from acts of the understanding can be had without making such a distinction; for an act of the understanding can signify something and can supposit for something just as well as any sign. Therefore, there is no point in postulating anything over and above the act of understanding.[5]

Thus, Ockham agrees that we can get below the distinction between discrete and common terms as it manifests itself in external, spoken language; but he wants to deny that what we reach is a distinction between kinds of things in the real order. What we reach on the contrary is the same old distinction now functioning within the context of a new sort of language. To bring out the force of his account, Ockham distinguishes between what he calls *first intentions* and *second intentions*. A mental word is a first intention if at least one of the things it signifies is not a mental word; whereas, a mental word is a second intention if it has at least one significatum and is not a first intention. Employing the distinction, Ockham tells us that the mental word *universal* is a term of second intention.

II

While plausible in isolation, Ockham's account of the role of general terms in predication appears more dubious when we confront the issue of abstract terms like 'paternity' and 'humanity'. Expressions of this sort surely appear to play essential roles in true propositions; but qua playing these roles they would seem to commit us to the existence of abstract entities, objects over and above individual substances like men and trees. But we are committed to Platonic entities in any event, so that there is no reason to strain at a Platonic analysis of predication. Like many reductionists Ockham finds the issue of abstract terms the major obstacle to a thorough-going nominalism. He spends more than half of Part I of the *Summa* providing an account of their role in language.

In Ockham the term 'abstract' is used in contrast with the term 'concrete'. The distinction here is purely syntactical. It is the distinction between normal predicative expressions like 'man', 'black', 'animal', and the nouns built from these by the addition in English of suffixes like '-ity', '-ness', '-hood', and '-kind'. The following examples illustrate the contrast in question: 'wise'— 'wisdom', 'triangular'—'triangularity', 'man'—'mankind', and 'black'—'black-ness'.[6]

As a syntactical distincton the dichotomy between abstract and concrete is relatively harmless, but as we have suggested the nominalist is likely to experience problems when he attempts to get at the semantics behind the distinction. These problems stem from what appears to be a perfectly natural interpretation of the dichotomy. It is natural, that is, when confronted with terms like 'wisdom' and 'wise' to say that whereas 'wisdom' signifies some characteristic or quality, 'wise' signifies the individuals who exhibit the qual-ity, signifying besides the characteristic or quality in question. Beginning with examples like this it is easy to generalize. Abstract terms, we are tempted to say, signify abstract entities; their concrete counterparts signify the individ-uals exhibiting those abstract entities, signifying, in addition, the abstract entities they exhibit.

In Ockham's terminology, this account of abstract and concrete terms amounts to the proposal to treat all abstract terms as *absolute* and all con-crete terms as *connotative*.[7] When he introduces this crucial dichotomy, Ock-ham tells us that while absolute terms have only primary signification, con-notative terms have both primary and secondary signification. So far, we have used 'signify' and its cognates very generally. We have said that a categore-matic term signifies an object in the sense that it is a sign of the object; and, following the medievals, we have interpreted the notion of a linguistic sign in a psychological idiom. In less overtly psychological terms, we have used the term 'signify' in such a way that a term 'x' signifies an object, a, just in case the use of 'x' has the effect of introducing a into discourse. Henceforth, I shall use the numerical subscript 'o' to mark this sense of 'signify'.[8]

As the definition suggests, to say that a term, 'x', signifies$_0$ an object, a, is to provide very general information about the semantical relationship be-tween 'x' and a. To provide more determinate information, we must employ the distinction between primary and secondary signification. Ockham never defines these notions; but from his use of the terms, it is clear that a term, 'x', signifies primarily (signifies$_1$) an object, a, just in case 'x' signifies$_0$ a and 'a is (an) x' is true. If we employ the term 'predicate' as Ockham does (so that both singular and general terms can function as predicates), we can say that a term signifies$_1$ all and only those objects of which it can be truly predicated.[9] Thus, 'man' signifies$_1$ the various individuals who are men, 'Socrates' signifies$_1$ Socrates, and 'triangular' signifies$_1$ all the objects which are triangular.

The notion of primary signification, however, points to only one way in which the use of a term can introduce an object into discourse; for terms can signify$_0$ objects which they do not signify$_1$. Suppose that there is such a thing as whiteness, that 'whiteness' signifies$_1$ whiteness. On that supposition, it seems plausible to think that the use of 'white', in some sense, directs the attention of our audience to whiteness. 'White', we want to say, just means 'object having whiteness'. But, then, 'white' signifies$_0$ whiteness. It does not, however, signify$_1$ whiteness; whiteness, to follow a long tradition, is not white; objects having whiteness are. Labelling the style of signification at work here, Ockham says that 'white' signifies secondarily (signifies$_2$) or connotes whiteness.

The secondary signification of 'white', unfortunately, is not paradigmatic. Most cases deviate from the pattern set out above. Not only does the relationship of signification$_2$ differ drastically in these cases, but the things that are signified$_2$ are also very different. Besides qualities like whiteness and wisdom, a term can signify$_2$ the constitutive parts of an object and even the truth of a contingent proposition. The best our account can be then is very general. Taking advantage of the vagueness of 'object', let us say that a term, 'x', signifies$_2$ an object, a, just in case 'x' signifies$_0$ a, but does not signify$_1$ a.[10]

With these notions under control we are tempted to follow Ockham's lead and define an absolute term as one that signifies$_1$ whatever it signifies$_0$ and a connotative term as one that signifies$_1$ some of the objects it signifies$_0$ and signifies$_2$ others among those objects. But while this works well in the case of absolute terms, it fails to capture the notion of a connotative term; for although he defines this notion in terms of both primary and secondary signification, Ockham's subsequent use of the term 'connotative' is such that terms which have significata$_2$ but no significata$_1$ can be connotative. Only in connection with simple cases like 'white' does Ockham stipulate that connotative terms have both primary and secondary significata. To take account of this fact, we must state our definitions as follows:

> A term, 'x', is absolute just in case the class of objects it signifies$_0$ is wholly composed of significata$_1$ of 'x'.

> A term, 'x', is connotative just in case at least one of the significata$_0$ of 'x' is a significatum$_2$ of 'x'.

We can now apply this distinction to what I have called the "natural" interpretation of abstract and concrete terms. That interpretation, I claimed, has the effect of converting all abstract terms into absolute terms and all concrete terms into connotative terms. In that interpretation a term like 'triangularity' is construed as an expression signifying$_1$ the abstract entity triangularity and signifying$_2$ nothing else; whereas, a term like 'triangular' is construed as signifying$_1$ the objects that have triangularity while signifying$_2$ the triangularity they have. More generally, the interpretation would claim that in the case of every pair of terms of the form '*F-ness*' and '*F*', the abstract form, 'F-ness', signifies$_1$ *F-ness* and the concrete form '*F*' signifies$_1$ *F-things* and signifies$_2$ *F-ness*.

To construe abstract and concrete terms in this way, I have claimed, is natural. To the extent that it clarifies what surely appear to be genuine referring uses of abstract terms, the construction is even plausible. But while natural and plausible, the interpretation carries with it a Platonic ontology, an ontology replete with abstract entities of every sort. The account offends against our desire for theoretical simplicity and should, if possible, be suppressed. But how? Although the existence of abstract terms is an undeniable fact, are we committed to treating all such expressions as absolute terms? If not, what sort of account is appropriate?

These questions isolate the problems Ockham sets himself in the central sections of the *Summa*. He is, however, suspicious of anything like a general solution to these problems. Since he thinks that there may be important differences among abstract terms, he insists on examining the issue by cases. What we need is some method for sorting out abstract terms. In this context Ockham fastens on Aristotle's categories. He claims the categories provide us with a natural ordering of abstract terms; they enable us to consider the ontological merits of abstract terms case by case.

Traditionally, Aristotle's categories have been interpreted as a list of the most general kinds to which objects can belong. If this interpretation is correct, there is something incoherent in Ockham's suggestion that we employ the categories as a framework for an investigation seeking to determine the extent of our ontic commitments. The categories in this interpretation are themselves the results of just such an investigation; they represent a list of all the objects to which we are ontologically committed. It is not surprising, then, that Ockham stands opposed to this traditional interpretation of the categories. The categories, he insists, involve a minimum of ontological presuppositions. They are not a classification of non-linguistic objects at all, but an attempt to classify categorematic terms according to what Ockham calls their *mode of signification*.

Ockham explicates this notion of the mode of signification by focusing on the various questions we can ask about an individual substance like Socrates. More specifically, he focuses on all those questions raised about an individual substance that are susceptible of one-word answers other than 'yes' and 'no'. Each of these questions can be answered meaningfully, even if falsely, by a large number of categorematic terms. Let us think of each such question as collecting all the categorematic expressions which can be meaningfully employed as answers to that question, and let us say that the terms collected by any given question constitute the answer-range of that question.

The answer-range of different questions will tend to overlap. Thus the terms constituting the answer-range of one question will constitute only a segment of the answer-range of another question. The answer-range of 'What color is he?', for example, constitutes only a part of the answer-range of 'How is he sensibly characterized?' The second question, we can say, is more general than the first; its answer-range is broader. We can, then, by moving to ever more general questions, generate answer-ranges that are ever more extensive. Ockham denies, however, that we can proceed to infinity in this manner; he also denies that we can reduce the multiplicity of answer-ranges to an absolute unity. In our search for ever more general questions about substance, we arrive, sooner or later, at ten very general questions. They constitute the most general questions we can raise about substances. Their answer-ranges, Ockham contends, are both mutually exclusive and collectively exhaustive. No categorematic term is included in the answer-range of more than one of these ten questions, and every categorematic term is included in the answer-range of one of the questions. According to Ockham the ten questions are: What is it? (Quid?); How is it qualified? (Quale?); How much is it? (Quantum?); How is it related to other things? (Cuius? or Ad Quid?); What is it doing? (Quid agit?); What is being done to it? (Quid patitur?); Where is it? (Ubi?); When is it? (Quando?); In what position is it? (In quo situ?); What does it have on? (In quo habitu?).[11]

Ockham identifies the answer-ranges of these ten questions with Aristotle's ten categories. Thus, the answer-range of 'What is it?' constitutes the category of substance; the answer-range of 'How is it qualified?', the category of quality and so on. According to Ockham each of the categories is composed of terms that convey one very general kind of information about substance. Thus all the terms included in the answer-range generated by 'What is it?' convey information about what substances are; whereas, the terms included in the answer-range of 'How is it qualified' convey information about the qualitative determinations of substances. Using Ockham's own terminology, the terms in a given category signify$_1$ substance in a particular mode. Terms from the category of substance signify$_1$ substances essentially or in the mode of substance; terms from the category of quality signify$_1$ substances qualitatively or in the mode of quality and so on.

But there is a difficulty with this account. Even if we accept the dubious claim that none of the ten questions can be reduced to any other questions in the list, we are likely to wonder just how the scheme accommodates the abstract terms that were the origin of our appeal to the categories. Employing Ockham's technique for classifying terms, we discover that all abstract terms fall under the category of substance. The only one of the ten very general questions that abstract terms can serve to answer meaningfully is the question, 'What is it?' All the other questions require concrete terms as answers. But clearly this is an unfortunate consequence. For one thing, we appealed to the Aristotelian categories because we wanted a framework for sorting out the various abstract terms. If, however, we employ Ockham's interpretative scheme, the categories are useless in this connection. But quite apart from our search for a classification of abstract terms, there is a difficulty surrounding the allocation of abstract terms to the category of substance. Terms in the category of substance supposedly all signify$_1$ substances. Indeed, it is precisely because abstract terms do not appear to signify$_1$ substances but other more problematic entities that we are engaged in the analysis. Abstract terms appear to be absolute, to signify$_1$ abstract entities, so that allocating them to the category of substance is inappropriate.

Ockham is aware of these difficulties. His response is to deviate from the scheme and simply to stipulate that abstract terms be placed in the same category as their concrete counterparts. He feels that this stipulation provides us with a natural ordering of abstract terms. It is only plausible to assume, he would claim, that the counterparts of terms exhibiting a particular mode of signification will be sufficiently similar to allow a uniform treatment. Furthermore, although Ockham would construe this stipulation as merely provisional, he wants to claim that the ensuing analysis will vindicate his move. In general, it will show that if abstract terms have any place in the system they belong with their concrete forms.

Ockham's treatment of substance focuses in large part on the problem of universals. His concern here is to provide a neutral account of Aristotle's distinction between first and second substances, but in a number of places Ockham examines the relationship between abstract and concrete terms from the category of substance. In these contexts, he attacks a view that is essentially an application of what I have called the 'natural' interpretation of abstract and concrete terms to expressions in the category of substance. On that view, abstract terms from this category signify$_1$ the essence or nature in virtue of which substances are what they are; whereas their concrete counterparts signify$_1$ the various individual substances while signifying$_2$ or connoting their essence. Ockham's attack on this view comes out in a number of arguments that are likely to appear hopelessly mysterious to the contemporary reader.[12] While I do not pretend to understand those arguments in detail, I find a common theme running throughout. Ockham, I want to suggest, is arguing that the proponent of this view can make his account intelligible only if he appeals to the notion of bare substrate. Essentially, Ockham is challenging the proponent of essences to locate the subject or bearer of the postulated essences. That subject must be something such that by adding the essence to it we get, for example, men. It might seem that the relevant subjects are the individual substances in question, but Ockham insists that this will not do. The individual substances already are men, so that there can be no question of adding something to them to make them men. More generally, the subjects of essence cannot be entities to which the sortal predicates in the category of substance apply. Such objects already possess whatever it is that an object needs to be a substance of this or that sort. The subject of essence, Ockham claims, must lie at a level below that at which substance sortals apply. What though would an object from that level be like? It would have to be an entity conforming to Locke's characterization of substrate, a "something I know not what." But surely, we can take Ockham to be claiming, a mysterious entity like bare substrate should play no role in our theory.

As I read him, Ockham is claiming that the proponent of this view is committed to bare substrate because he distinguishes between substance and essence. Ockham's counter is simply to identify the two. But having identified substances and their essences, he cannot construe the relevant abstract terms as expressions signifying$_1$ (and their concrete counterparts as terms signifying$_2$) objects distinct from substances. His account of concrete terms from the category of substance is straightforeward. Ockham claims they are absolute terms; the only objects they signify$_0$ are their significata$_1$ —the various individual substances.[13] Abstract terms, he suggests, present more serious difficulties. The above claim that they do not signify$_1$ anything distinct from individual substances suggests that their role is precisely the same as that of their concrete counterparts. But this is to say that they are synonymous with their concrete counterparts, and that is surely wrong. Ockham is fairly liberal in his use of the term 'synonymous'. He claims that two terms 'x' and 'y' are synonymous if and only if (1) 'x' and 'y' are mutually intersubstitutable and (2) 'x' and 'y' are mutually predicable of each other, and as Ockham is quick to point out the abstract and concrete terms in question fail to satisfy either (1) or (2). Thus, in violation of (1), while 'Man runs' is true, 'Humanity runs' is false; and in violation of (2), both 'Man is humanity' and 'Humanity is a man' are absurd.[14]

What Ockham feels he needs here is an account of the role of abstract terms from the category of substance that will accommodate his reductive analysis of that category while preserving the conceptual gulf between abstract and concrete. The account he presents is ingenious. Ockham tells us that a term like 'humanity' incorporates one or more syncategorematic elements in its meaning. Here it differs from its concrete counterpart so that, in a quite ordinary sense, the two differ in meaning. Thus, 'humanity' unlike 'man' is what Russell called an incomplete symbol. Its meaning cannot be explicated in isolation—simply by pointing to one or more objects. What we must do if we are to exhibit the meaning of an abstract term like 'humanity' is to indicate the various propositions in which it can occur. Ockham is not altogether clear about the structure of these propositions; but he appears to hold that they all involve the concept of necessity, that (in the case of 'humanity') they incorporate a context of the following sort: 'Men . . . necessarily. . . .' Thus 'humanity' is not a device for referring to objects over and above the individuals that are men, but neither is it simply a device by which we refer to men. It is an expression which provides us with an abbreviated way of making claims about what necessarily is true of men qua men.

Thus, even though abstract terms from the category of substance introduce no new entities, they are not synonymous with their concrete counterparts. But in showing this Ockham provides us with a technique for eliminating from discourse all abstract terms in the category of substance. We cannot simply replace an abstract term, '*F-ness*', with its concrete counterpart '*F*', but we can employ the scheme hinted at above. Thus, all contexts of the form '*F-ness* . . .' can be supplanted by modal contexts of the form '*F*-things necessarily . . .' There are, of course, gaps in Ockham's account. His schema tells us how to handle expressions of the form '*F-ness*', but it would seem that the move from '*F-ness* . . .' to '*F-things* necessarily . . .' will involve changes in one or more expressions occurring in that part of the context '*F-ness* . . .' that is designated by '. . . . .'; for presumably at least some of the expressions that are syntactically and semantically suited for predicative union with abstract terms cannot enter into the subject-predicate nexus with concrete expressions.

While it remains incomplete, the schema sketched above highlights the fact that abstract terms from the category of substance do not add to the significative power of language. As the schema shows, abstract terms provide short-hand ways of saying things that could be said exclusively with the use of concrete terms. But since abstract terms from the category of substance do not play purely significative roles, they cannot, strictly speaking, be either connotative or absolute. They do not signify$_0$ objects at all; they merely point to propositional contexts. Those contexts do, however, incorporate significative expressions—the concrete forms which signify$_1$ individual substances. This, I take it, is all that Ockham means when, summarizing the results of his account, he tells us that abstract terms from the category of substance signify$_1$ individual substances. Although he appears to be saying that abstract terms are absolute, he is really just pointing to the possibility of eliminating from language all the abstract terms in the category of substance. While not significative themselves, these abstract terms give way, under analysis, to propositional contexts incorporating terms that signify$_1$ substances.[15]

The category of quality incorporates, in the first instance, all such terms as can meaningfully serve to answer the question, 'How is it qualified?' and in the second instance the abstract counterparts of these terms. The speaker of English is likely to have a difficult time with this category. I have translated the Latin 'Quale?' as 'How is it qualified?', but the two are not really equivalent. English simply has no interrogative with the force of the Latin 'Quale?' The English abstract term 'quality', on the other hand, is more general than its Latin counterpart. In philosophical contexts the term is frequently employed as a general term covering all non-relational properties. But while the Latin term 'qualitas' is more selective, it is difficult to point to the principle of selectivity at work. This category incorporates what to the speaker of English must appear a very heterogenous group of terms. Among its abstract forms there are expressions (like 'sweetness' and 'whiteness') that purport to signify$_1$ the various sensible properties of objects, expressions (like 'courage' and 'wisdom') that purport to signify$_1$ overtly dispositional features like virtue and knowledge, and expressions (like 'straightness' and 'curvature') that purport to signify$_1$ the shape and form of substances.[16]

Given the heterogeneity of these terms, we are not surprised to find Ockham rejecting any single account of all the abstract terms in the category of quality. He wants to claim, on the contrary, that while some of the pairs of abstract and concrete terms from this category do conform to the "natural" interpretation outlined above, others do not. For some expressions in this category, then, the abstract-concrete and absolute-connotative dichotomies run parallel. Roughly, the pairs in question are those associated, on the one hand, with the perceptible qualities of objects and, on the other, with dispositional qualities. In both of these cases, Ockham wants to grant that abstract forms signify$_1$ objects distinct from substances; their concrete counterparts signify$_1$ the substances exhibiting these objects while signifying$_2$ the objects they exhibit.

In the case of abstract terms of this sort surface grammar does not altogether mislead us. They appear to signify$_1$ abstract objects and actually do. Nonetheless, if we attend only to surface grammar we are likely to construe these expressions as discrete terms. They are after all generally employed in this way in ordinary language. But it is very tempting to move from this fact of usage to the claim that terms like 'whiteness' and 'courage' each signify$_1$ objects that can be exhibited simultaneously by several different objects. Thus, the surface grammar of these terms tempts us to employ the term 'universal' as a term of first rather than second intention, as a term marking a distinction in the real order.

But it takes merely a moment's reflection to see that such a move is unsatisfactory. Suppose, for example, that whiteness were an object exhibited by all white things. Whiteness would, at any given time, be present in each of several non-continuous regions of space; but that Ockham contends is impossible. An object occupying two discontinuous regions of space at any given time would be divided from itself; it would be two objects and not one. The premise at work here is one that recurs in Ockham's treatment of the categories. Essentially, it is the claim that if at any time, t, an object, a, is in a place, p_1, and an object, b, in a place, p_2 (where p_1 and p_2 are numerically different non-continuous regions, neither of which is a part of the other), then a and b are numerically different objects.[17] But applying this premise in the present case we are forced to conclude that there can be no one object that is present in all white things. Our only alternative, Ockham wants to claim, is to deviate from ordinary usage and to treat absolute terms from the category of quality as common terms. If we follow Ockham's proposal we must say that there are as many whitenesses as there are white things and that each of these is signified$_2$ by 'whiteness'.

But while Ockham wants to accept at least part of the "natural" interpretation for terms like 'whiteness' and 'courage', he resists a parallel treatment of
terms expressive of figure and form. These expressions, he contends, are not
absolute terms signifying$_1$ entities in virtue of which substances are said to be
straight, curved, and the like. There simply are no such entities. The form of argument at work here is characteristic of Ockham's treatment of the "natural"
interpretation. According to the "natural" interpretation a substance is curved
in virtue of possessing the entity curvedness. But is this the end of the story?
Ockham thinks not. Even if a substance possesses the relevant entity it can be
curved only if its parts are arranged in a certain way. That the parts of the substance be arranged in this way, then, is a necessary condition of the applicability
of the predicate 'curved'. Ockham wants to claim, however, that it is also a
sufficient condition. Suppose some substance were to lack the relevant entity.
That substance nevertheless would be curved provided that its parts are arranged
in the requisite way. The absence of curvedness would be irrelevant to the applicability of the predicate 'curved'. But the appeal to that entity is superfluous,
and since it is superfluous the account should be avoided. The principle at work
here is, of course, the principle of theoretical parsimony that has come to bear
Ockham's name. As he says in a different context, "One ought not postulate
many things when he can get by with fewer."

But we need an alternative account of expressions associated with figure
and form. The concrete terms, Ockham tells us, are connotative. They sig-
nify$_1$ substances and such qualities as can be meaningfully said to have a shape
or figure. Qua connotative they signify$_2$, but their significata$_2$ are not non-
linguistic entities. A term like 'curved', Ockham claims, signifies$_2$ the truth
of the contingent proposition which states that the conditions for the applicability of that term are satisfied. The proposition says in effect that the signified$_1$
substance or quality has its parts arranged in such and such a way.

Sometimes Ockham says that abstract terms expressive of figure and form
are connotative terms synonymous with their concrete counterparts; nevertheless this claim runs counter to what seems to be his "official" position. It is I
think merely a short-hand way of summarizing his views on figure and form.
The "official" view is that abstract forms like 'straightness' and 'curvature' are
terms only from a syntactical point of view. Semantically, they are like abstract
terms from the category of substance; they are incomplete symbols which can
be explicated only in terms of propositional contexts. As in the case of substance-
words the relevant contexts appear to involve the modal concept of necessity. An
abstract term like 'straightness' is a device for making claims about what is necessarily true of straight objects qua straight. Such terms are all, via the relevant
modal contexts, eliminable in favor of the more familiar concrete forms.[18]

We have distinguished between terms that are and terms that are not expressive of figure and form. Ockham provides a more manageable criterion for de-

termining when abstract terms from the category of quality are to be construed as absolute. Where '*F-ness*' and '*F*' are terms from the category of quality which are related as abstract and concrete, Ockahm's criterion tells us that '*F-ness*' is absolute just in case it is impossible some object *a*, which does not satisfy '*F*' at t_1 come to satisfy '*F*' at t_{1+n} merely as the result of a change in place. Thus, Ockham wants to construe 'whiteness' as an absolute term, for he holds that an object that is not white cannot come to be white merely by undergoing local motion; but 'straightness', he would hold, is connotative. A curved bow, for example, can become straight merely as the result of the spatial rearrangements of its parts.

Ockham follows Aristotle in distinguishing terms expressive of *continuous quantity* and terms expressive of *discrete quantity*. The distinction between continuous and discrete quantities, at least as it functions in Aristotle, is the distinction between quantities (like the line) which have parts that are spatially contiguous and quantities (like the numbers) where the question, 'Where do its parts join?' makes no sense. Ockham and Aristotle both claim that terms expressive of continuous quantity point to the subject matter of geometry; whereas, it is among the terms expressive of discrete quantities that we find the expressions crucial in arithmetic.

Ockham's account of this distinction is, like his analysis of figure and form, reductionistic. He contends that neither geometry nor arithmetic presuppose entities over and above substances and qualities. He presents a large number of arguments in support of this claim. Many of these arguments parallel the argument I outlined in my discussion of figure and form: the relevant entities are useless as explanatory entities and should consequently be eliminated from our theory. Nevertheless, some of these arguments are meant to exhibit intrinsic difficulties in the notion of a uniquely mathematical object. In particular Ockham wants to point to difficulties involved in specifying subjects for these objects.

In the case of geometrical objects he argues that since points, lines, figures, and solids are not themselves substances, they must exist in something else. The obvious candidate here is material substance, but if we look to the case of geometrical points we see that this account is unsatisfactory. Points are indivisible in all dimensions; and according to Ockham, to locate the immediate subject of a point—"where" a point is—is to locate something that is itself indivisible in all dimensions. But since material substance and the parts of material substance are divisible in all dimensions, they cannot function as the subjects of points. The view that would make lines the subjects of points, Ockham also finds unsatisfactory. Lines, he points out, are divisible in one dimension. Besides, lines need subjects; and, according to Ockham, they must agree with lines in being indivisible in two dimensions. But neither material substances nor their parts can be the "where" of lines. Since they are divisible in breadth, surfaces cannot play this role either; but even if they could, surfaces require subjects, subjects that are indivisible in depth; and both material substances and geometrical solids fail to meet this requirement. But in any event geometrical solids require subjects and the only possible candidates here are material substances. We could provide subjects for geometrical solids by stipulating that the subject of a geometrical solid, x, be some material substance that is exactly congruent with x. But if we make this stipulation, Ockham concludes, the need for geo--metrical solids disappears. Whatever purpose a given solid is meant to serve, the material substance that is its subject serves as well.

A similar difficulty arises in the case of discrete quantities. Where, for example, does the duality of the two men I have just counted exist? According to Ockham it is not a self-subsistent entity: it must exist in some subject. Ockham would agree that in a general way it is easy to specify the subject of this entity—the two men. Difficulties arise when we try to be more specific. The duality of the two men cannot exist in just one of the men; it is the duality of both men. But neither can it exist in both of the men. The men are spatially discontinuous objects; and for Ockham we have seen it is a necessary truth that one and the same object cannot exist in spatially discontinuous subjects.[19]

According to Ockham the concrete terms from the category of quantity are, like the concrete forms expressive of figure and form, connotative expressions signifying$_1$ substances and qualities while signifying$_2$ the truth of some contingent proposition. In each case the connoted proposition states that the conditions required for the applicability of the term in question have been satisfied, and invariably these conditions focus on the results of some procedure of measurement or counting. Their abstract counterparts receive the form of treatment that by now should be familiar; they are construed as incomplete symbols to be analyzed in terms of contexts involving necessity. They are simply devices for making statements about what is necessarily true of substances and qualities qua satisfying the various concrete terms from this category. To speak then of continuous quantities is simply to make claims about substances and qualities qua long, triangular, etc., and to speak of discrete quantities is to speak of substances and qualities qua enumerable as two, three, four, etc. But, then, neither geometry nor arithmetic require entities over and above substances and qualities; the subject matter of mathematics is wholly constituted by these objects qua satisfying the relevant quantitative predicates.

When Ockham introduces the categories he tells us that there is no interrogative in Latin that is syntactically suited to collect all and only the concrete terms from the category of relation; thus, when he deals with the category in isolation he attempts to provide a more detailed analysis of relative expressions. He tells us that the various concrete forms in the category come in pairs such that an object, a, can satisfy one of the predicates from the pair only if there exists some other object, b, such that a satisfies the relevant predicate with respect to *b* and *b* in turn satisfies the other predicate in the pair with respect to *a*.[20] 'Father' and 'son' are examples. If an individual is to be a father there must be some other individual whose father he is, and that individual in turn must be his son. .

Philosophers have frequently claimed that the individuals *a* and *b*, which pairwise satisfy expressions of this sort, are themselves related or relatives and that there is some third entity that serves to bring them together, to relate them. Ockham rejects out of hand the suggestion that some third entity is involved here. That object would have to exist in something. If we focus on the case of a father and son we see that the relevant entity could not exist in just one of these men, for it supposedly brings the *two* of them together. Neither could it exist in both men, for the men are spatially discontinuous objects and cannot be the subject of numerically one entity.

To the claim that a third entity is *required* to tie the related individuals together Ockham responds with an argument that in some ways reminds us of Bradeley's argument against relations. If we are told that two objects can be relationally tied together only by the mediation of some third entity, we must ask, Ockham claims, how that entity is related to the original two entities. Is it related to them immediately—without the mediation of additional entities? If it is then objects can be related immediately so that there was no need to postulate such an entity in the first place. If it is not then additional entities must be introduced into the analysis; and, of course, the same question will arise with respect to these entities. Now, either we will at some point arrive at a relating entity that is immediately related to the objects it relates or we will not. If we do it is possible that there be immediately relatable objects. But in that case it seems that relations in general are unnecessary, for, as we have said, we could have construed our original objects as immediately relatable. If, on the other hand, we do not arrive at immediately relatable objects, we are faced with an infinite regress in which case relating entities are powerless to do the job assigned them.[21]

Not only does he reject the notion of relations, but Ockham finds it dangerous to speak of the individuals signified$_2$ by relative terms as related or relatives. It can lead us to think that there is something in the being of those objects that is merely relative, and that Ockham thinks is absurd. It is better, he suggests, to reserve the term 'relative' for the various concrete terms in the category. This amounts to the proposal to treat the term 'relative' as a term of second intention, as a term predicable exclusively of linguistic objects.[22] As regards the abstract counterparts of relatives, Ockham again follows the general procedure introduced in the case of substance. The expressions are mere *facons de parler*; they provide us with shorthand ways of saying things that could be said exclusively with the use of the less problematic concrete forms.

Ockham's treatment of the remaining six categories is relatively brief. The same general pattern is exhibited throughout. In each case Ockham rejects the "natural" interpretation outlined earlier. On his view, the concrete forms from the various categories are to be construed as connotative terms signifying$_1$ only substances and qualities while signifying$_2$ the truth of contingent propositions which state that the conditions required for the applicability of the relevant predicates have been met. The abstract forms do not, of course, introduce any new entities, and this tempts us to say that there are synonymous with their concrete counterparts. But while Ockham sometimes says this, his considered view is that they are not terms at all but incomplete symbols to be parsed along the lines suggested above.

But if we think back to Ockham's account of the categories, we see that his analysis alters his original conception of the classification. The categories were first presented as a classification of categorematic terms according to the mode in which they signify$_1$ substances, and at that point all abstract terms seemed to cast doubt on Ockham's account. The subsequent analysis, however, has shown that most abstract terms are eliminable so that their inclusion in the categories is not really problematic at all. Although they cannot serve to answer the various category-generating questions, they are analyzable in terms of expressions that can.

But while most abstract terms are eliminable those that purport to signify$_1$ sensible and dispositional qualities are absolute and, therefore, essential to the significative power of language. But it turns out to be a mistake to construe the categories as a classification of terms according to the mode in which they signify$_1$ substances. For one thing abstract qualitative terms do not signify$_1$ substances at all; for another the various concrete terms from the adjectival categories can, as Ockham's analysis of those categories indicates, signify qualities as well as substances, Patches of color, for example, can be round or square; can be of such and such a length; can be in this or that place; etc.

Thus, we must broaden our conception of the categories and construe them as a classification of terms according to the mode in which they signify$_1$ objects (where 'object' is neutral as between substances and qualities). But, then, although Ockham himself never makes the move, there would be good reason for subsuming the various non-eliminable abstract terms from the category of quality under the category of substance. Such terms do not signify$_1$ anything at all in the mode of quality, so that they do not belong in that category; and although they do not signify$_1$ substance, they agree with terms like 'man' in signifying$_1$ their significata$_1$ in the mode of essence or substance—by telling us what those significata$_1$ are. Given the broadened conception of the categories to which Ockham's analysis has driven us, this entails that abstract terms like 'whiteness' and 'courage' belong in the category of substance.[23]

But this is not to say that substances and qualities are not very different sorts of things. Ockham is clear on this point. Whereas substances are independent entities which can exist of and by themselves, qualities can only exist in another. But while Ockham wants to preserve the distinction between substances and qualities, he stands opposed to a view that dominates the traditional interpretation of Aristotle's categories. On that view transcendental terms— universally predicable expressions like 'object', 'entity', and 'thing'—are not univocally predicable of everything. They have different meanings when they are predicated of things as different as substances and qualities. Ockham pays lip service to this view—doubtless because it is a view that Aristotle is fairly explicit about defending;[24] nevertheless, his considered opinion is that the view is wrong.

Ockham's account of ambiguity or, as he calls it, equivocality, takes as its background the theme that spoken language is an extension of mental language. He tells us that a term is *univocal* if it is subordinated to or an extension of just one mental word; whereas, expressions that serve as extensions of different mental words are *equivocal.* 'Bat', for instance, plays in different contexts the roles of two quite different natural signs and consequently is equivocal. Now Ockham tells us that there is at least one transcendental expression which is, in its application to all objects, subordinated to just one mental word. That in effect is to say that at least one transcendental term is univocally predicable of all things.

Ockham's most detailed defense of this claim is found in that section of the *Summa Logicae* that immediately precedes his analysis of the categories. At first glance it appears that he is presenting us with an argument here, but if we look closer it becomes clear tht he is merely *stipulating* that there is one mental word that is predicable of all objects. Given the context, however, we need not construe Ockham's stipulation as arbitrary; we can, on the contrary, construe him as stating a presupposition for the ensuing analysis of the categories. That analysis is an ontological investigation; it is an attempt to determine what there is. Ockham can be interpreted as saying that unless some one expression is univocally predicable of all things, we can make no sense of that investigation. Ontology has maximal generality of scope; there is nothing that is not incorporated in its subject matter, for the task of the ontologist is to determine what objects, entities, or things there are. But notice that unless there is some one expression that is univocally predicable of all things, we cannot say this. To specify the subject matter of ontology we need some term like 'entity', 'object', or 'thing' that can in one sense be applied to everything. As I interpret him Ockham is telling us that there must be one universally predicable mental word to which at least one conventional transcendental is subordinated. Without this the analysis that follows makes no sense.

NOTES

1. Although Ockham defines the term 'syncategorematic' more narrowly than this in chapter 4, his subsequent use of the term converges with mine. See, for example, chapter 69.

2. To be accurate here we would have to employ the distinction between primary and secondary signification that I outline later. Employing that distinction we would have to say that a proposition of this sort is true just in case the subject is numbered among the primary significata of the predicate; otherwise it is false. This issue of truth conditions is pursued in the second paper, "Ockham on Generality."

3. Of course it may be that other entities are involved, but Ockham wants to claim that if this is so the analysis of predication will never reveal it. The pressure to postulate additional entities must come from other quarters. As it turns out, additional entities (albeit individuals) are involved in the use of some predicates from the category of quality; but as the second part of this paper shows, it is the analysis of abstract terms and not predication that establishes this fact.

4. There is, of course, one sense of 'particular' in which 'particular' designates real, i.e. non-linguistic entities, but in that sense it is not opposed to 'universal'. See chapters 14 and 19 for an account of this sense of the term.

5. This account is likely to remind the reader of Wilfrid Sellars' account of intentionality. Sellars himself admits his debt to medieval philosophy in general in "Being and Being Known" in *Science, Perception, and Reality* (New York: Humanities Press, 1963), 41-59 and to Ockham, in particular, in "Towards a Theory of Categories" in *Experience and Theory,* Lawrence Foster and J. W. Swanson, eds. (Amherst: University of Massachusetts Press, 1970), 55-78.

6. Ockham himself introduces this dichotomy as a distinction among names, a grammatical category incorporating both nouns and adjectives. Nonetheless, this same sort of phenomenon is at work in the case of other parts of speech, e.g., verbs and their gerund-forms ('run' and 'running'). Fastening on this fact I speak not of concrete and abstract names but of concrete and abstract terms.

7. Again, Ockham presents this dichotomy as a distinction among names; but here he clearly is tempted to extend the distinction beyond that grammatical category. Thus, he speaks of verbs, adverbs, etc. as connoting this or that about substance and quality. Following out these hints, I speak of absolute and connotative terms rather than names.

8. 'Signify$_0$' is neutral as between the four senses of 'signify' outlined in chapter 33. In place of this sense of 'signify', Ockham frequently employs the term 'importare'. Literally this means "to carry into" and conveys clearly the notion of introducing into discourse.

9. 'Signify$_1$' is roughly equivalent to the first sense of 'signify' discussed in chapter 33; and one could easily expand my account in such a way that the term could also fit the second sense of 'signify' found in that chapter. In the interests of brevity, I do not engage in the relevant expansion here.

10. 'Signify$_2$' covers both the third and fourth senses of 'signify' found in chapter 33.

11. Ockham tells us that this account of the categories originates with Averroes. Readers will find a very similar explication of Aristotle's categories in Gilbert Ryle's classic paper "Categories," reprinted in Flew, A. G. N., *Logic and Language,* 2nd series (Oxford: Basil Blackwell, 1953), 65-81.

12. See in particular chapters 7 and 16.

13. In dealing with the category Ockham does not consider the case of concrete terms like 'unicorn' that have no significata$_1$. It seems, however, that he would want to construe them as connotative terms signifying$_2$ the truth of some proposition.

14. Ockham does not provide much commentary here. He seems to think that our natural linguistic intuitions will substantiate his claim. See, for example, chapter 8.

15. The account presented here is clearly Ockham's. The difficulty, as I suggest, is that Ockham sometimes says things that are inconsistent with this analysis. My own inclination is to emphasize the revolutionary rather than the reactionary side of Ockham's account.

16. If it is to be construed as anything more than a general way of pointing to the contents of the category of quality, this technique for dividing the category is inadequate. Thus, there are terms like 'light' that do not naturally fit any of these divisions. Actually, the only division that Ockham finds crucial is that between terms expressive of figure and form, on the one hand, and all the remaining terms in the category, on the other.

17. This premise is never stated as explicitly as I suggest here. It is rather implied as it is, for example, in chapter 44.

18. My account deviates from Ockham in order of presentation. He deals with the category of quality after he deals with the categories of quantity and relation. His analysis of figure and form, then, is far briefer than my account would suggest. He merely applies the results of his analysis of these two categories to abstract terms expressive of figure and form and concludes with little commentary that these terms are not absolute. Since I want to bring to the fore the real existents (substances and qualities) in terms of which Ockham analyzes quantity and relation, I introduce Ockham's reductionism in terms of figure and form. What I have done is expand his own treatment of this species of quality in terms of his analysis of quantity and relation.

19. This argument is found in Ockham's *Commentary on the Categories* which exists only in early editions.

20. This account holds only in the case of natural signs or intentions. Both Ockham and Aristotle want to claim that given the poverty of conventional languages, a term, 'T_1', can be a relative even though there is no term, 'T_2', such that 'T_2' is the relative of 'T_1'. My account requires expansion, then, to handle this case. In the interests of brevity I omit the expansion here.

21. Since this argument is found in chapter 51, it is not from Ockham's own hand; nonetheless, it is sufficiently like other arguments found in authentic sections of the text to warrant the label "Ockhamistic."

22. My use of the term 'second intention' deviates from my analysis of that term in the first part of this paper. There I define second intentions as a subclass of intentions of the soul. Although Ockham construes this as the proper meaning of the term, he extends his use of the term as I do here, to cover conventional signs as well.

23. Of course, if we make this modification in the Ockhamistic theory of categories, the term 'substance' hardly does justice to the richness of this category. A new term would have to be introduced to capture the ontological force of the expanded category.

24. See Ockham's *Commentary on Porphyry*, chapter 3, Ernest Moody, ed. (St. Bonaventure, New York: Franciscan Institute Publications, 1965), 44-45. Ockham refers to this passage in chapter 38 of the *Summa*.

Ockham on Generality

Michael J. Loux

Contemporary accounts of propositions like

(1) Every philosopher reads Aristotle

and

(2) Some Greeks are sailors

tend to stress the role of the expressions 'every' and 'some'. Philosophers
see the apparatus of quantification beneath these expressions and attribute
the generality of reference ingredient in propositions like (1) and (2)
to the unique role played by the quantifier. Ockham, like other medieval
logicians, takes a quite different approach. He contends that expressions
like 'every' and 'some' are completely lacking in referential force. According to Ockham, it is only non-logical or categorematic terms that can play
genuinely referring roles, so that generality of reference must ultimately
be secured by the categorematic terms embedded in general propositions
rather than by expressions like 'some' and 'every' which introduce them.
This theme plays a central role in Ockham's metaphysics and logic, and
in this paper I would like to consider its elaboration in the *Summa Logicae*.

I

The framework for Ockham's treatment of generality is his theory of
supposition. As Ockham explains it, supposition is a semantical property
that agrees with signification in involving a word-thing relation; but whereas signification is a property that is invariantly associated with a categorematic term, supposition is a property a term exhibits only within the context
of a proposition.[1] Its role in his semantics is not unlike that played in
contemporary theories by the notion of reference. To say that a term
supposits for an object in a proposition is to say that the term so functions
in that proposition as to stand for or denote the object in question.

23

Now, Ockham holds that one and the same term can, in different propositional settings, refer to or supposit for categorically different objects. This view is developed in his claim that there are three different kinds of supposition He calls these *material, simple,* and *personal supposition.* Material supposition is the kind of reference a term has when it is used to refer to itself. 'Man', for example, has material supposition in ' "Man" is a three-letter word'. Although it is a general term, it is functioning there as a singular term taking itself as referent or suppositum. In simple supposition, on the other hand, a term supposits for a concept or intention of the soul. Thus, 'man' supposits simply in *'Man* is a species'. In characterizing simple supposition we can mobilize Ockham's theory of thinking as a kind of inner speech and say that when a term supposits simply, it functions as a singular term suppositing for that conceptual word which in the inner language of the soul plays the same role that it plays in overt speech.[2]

Ockham construes both material and simple supposition as deviant forms of supposition; together they stand opposed to the normal referential use of terms in personal supposition. He explicates the notion of personal supposition in terms of the concept of signification$_1$. As we defined the notion earlier a term signifies$_1$ all and only those objects of which it can be truly predicated. Ockham tells us that a term supposits personally when it supposits for the object or objects it signifies$_1$.[3] Thus, 'Socrates' has personal supposition in 'Socrates is wise' since it supposits in that proposition for the individual that is its bearer—Socrates, and 'man' supposits personally in 'Every man is an animal'; for according to Ockham it so functions in that proposition as to refer to the various objects of which it can be truly predicated.

These two examples exhibit the two kinds of personal supposition— *discrete supposition,* where the suppositing expression is a singular term referring to its sole significatum$_1$, and *general supposition,* where a general term supposits for all its significata$_1$. Ockham says little about the former. It is the case of general supposition that receives his detailed attention, and the focus of his attention is the fact that with general supposition, generality of the sort we want to consider enters language.

II

When he first considers the notion of general supposition Ockham provides an account that is meant to handle a narrow range of cases, and his consideration of even these cases is subject to an idealizing restriction that is only later lifted.[4] He limits himself to the supposition of general terms in propositions which involve exclusively the use of present tense verbs and which are through-and-through assertoric; the idealizing restriction is the contrafactual assumption that all general terms have non-empty extensions.

In the interests of clarifying the scope of Ockham's initial account of supposition it will prove useful to consider an imaginary language, E^*. Although it is a much weaker language, E^* has much in common with English. Indeed, we can think of E^* as that fragment of English which remains when we eliminate (a) propositions which involve verbs in any of the past or future tenses, (b) propositions which incorporate, even if only implicitly, terms expressing the modalities, and (c) propositions consisting of one or more categorematic terms with empty extensions. Ockham's initial presentation of the concept of general supposition can be construed as the attempt to explicate the way in which general terms in E^* supposit.

As we have described E^*, all of its general terms have non-empty extensions. Employing the concept of signification$_1$, we can say that every general term in E^* has at least one significatum$_1$. Since E^* has no resources for incorporating these general terms into propositions that involve, even implicitly, the modal notions of necessity or possibility, we can think of these non-empty extentions as consisting exclusively of actualized objects; and since the propositions of E^* are all in the present tense the extensions of the general terms of E^* can be construed as incorporating only presently existing objects.

Let us think of these extensions as domains for the terms in question. Associated with each general term in E^*, then, there is a non-empty domain consisting of all and only those actual, presently existing objects that are significata$_1$ of the term in question. Philosophers before Ockham frequently called the objects of each such domain the *appellata* of the term whose domain they constitute.[5] Employing this piece of jargon, I shall call these non-empty domains *appellative domains,* and I shall employ the symbol $\{AD/\text{'}T\text{'}\}$ to mark the class of objects that constitute the appellative domain for a term, 'T'.

Now, Ockham holds that when a term in E^* supposits generally, it supposits for all the elements in its appellative domain; nonetheless, he wants to maintain that general terms can supposit for these objects in a variety of styles. His claim is that by specifying these different styles of supposition, we can generate a set of semantical relationships rich enough to provide an account of the logical structure of all the general propositions of E^*.

The first style of general supposition which Ockham considers he calls *determinate supposition.* He describes it as follows:

. . . whenever it is possible to descend to the particulars under a general term by way of a disjunctive proposition and whenever it is possible to infer such a proposition from a particular, the term in question has personal determinate supposition.

Ockham explicates determinate supposition in terms of the inference patterns which the use of an expression exhibiting this form of supposition licenses for the proposition in which it is embedded. The claim here is that where a term supposits determinately in E^*, we can "descend" from the proposition embedding the term to a certain disjunction of singular propositions and we can "ascend" from any one of the singular propositions in the disjunction to the embedding proposition.[6] Talk of warranted "descent" and "ascent" is clearly talk about entailment, and the examples Ockham employs indicate that the singular propositions in question are propositions differing from the embedding proposition only in replacing the term suppositing determinately (along with any syncategorematic terms welded to it) by singular terms suppositing discretely for the various elements in the appellative domain of the suppositing term. I shall call these propositions *singular instantiations* of the embedding proposition and shall say that they instantiate it with respect to the suppositing term. The view, then, is that where a term supposits determinately in E^*, it so functions that the proposition in which it is embedded entails the disjunction of all those propositions that instantiate it with respect to the suppositing term and is entailed by any one of these propositions. Since, however, to be entailed by any one singular instantiation is to be entailed by the disjunction of all of them, we can say that

A term, 'T', in E^* supposits determinately in a context $(\ldots\ldots T\ldots\ldots)$ just in case $(\ldots\ldots T\ldots\ldots)$ entails and is entailed by $[(\ldots\ldots T_1\ldots\ldots)$ $\vee (\ldots\ldots T_2\ldots\ldots) \vee \ldots\ldots \vee (\ldots\ldots T_n\ldots\ldots)]$ (where 'T_1' - 'T_n' are singular terms whose significata₁ exhaust $\{AD/\text{'}T\text{'}\}$).

Ockham's example is the term 'man' as it functions in the E^* proposition 'A man is an animal'. The referential force of 'man' in this proposition is such that 'A man is an animal' entails and is entailed by 'This man is an animal, or that man is an animal, or . . . .' Thus, while 'man' is suppositing for all the elements in $\{AD/\text{'man'}\}$ it is suppositing for them in a special style. We can call it a propositionally inclusive style of supposition: in the E^* proposition 'A man is an animal', 'man' so supposits for the elements in its appellative domain that the use of the term has the effect of reiterating the context '. . . is an animal' over each of the elements in that domain. But while it is a propositionally inclusive style of supposition, 'man' supposits only disjunctively in 'A man is an animal'; for the use of 'man in this proposition has the effect of reiterating the embedding context only disjunctively across $\{AD/\text{'man'}\}$.

Terms which exhibit determinate supposition in E^*, then, supposit in a propositionally inclusive, yet merely disjunctive way. Opposed to determinate supposition, we have what Ockham calls *confused supposition*. Actually, this is not a single style of general supposition, but two quite different styles which agree only in lacking one of the two properties which are constitutive of determinate supposition One, *confused and distributive supposition,* is a propositionally inclusive style of reference that is not merely disjunctive; whereas, the other, *merely confused supposition,* is disjunctive, but not propositionally inclusive.

Let us consider confused and distributive supposition first. Ockham says,

> Confused and distributive supposition occurs when . . . it is possible . . . to descend by a conjunctive proposition and impossible to infer the original proposition from any of the elements in the conjunction.

Again, this style of supposition is defined with reference to the inferential moves which terms exhibiting it license; and once again, these moves bear, on the one hand, on the proposition in which the suppositing term is embedded and, on the other, on the propositions which instantiate it with respect to the suppositing term. Where a term in E^* has confused and distributive supposition, it is possible to "descend" from its embedding proposition to the conjunction of all the relevant singular instantiations. Ockham tells us that no one of those instantiations warrants an "ascent" to the embedding proposition, but it is clear that the conjunction of all of them does, so that

> A term, 'T', in E^* has confused and distributive supposition in a context $(\ldots\ldots T\ldots\ldots)$ just in case $(\ldots\ldots T\ldots\ldots)$ entails and is entailed by $[(\ldots\ldots T_1\ldots\ldots) \wedge (\ldots\ldots T_2\ldots\ldots) \wedge \ldots\ldots \wedge (\ldots\ldots T_n\ldots\ldots)]$ (where T_1-T_n exhaust $\{AD/\text{'}T\text{'}\}$).[7]

An example is the subject in the E^* proposition 'Every man is an animal'; here, 'man' so supposits that 'Every man is an animal' entails and is entailed by the conjunctive reiteration of '. . . is an animal' across $\{AD/\text{'man'}\}$. Confused and distributive supposition, then, is a style of supposition that is like determinate supposition in being propositionally inclusive, but unlike it in being conjunctive rather than merely disjunctive.

Merely confused supposition, on the other hand, is neither propositionally inclusive nor conjunctive. Defining it, Ockham says,

> Merely confused supposition occurs when a common term supposits
> personally and it is impossible . . . to descend to particulars by way of
> a disjunctive proposition, but it is possible to descend by way of a
> proposition with a disjunctive predicate and it is possible to infer the
> original proposition from any particular.

The claim is that where a term in E^* has merely confused supposition, its
embedding proposition is entailed by any proposition which instantiates it
with respect to the suppositing term; but while granting this, Ockham
denies that the use of a term to supposit in this way licenses even the disjunctive reiteration of the embedding context across its appellative domain.
Where a term has merely confused supposition, however, we can make a
"descent" to a kind of disjunction—what we might call a terminal disjunction. An expression with this form of supposition so functions that
singular terms suppositing discretely for each of the elements in its domain
can be disjunctively reiterated within the embedding context. Ockham's
definition suggests that only the predicate-terms of E^* propositions can
exhibit merely confused supposition, but in other contexts he explicitly
tells us that the notion has a more general application. Consequently, if we
employ a new symbol (v as opposed to V) to signal terminal disjunction,
we can say that

> A term, 'T' in E^* has merely confused supposition in a context
> (. . . . . T . . . . .) just in case (. . . . . T . . . . .) entails and is entailed by
> (. . . . . T_1 v T_2 v . . . . . v T_n . . .) (where T_1-T_n exhaust $\{AD/'T'\}$).[7]

'Animal' has merely confused supposition in the E^* proposition
'Every man is an animal'. The use of this term does not license the reiteration of 'Every man is . . .' across the domain of animals either conjunctively or disjunctively; for if we assume that the number of men is greater
than one, then there is no one animal that they all are. Nevertheless,
'animal' so functions in 'Every man is an animal' that it warrants the inference from its embedding E^* proposition to the E^* proposition 'Every man
is this animal or that animal or . . .'[8]

According to Ockham, determinate, confused and distributive, and
merely confused supposition exhaust the styles of general supposition.[9] His
contention is that with these three styles of general supposition in hand, it
is possible to exhibit the logical structure of all the general propositions in
E^*; and after distinguishing these styles, Ockham provides us with a set
of rules which enable us to move from the syntactical characterization of
a term in such a proposition to the conclusion that it exhibits one and only
one of these three styles. These rules tell us, for example, that if a term in

E^* immediately follows the expressions 'every' or 'no', it has confused and distributive supposition; but while helpful, Ockham's rules tend to be something of a hodge-podge. Consequently, I shall not attempt to systematize or even summarize them. I shall, on the contrary, display the semantical structure which these rules dictate for the familiar $A, E, I,$ and O forms of the traditional square of opposition as these forms appear in E^*.

In Ockham's analysis, all A-propositions in E^* are composed of a subject exhibiting confused and distributive supposition and a predicate with merely confused supposition, so that an E^* proposition of the form 'Every A is B' comes out as

$(A_1$ is $B_1 \vee B_2 \vee \ldots \vee B_n) \wedge (A_2$ *is* $B_1 \vee B_2 \vee \ldots \vee B_n) \wedge \ldots$
$\wedge (A_n$ is $B_1 \vee B_2 \vee \ldots \vee B_n)$ (where A_1-A_n and B_1-B_n exhaust $\{AD/\text{'A'}\}$ and $\{AD/\text{'B'}\}$ respectively).

In the E-propositions of E^*, both subject and predicate have confused and distributive supposition. Thus, E^* propositions of the form 'No A is B' receive the following treatment:

$[(A_1$ is not $B_1) \wedge (A_1$ is not $B_2) \wedge \ldots \wedge (A_1$ is not $B_n)] \wedge$
$[(A_2$ is not $B_1) \wedge (A_2$ is not $B_2) \wedge \ldots \wedge (A_2$ is not $B_n)]$
$\wedge \ldots \wedge [(A_n$ is not $B_1) \wedge (A_n$ is not $B_2) \wedge \ldots$
$\wedge (A_n$ is not $B_n)]$ (where A_1-A_n and B_1-B_n exhaust $\{AD/\text{'A'}\}$ and $\{AD/\text{'B'}\}$ respectively).

I-propositions have both subject and predicate suppositing determinately, with the result that an E^* proposition of the form 'Some A is B' is exhibited as

$[(A_1$ is $B_1) \vee (A_1$ is $B_2) \vee \ldots \vee (A_1$ is $B_n)] \vee [(A_2$ is $B_1) \vee$
$(A_2$ is $B_2) \vee \ldots \vee (A_2$ is $B_n)] \vee \ldots \vee [(A_n$ is $B_1) \vee (A_n$ is $B_2)$
$\vee \ldots \vee (A_n$ is $B_n)]$ (where A_1-A_n and B_1-B_n exhaust $\{AD/\text{'A'}\}$ and $\{AD/\text{'B'}\}$ respectively).

Finally, while the subject of an O-proposition in E^* has determinate supposition, the predicate has confused and distributive supposition. Consequently, E^* propositions exhibiting the form 'Some A is not B' can be displayed as follows:

$[(A_1$ is not $B_1) \wedge (A_1$ is not $B_2) \wedge \ldots \wedge (A_1$ is not $B_n)] \vee$
$[(A_2$ is not $B_1) \wedge (A_2$ is not $B_2) \wedge \ldots \wedge (A_2$ is not $B_n)] \vee \ldots$
$\vee [(A_n$ is not $B_1) \wedge (A_n$ is not $B_2) \wedge \ldots \wedge (A_n$ is not $B_n)]$ (where A_1-A_n and B_1-B_n exhaust $\{AD/\text{'A'}\}$ and $\{AD/\text{'B'}\}$ respectively).

Now, Ockham maintains that these expansions provide us with an analysis of the meaning of E* propositions of the relevant forms, but he also contends that they provide the machinery for specifying the truth conditions for general propositions of E^*. Given a general proposition exhibiting one of the four forms, we can say that it is true just in case the relevant expansion is true. But, then, the truth value of a general proposition in E* turns out to be truth functionally dependent upon the truth values of the singular instantiations which comprise the different expansions. This should be immediately obvious in the case of the I, E, and O forms, for in these cases the expansions involve only truth functional connectives. It is less clear in the case of A-propositions in E^*, for there our expansion incorporates the terminal connective, v, and we have not provided any general directions for reducing that connective to propositional connectives. Now, it may be that no such general directions are possible; but within the context of our expansions, such a reduction is clearly legitimate, for 'A_1 is B_1 v B_2 v . . . . . v B_n' is equivalent to

$$(A_1 \text{ is } B_1) \text{ V } (A_1 \text{ is } B_2) \text{ V } . . . . . \text{ V } (A_1 \text{ is } B_n)$$

where v gives way to the truth functional V. But, then, even in this case, the truth value of a general proposition turns on the truth value of a truth functional compound of singular propositions.

The significance of this point should be clear. Given any general proposition in E*, the expansions enable us to reduce questions about the truth of that proposition to more manageable questions about the truth of singular propositions in E^*.[10] The questions are all the more manageable since the relevant singular propositions are uniformly identity-statements or the negations of such, and Ockham thinks that the truth-conditions for propositions of that sort can be specified in a straightforward way. He tells us that an affirmative proposition of the form '$A_1 = B_1$' is true in E^* just in case the object for which 'A_1' supposits is numerically identical with the object for which 'B_1' supposits; whereas, an E* proposition of the form '$A_1 \neq B_1$' is true just in case '$A_1 = B_1$' is false. But, then, having applied this schema to all the singular instantiations comprising our expansions, we need only consult the logic of truth functions to determine the conditions under which a general proposition in E* comes out true.[11]

The reader is likely to see an analogy here between Ockham's account and the account which the contemporary logician provides for quantificational formulae as they bear on finite domains. Where finite domains are involved, the logician tells us that $(x)Fx$ and $(Ex)Fx$ can be construed as mere abbreviations for truth functional compounds of singular propositions of the form 'Fa'. There are, of course, important differences in the two accounts. For one thing, the contemporary logician employs the function-argument schema and, consequently, his analysis makes no attempt to eliminate all vestiges of general terms. But even when we point to such differences the analogy remains strong.[12] It is an important analogy, inasmuch as it shows that Ockham's account of generality is meant to handle the use of general terms only where their appellative domains are finite. Ockham's account hinges on the various expansions we have presented. Now, those expansions presuppose the possibility of providing a list incorporating each of the various objects falling within the appellative domain assigned to a term, and where the objects constituting those domains are infinite in number, no such list is possible. Nor is the demand that the domains be finite an idiosyncrasy of Ockham's treatment of E^*; for even when we extend the account beyond the limited resources of E^* to handle the case of general terms without supposita, the case of modal propositions, and the case of propositions involving the past and future tenses, Ockham's account presupposes that the domains over which general terms range are finite.

It is tempting to convert the analogy into an objection; for whereas the apparatus of quantification can be extended to handle domains that are not finite, Ockham's account cannot be extended in the same way. But, of course, if the system was not meant to be extended in that way, it hardly constitutes an objection to point this out. The objection would have to be reformulated to show that there are contexts (such as those provided by the work of the mathematician) which require the assumption of non-finite domains. My suspicion is that Ockham would repudiate this claim, but how he would frame his defense to handle the contexts in question is not altogether clear.[13]

A related, yet different objection, would focus on the fact that all of the expansions provided by Ockham's analysis require supplementation by means of clauses of the form

(where A_1-A_n and B_1-B_n exhaust $\{AD/'A'\}$ and $\{AD/'B'\}$ respectively).

What such clauses amount to is the claim that A_1-A_n and B_1-B_n are *all* the A's and *all* the B's that there are, but this is to say that implicit in the supplementary clauses is the syncategorematic expression 'all'. The objection, then, would be that although Ockham's analysis is meant to eliminate the syncategorematic signs of generality, the expansions employed to eliminate these expressions implicitly contain them.

Now, it may be that Ockham's analysis is meant to show the dispensability of the various signs of generality. If it is, this is a very powerful objection. But in defense of Ockham, it might be urged that nothing in the text forces us to impute this sort of aim to him. Indeed, if the expansions he points to require the quantifiers, it would seem to be sound interpretation to conclude that he wasn't trying to show their dispensability. What is clear from the text is that Ockham means to provide an account of generality according to which the referring devices in general propositions are general terms and not the syncategorematic expressions welded to them. It seems to me that Ockham could have held that it is general terms which play the referring role in propositions like our original (1) and (2) while granting the non-eliminability of the quantifiers, and if this is what Ockham is maintaining, the objection loses its force.

III

However interesting it may be as a model, the account of generality in E^* represents only the rudiments of an adequate theory of supposition. What we want, in the end, is a theory which can handle the case of propositions incorporating the various modalities, the full range of tenses, and general terms with empty appellative domains. To display the relevant extensions in Ockham's theory, let us imagine successive enrichments in the resources of E^*. Let us suppose, first of all, that the vocabulary of our imaginary language is increased to include categorematic terms with empty appellative domains. To simplify matters, let us think of this enriched version of E^* as that fragment of English containing, in addition to the propositions of E*, all of the present tensed, assertoric propositions of English which incorporate categorematic terms with empty appellative domains; and let us call the result of so enriching E^*, E^{**}.

Our problem, then, is one of extending the theory of supposition for E^* to handle the supposition of terms in those propositions wherein E^* and E^{**} differ. We want, that is, a generalized account of supposition, one that covers indifferently the use of general terms in E^* and E^{**}. Initially, such an account might seem unattainable. Indeed, it might even seem that when we confront the new propositions of E^{**}, the term 'supposition' ceases to be applicable. As we have presented (and as Ockham himself presents) the notion of supposition, suppositing terms always supposit for something. Where there is no suppositum, one wants to say, there can be no supposition. Ockham is aware of this difficulty; his response is simply to extend the notion of supposition, so that even terms with empty appellative domains can be said to supposit.

Now, we might be willing to accept this extension of the notion of supposition; but when we find Ockham telling us that the problematic terms of E^{**} can supposit in the various styles outlined, we are bound to become anxious. It is simply not clear how our original definitions of the various styles of general supposition can have any application where terms have empty appellative domains. Those definitions stipulate that where a term exhibits one of the three styles of general supposition, its use warrants an expansion for the embedding proposition, an expansion involving the various objects which comprise the appellative domain of the suppositing term. But if there are no such objects, then the relevant expansions would appear to be impossible and the definitions inapplicable.

Actually, there is not just one difficulty here, but several. The first concerns the possibility of a proposition's having instantiations with respect to a term lacking significata$_1$. But is this a genuine difficulty? I think not; for suppose $(\ldots\ldots T \ldots\ldots)$ is a proposition in E^{**} incorporating a general term, 'T', with an empty appellative domain. Just because there are no T's it does not follow that we cannot construct E^{**} propositions of the form $(\ldots\ldots T_1 \ldots\ldots)$ and $(\ldots\ldots T_2 \ldots\ldots)$. Given our description of E^{**}, there seems to be no difficulty in this at all; we could simply invent singular terms to form the required instantiations.

But allowing such deviant forms, new questions arise. How are the propositions we have constructed to be treated? Are they to be construed as true? False? Should we assign them a truth value at all? Although it is difficult to be certain how Ockham would answer these questions, it is tempting to construe him as a Russellian; for he frequently talks as though non-modal, present tensed propositions with singular terms lacking a suppositum are false. But if we are willing to see beneath such remarks a developed position, it seems less clear that our definitions are inapplicable. As we stated them the definitions stipulate that a term supposits determinately, for example, just in case the proposition embedding the suppositing term entails and is entailed by a disjunctive proposition, one whose disjuncts instantiate the embedding proposition with respect to the suppositing term. But if Ockham is the Russellian it is tempting to think he is, all these disjuncts come out false; so also, then, does their disjunction. Now, presumably the entailment at work in our definition is the standard form of entailment. Presumably we were using the term 'entails' in such a way that one proposition entails another just in case it is impossible for the first to be true and the second false. But, then, so long as we stipulate that all the propositions of E^{**} which incorporate terms with determinate supposition but no supposita are false, our definition remains intact; and clearly the same point will hold for our definitions of the

other forms of general supposition. Thus, if Ockham is willing to grant
that all general propositions incorporating general terms with empty
domains come out false, his original definitions turn out to be general
definitions holding not only for the propositions of E^*, but for the propositions of E^{**} as well.

Unfortunately, Ockham's view does not prove to be so accommo-
dating; for while, in the case of A- and I- propositions, he agrees that the
use of general terms with empty domains results in the falsity of the
embedding proposition, he wants to deny that this is so in the case of E-
and O-propositions. Thus, although Ockham holds that the E^{**} proposition 'Every man is an animal' is true only if there are both men and
animals, he contends that the E^{**} propositions 'No rhinoceros is a dinosaur' and 'Some rhinoceros is not a dinosaur' come out true even in the
case where there are no rhinoceri.

We need new definitions, then, for the styles of supposition as they
appear in the negative propositions of E^{**}. Ockham never states these
new definitions explicitly, but from a number of his remarks it is clear how
they are to go. Determinate supposition in negative propositions, for
example, is to be defined as follows:

A term 'T' in E^{**} has determinate supposition in the negative context
$(-\ldots.T\ldots.-)$ just in case $(-\ldots.T\ldots.-)$ entails and is entailed
by [(There are no T's) or $<(-\ldots.T_1\ldots.-) \vee (-\ldots.T_2\ldots.-)$
$\vee \ldots. \vee (-\ldots.T_n\ldots.-)>]$ (where T_1-T_n exhaust $\{AD/\text{'}T\text{'}\}$).

The original definitions for merely confused and confused and distributive
supposition require parallel reformulations. In each case the definition
stipulates that the negative proposition in E^{**} which embeds the suppositing term entails and is entailed by a disjunctive proposition, whose disjuncts are (a) the proposition that there are no supposita for the suppositing term and (b) the proposition expressing the expansion specified by
the original definition.

Our original definitions of the three styles of supposition could remain
unaltered for the case of affirmative propositions, but to make explicit
the existence requirement underlying this form of supposition we could
so revise the original definitions that a term, 'T' in E^{**} is said to supposit
in one of those ways just in case its embedding proposition $(\ldots.T\ldots.)$
entails and is entailed by the conjunctive proposition whose conjuncts are
(a) the proposition that there are T's and (b) the proposition expressing
the relevant expansions.

When we apply these new definitions to the case of E^{**}'s $A, E, I,$
and O forms, we get results that depart radically from the treatment these

forms receive at the hands of the contemporary logician. There is, however, a rationale behind Ockham's interpretation of the different forms. To bring this out I shall begin with the case of E^{**} propositions of the I-form, for here Ockham's account does not deviate from the contemporary analysis. Then, moving from the case of I-propositions to the case of A, O, and E propositions, I shall try to exhibit the reasoning that led him to interpret the remaining forms in the way that he did.

Ockham stipulates that no I-proposition in E^{**} can be true unless both its subject and predicate have non-empty domains; but since the relevant expansions can hold only if the predicate term has a non-empty appellative domain, we can say that an E^{**} proposition of the form

Some A is B

is true just in case

(1) $\{AD/`A`\}$ is non-empty; and
(2) $[<(A_1$ is $B_1) \lor (A_1$ is $B_2) \lor \ldots \ldots \lor (A_1$ is $B_n)> \lor$
   $<(A_2$ is $B_1) \lor (A_2$ is $B_2) \lor \ldots \lor (A_2$ is $B_n)> \lor \ldots$
   $\lor <(A_n$ is $B_1) \lor (A_n$ is $B_2) \lor \ldots \lor (A_n$ is $B_n)>]$ is true
   (where A_1-A_n and B_1-B_n exhaust $\{AD/`A`\}$ and $\{AD/`B`\}$
   respectively);

and this is just not that different from the contemporary claim that (Ex) $(Ax \land Bx)$ is true just in case there is some object that satisfies both 'A' and 'B'.

Ockham, like most medievals, wanted to preserve an inferential link between 'every' and 'some'. He wanted, that is, to guarantee all entailments of 'Some . . . . .' by 'Every . . . . .'; but if this inferential link is to be preserved, the existence requirement must be written into the truth-conditions for A-propositions. Thus, Ockham maintains that E^{**} propositions of the form

Every A is B

are true just in case

(1) $\{AD/`A`\}$ is non-empty; and
(2) $[(A_1$ is $B_1 \lor B_2 \lor \ldots \lor B_n) \land (A_2$ is $B_1 \lor B_2 \lor \ldots \lor B_n)$
   $\land \ldots \land (A_n$ is $B_1 \lor B_2 \lor \ldots \lor B_n)]$ is true (where
   A_1-A_n and B_1-B_n exhaust $\{AD/`A`\}$ and $\{AD/`B`\}$
   respectively);

and here we have an obvious departure from the contemporary treatment

of A-propositions according to which 'Every '*A* is *B*' comes out true even
in the case where there are neither *A*'s nor *B*'s.

The second major departure is in Ockham's interpretation of *O*-
propositions in E^{**}. Here Ockham allows a proposition to come out true
even in the case where its subject term has an empty appellative domain.
But why? Well, the medievals construed *O*-propositions as the contradictories of *A*-propositions. As Ockham interprets it 'Some *A* is not *B*' is
simply 'It is not the case that every *A* is *B*', but, then, the truth conditions
for the *O*-propositions of E^{**} can be obtained merely by negating the
truth conditions for *A*-propositions in E^{**}. In (2) of the truth conditions
for A-propositions, we have a formula incorporating terminal disjunction;
but as we have seen the terminal disjunction operating there can be eliminated in favor of propositional disjunction, so that the expansion specified
in (2) above can be read as

$$[(A_1 \text{ is } B_1) \vee (A_1 \text{ is } B_2) \vee \ldots \vee (A_1 \text{ is } B_n)] \wedge$$
$$[(A_2 \text{ is } B_1) \vee (A_2 \text{ is } B_2) \vee \ldots \vee (A_2 \text{ is } B_n)] \wedge \ldots \wedge$$
$$[A_n \text{ is } B_1) \vee (A_n \text{ is } B_2) \vee \ldots \vee (A_n \text{ is } B_n)].$$

Once we make this transformation we can see how Ockham's account of
O-propositions follows directly from his account of the truth conditions for
A-propositions, for he tells us that E^{**} propositions of the form

Some *A* is not *B*

are true if and only if it is not the case that either $\{AD/{}^{\epsilon}A'\}$ is non-
empty or the expansion just mentioned holds; but employing truth functional equivalences, this is simply to say that E^{**} propositions of the form

Some *A* is not *B*

are true just in case

(1) $\{AD/{}^{\epsilon}A'\}$ is empty; or
(2) $[<(A_1 \text{ is not } B_1) \wedge (A_1 \text{ is not } B_2) \wedge \ldots \wedge$
       $(A_1 \text{ is not } B_n)> \vee <(A_2 \text{ is not } B_1) \wedge (A_2 \text{ is not } B_2)$
       $\wedge \ldots \wedge (A_2 \text{ is not } B_n)> \vee \ldots \vee <(A_n \text{ is not } B_1) \wedge$
       $(A_n \text{ is not } B_2) \wedge \ldots \wedge (A_n \text{ is not } B_n)>]$ is true (where
       A_1-A_n and B_1-B_n exhaust $\{AD/{}^{\epsilon}A'\}$ and $\{AD/{}^{\epsilon}B'\}$
       respectively).

Ockham's interpretation of *E*-propositions in E^{**} does not differ from
that provided by the contemporary logician, nor should this surprise us.
On both accounts *E*-propositions are taken to be the contradictories of
I-propositions; and since *I*-propositions receive the same treatment on both

accounts, their contradictories will as well. To construct the truth conditions for E-propositions in E^{**} we need merely negate the truth conditions for I-propositions, so that E^{**} propositions of the form

No A is B

come out true just in case either

(1) $\{AD/`A`\}$ is empty; or

(2) $[<(A_1 \text{ is not } B_1) \wedge (A_1 \text{ is not } B_2) \wedge \ldots \wedge (A_1 \text{ is not } B_n)> \wedge <(A_2 \text{ is not } B_1) \wedge (A_2 \text{ is not } B_2) \wedge \ldots \wedge (A_2 \text{ is not } B_n)> \wedge \ldots \wedge <(A_n \text{ is not } B_1) \wedge (A_n \text{ is not } B_2) \wedge \ldots \wedge (A_n \text{ is not } B_n)>]$ is true (where A_1-A_n and B_1-B_n exhaust $\{AD/`A`\}$ and $\{AD/`B`\}$ respectively).

And by interpreting E-propositions in this way the tie between 'no' and 'some $\ldots$ not' is preserved in the bargain.

We have so far interpreted these accounts as statements of truth conditions, but when we eliminate their meta-linguistic overtones, we get what Ockham construes as analyses of the meaning of the A, E, I and O propositions of E^{**}. Thus, he takes it to be part of the meaning of the E^{**} proposition 'Every A is B' that there be A's; and he thinks that 'No A is B', as it appears in E^{**}, is to be analyzed as the disjunctive proposition that either there are no A's or that every A is such that it is not B.

IV

But, of course, E^{**} is not our language. To arrive at a theory of supposition that can handle the complete range of propositions we employ, we must extend the account to handle the supposition of terms in past and future propositions and in modal contexts. In closing I want to consider the resources in Ockham's analysis for dealing with these cases.

Once again let us begin by enriching our imaginary language. Let us increase the propositional resources of E^{**} by the addition of all the non-modal propositions of English which incorporate the past and future tenses, and let us call this new language E^{***}. Now, it might seem that the new cases which E^{***} brings to the scene could be handled in a straightforward way. We could begin by assigning new domains to our general terms (i.e., domains of past objects and domains of future objects); then, retaining the definitions of the various modes of supposition as they function in E^{**}, we could make explicit in our applications of these definitions to the deviant cases that the domains in question are the new domains. Thus, to handle E^{***} propositions of the form 'Some A was B', we could assign to 'A and 'B' domains consisting of all and only those objects that were A and were B at any moment prior to the present— preterite domains for 'A' and 'B' ($\{PD/'A'\}$ and $\{PD/'B'\}$). These new domains would incorporate some, but perhaps not all of the objects comprising $\{AD/'A'\}$ and $\{AD/'B'\}$ and, presumably many other objects as well. Having identified these new domains we could say that E^{***} propositions of the form

> Some A was B

are true just in case

(1) $\{PD/'A'\}$ is non-empty; and
(2) $[<(A_1$ was $B_1) \lor (A_1$ was $B_2) \lor \ldots \ldots \lor$
       $(A_1$ was $B_n)> \lor <(A_2$ was $B_1) \lor (A_2$ was $B_2)$
       $\lor \ldots \lor (A_2$ was $B_n)> \lor \ldots \lor <(A_n$ was $B_1) \lor$
       $(A_n$ was $B_2) \lor \ldots \lor (A_n$ was $B_n)>]$ is true
       (where A_1-A_n and B_1-B_n exhaust $\{PD/'A'\}$ and $\{PD/'B'\}$
       respectively).

Although this sort of account appears plausible, Ockham finds it unsatisfactory. In informal terms the account construes the E^{***} form 'Some A was B' as the claim that at some time in the past something was simultaneously both A and B, and while this analysis does justice to many E^{***} propositions there are others that resist it. The E^{***} proposition 'Some good man was evil', for example, is quite likely true, but in the account just presented it can be true only if at some time in the past the inconsistent proposition 'This good man is evil' was true. In fact all that is required for the truth of 'Some good man was evil' is the existence of at least one man who, while now good, was formerly evil. Ockham takes this as his clue for dealing with the past tense propositions of E^{***}. He contends that 'Some A was B' is implicitly the disjunctive proposition 'Either some object that now is A was formerly B, or some object that was formerly A was formerly B'; and he insists on writing the disjunctive character of the proposition into the statement of its truth conditions, so that E^{***} propositions of the form

> Some A was B

are true just in case

either (1) $\{AD/'A'\}$ is non-empty; and

        (2) $[<(A_1$ was $B_1)$ ∨ $(A_1$ was $B_2)$ ∨ $\ldots$ ∨
$(A_1$ was $B_n)>$ ∨ $<(A_2$ was $B_1)$ ∨ $(A_2$ was $B_2)$
∨ $\ldots$ ∨ $(A_2$ was $B_n)>$ ∨ $\ldots$ ∨
$<(A_n$ was $B_1)$ ∨ $(A_n$ was $B_2)$ ∨ $\ldots$ ∨
$(A_n$ was $B_n)>]$ is true (where A_1-A_n and
B_1-B_n exhaust $\{AD/'A'\}$ and $\{PD/'B'\}$
respectively);

or   (1) $\{PD/'A'\}$ is non-empty; and

        (2) $[<(A_1$ was $B_1)$ ∨ $(A_1$ was $B_2)$ ∨ $\ldots$ ∨ $(A_1$ was $B_n)>$∨
$<(A_2$ was $B_1)$ ∨ $(A_2$ was $B_2)$ ∨ $\ldots$ ∨ $(A_2$ was $B_n)>$
∨ $\ldots$ ∨ $<(A_n$ was $B_1)$ ∨ $(A_n$ was $B_2)$ ∨ $\ldots$ ∨
$(A_n$ was $B_n)>]$ is true (where A_1-A_n and B_1-B_n
exhaust $\{PD/'A'\}$ and $\{PD/'B'\}$ respectively).

Past tense propositions of the A, E, and O forms can be treated in precisely the same way, and a parallel form of analysis will accommodate the various general propositions of E^{***} whose main verb is in the future tense. According to Ockham such propositions are implicitly disjunctive; but if we are to exhibit the character of the disjunction, we must assign to each general term a domain consisting of all and only those objects which at any time later than the present will be its significata$_1$. Employing these future domains ($\{FD/'T'\}$) we can say, for example, that E^{***} propositions of the form

No A will be B

are true just in case

either (1) $\{AD/'A'\}$ is empty; or
$[<(A_1$ will not be $B_1)$ ∧ $(A_1$ will not be $B_2)$
∧ $\ldots$ ∧ $(A_1$ will not be $B_n)>$ ∧ $<(A_2$ will
not be $B_1)$ ∧ $(A_2$ will not be $B_2)$ ∧ $\ldots$ ∧
$(A_2$ will not be $B_n)>$ ∧ $\ldots$ ∧ $<(A_n$ will not
be $B_1)$ ∧ $(A_n$ will not be $B_2)$ ∧ $\ldots$ ∧
$(A_n$ will not be $B_n)>]$ is true (where A_1-A_n
and B_1-B_n exhaust $\{AD/'A'\}$ and $\{FD/'B'\}$
respectively).

or   (2) $\{FD/'A'\}$ is empty; or
$[<(A_1$ will not be $B_1)$ ∧ $(A_1$ will not be $B_2)$ ∧ $\ldots$ ∧
$(A_1$ will not be $B_n)>$ ∧ $<(A_2$ will not be $B_1)$ ∧
$(A_2$ will not be $B_2)$ ∧ $\ldots$ ∧ $(A_2$ will not be $B_n)>$ ∧

$\ldots\ldots \wedge <(A_n$ will not be $B_1) \wedge (A_n$ will not be $B_2) \wedge$
$\ldots\ldots \wedge (A_n$ will not be $B_n)>]$ is true (where A_1-A_n
and B_1-B_n exhaust $\{FD/{}^{\prime}A^{\prime}\}$ and $\{FD/{}^{\prime}B^{\prime}\}$ respectively).

Now, it is tempting to think that the truth conditions for the singular propositions incorporated in this schema (as well as that provided in the case of 'Some A was B') are self-explanatory; for it seems only plausible to think that 'A_1 was B_1' is true just in case 'A_1 is B_1' was true at some time in the past and that 'A_1 will not be B_1' is true just in case 'A_1 is not B_1' will be true at some point in the future. But appealing as it is, Ockham rejects this sort of account. We can get at his reasons for rejecting it if we reflect on the fact that expressions of the form 'A_1' and 'B_1' can be supplanted by a variety of kinds of singular terms. They deputize not only for proper names, but also for demonstratives, and demonstratives-cum-general terms (i.e., by expressions like 'this A' and 'this B' where 'A' and 'B' are the general terms which 'A_1' and 'B_1' limit).[14] When we stated the truth conditions for the identity statements in E^* and E^{**}, it was unnecessary to take account of this fact; but in the case of E^{***} propositions, we must be more discriminating.

The claim that a past or future tensed identity statement is true just in case the corresponding present tensed identity statement was or will be true works well enough where the singular terms embedded in the past or future tensed identity statement are proper names or demonstratives; but our experience with 'Some good man was evil' suggests that the account will yield unsatisfactory results when we confront past and future tensed identity statements whose singular terms are demonstratives-cum-general terms. To stick with our example, 'This good man was that evil individual' is of the form 'A_1 was B_1'; but while it may well be true, the corresponding present tensed proposition ('This good man is that evil individual') was never true. This is not to say that the present truth of 'This good man was that evil individual' does not presuppose the past truth of any present tensed identity statement; the point is rather that the present tensed identity statement in question cannot be one in which the demonstrative-cum-general term 'this good man' plays any role. Ockham exploits this insight and tells us that 'A_1 was B_1' is true just in case 'a is B_1' (where 'a' is a demonstrative or proper name whose suppositum is identical with the suppositum of 'A_1') was true at some time in the past and that 'A_1 will be B_1' is true just in case 'a is B_1' (where parallel restrictions are placed on 'a') will be true at some time in the future.[15]

To conclude our succession of imaginary languages, let us add to E^{***} the various propositions of English which incorporate the modal notions of possibility and necessity. Now, if it is clear how we are to extend Ockham's analysis to cover general propositions incorporating past and future tenses, it is less easy to be certain how his account handles the propositions proper to our new language, $E{***}$. The difficulty is that Ockham's remarks on this topic are sparse; and where he does consider examples, they tend to be propositions the contemporary philosopher would be reluctant to construe as modal. The examples are generally propositions of the form 'Some A can be B' or 'Every A is capable of being B'. Ockham's strategy with propositions of these forms is to invoke the kind of analysis to which he subjects supposition in past and future propositions. We are told to assign domains of possibilia to 'A' and 'B' ($\{\Diamond D/\text{'}A\text{'}\}$ and $\{\Diamond D/\text{'}B\text{'}\}$). Ockham never tells us precisely which entities we are to admit into these domains; but presumably he wants $\{\Diamond D/\text{'}A\text{'}\}$, for example, to include not only all of the objects constituting $\{PD/\text{'}A\text{'}\}$, $\{AD/\text{'}A\text{'}\}$, and $\{FD/\text{'}A\text{'}\}$, but other "objects" as well— "objects" that will never be actualized but are such that (a) their being actualized entails no impossibility and (b) were they to be actualized, they would be A. Employing domains of this sort we are told to treat 'Every A can be B' in the way we treated 'Some A was B' and 'No A will be B'— as an implicitly disjunctive proposition, so that 'Every A can be B' is parsed as 'Either every object in $\{AD/\text{'}A\text{'}\}$ can be an object in $\{\Diamond D/\text{'}B\text{'}\}$, or every object in $\{\Diamond D/\text{'}A\text{'}\}$ can be an object in $\{\Diamond D/\text{'}B\text{'}\}$ '.

Apart from the new domains, then, the machinery required to handle 'Every A can be B' is simply the machinery at work in Ockham's treatment of the propositions peculiar to $E{***}$. When we turn to propositions that are more explicitly modal, Ockham seems to think that the same type of analysis applies. Thus, $E{****}$ propositions of the form 'Every A is possibly B' are to receive precisely the same treatment accorded 'Every A can be B'. Indeed, the text suggests that Ockham construes 'Every A is possibly B' as synonymous with 'Every A can be B'; and although the textual evidence is weaker, Ockham seems to think that a parallel analysis holds in the case of $E{****}$ propositions of the form 'Every A is necessarily B'. There are no reliable clues as to the domains 'A' and 'B' are to be assigned in this case; but perhaps Ockham again wants these to be $\{AD/\text{'}A\text{'}\}$, $\{\Diamond D/\text{'}A\text{'}\}$, and $\{\Diamond D/\text{'}B\text{'}\}$ respectively, so that $E{****}$ propositions which exhibit the form 'Every A is necessarily B' are to be analyzed as 'Either every object in $\{AD/\text{'}A\text{'}\}$ is necessarily an object in $\{\Diamond D/\text{'}B\text{'}\}$, or every object in $\{\Diamond D/\text{'}A\text{'}\}$ is necessarily an object in $\{\Diamond D/\text{'}B\text{'}\}$ '.

The various disjunctions which explicate the general propositions peculiar to $E****$ give way to singular propositions like 'A_1 can be B_1', 'A_1 is possibly B_1', and 'A_1 is necessarily B_1'; and Ockham's account of the truth conditions for these propositions parallels that provided in the case of propositions like 'A_1 was B_1'. There, the move was to interpret the present truth of past and future tensed identity statements in terms of the past or future truth of present tensed identity statements. In the same way, in dealing with identity statements incorporating the modalities, Ockham wants to claim that a proposition like 'A_1 is possibly B_1' is true just in case some assertoric identity statement is possible. Our difficulties with 'A_1 was B_1' and 'A_1 will be B_1', however, should alert us to the fact that where 'A_1 is possibly B_1' is the proposition whose truth conditions are to be stated, the relevant assertoric proposition cannot, in general, be 'A_1 is B_1'. 'This white man is possibly black', for example, may well be true; but the proposition 'The white man is black' is impossible. Once again, it is demonstratives-cum-general terms that cause problems, and Ockham handles these problems in just the way he handled them within the context of $E***$. He tells us that 'A_1 is possibly B_1' is true just in case 'a is B_1' (where 'a' is a demonstrative or proper name whose suppositum is identical with the suppositum of 'A_1') is possible; and he holds that a parallel account works in the case of identity statements embedding the adverb 'necessarily'.

But this technique of moving the modality from the inside to the outside of a proposition suggests that even if my account is faithful to Ockham's treatment of the propositions peculiar to $E****$, it handles only half the difficulties associated with supposition in this language. The technique reminds us that the modalities can enter discourse either in their *de re* form (where they intervene adverbially between subject and predicate) or in their *de dicto* form (where they are predicated of propositions taken as wholes), and my account covers only the supposition of terms in $E****$ propositions which engage modalities *de re*.

Unfortunately, Ockham's discussion of supposition is of no help in filling in this gap; for in that section of the *Summa*, he completely ignores the supposition of terms in contexts which involve modality *de dicto*. In a later section of the *Summa,* where Ockham actually treats the distinction between modality *de re* and modality *de dicto,* he once again fails to relate the distinction to his theory of supposition.[16] What I would like to suggest is that his failure to do this may not be a mere oversight on Ockham's part.

In discussing the case where a modality is predicated of a general proposition, Ockham asks whether the resulting proposition is properly classified as general. He never provides any determinate answer to the question; but he expresses doubt about the view that propositions of the form ' "Every A is B" is necessary' are to be construed as universal affirmative propositions. The grounds of his doubt here are perhaps revealed in an earlier passage, where Ockham argues that truly predicating a modal expression of a general proposition does not guarantee that the same modal expression can be truly applied to any instantiation of that proposition. His example is the $E****$ proposition ' "Every true contingent proposition is true" is necessary'; and he contends that while this proposition is true, its instantiations (e.g., ' " 'Nixon is president' is true" is necessary') are obviously false. The force of this example should be clear: when a modality is predicated of a general proposition, the patterns of "descent" and " ascent" which dominate Ockham's theory of supposition do not apply. But since Ockham construes those patterns as definitive of the concept of a general proposition, it is plausible to think that he sees in their inapplicability to the case of modality *de dicto* grounds for doubting that the propositions in question are properly construed as general.

But if they are not general, it is reasonable to ask just how they are to be construed. Ockham is reluctant to commit himself on this point, but occasionally he implies that they are to be treated as singular propositions. Although he never deals with the point in any detail, it is easy enough to see why Ockham finds such an account appealing. The double quotes suggest that 'Every true contingent proposition is true' has not personal, but material supposition in ' "Every true contingent proposition is true" is necessary'. Now, if we take this suggestion seriously, we will be inclined to say that in the relevant context 'Every true contingent proposition is true' is functioning as a singular term taking itself as suppositum; and, consequently, we will be tempted to think of the proposition whose subject it is as a singular proposition. But if this line of reasoning represents an accurate reconstruction of Ockham's position, then the fact that he never confronts this sort of case with his theory of general supposition has a ready explanation: the theory simply does not apply there. General terms which (like 'true contingent proposition' and 'true' in our example) come under the scope of a modality *de dicto* are not suppositing personally and so, a fortiori, are not suppositing in any of the three styles which are exhaustive of Ockham's notion of general supposition.[17]

Now, while $E****$ is either English or something quite close to English, my account of Ockham's treatment of $E****$ hardly handles all of the difficulties which arise with regard to that language. I have, for example, considered only generality in propositions that can be plausibly interpreted on the subject-predicate model. I have not considered the supposition of general terms within the context of propositions where one or more quantifiers come under the scope of some other quantifier. Neither have I considered the difficulties associated with supposition in epistemic contexts. That I have not dealt with these and other problems about supposition is traceable, in part, to the aim of the paper — to provide a brief reconstruction of Ockham's theory; it is also traceable to Ockham's failure to treat these problems in any detailed way. But despite its short-comings, my account has, I hope, shown the rigor and sophistication of Ockham's theory of generality. Perhaps, too, it has done something to dispel the myth that logic was born at the hands of Russell and Whitehead.

NOTES

[1]As Ockham employs the term, a proposition is an indicative sentence possessing a truth value. I shall use the term in the same way.

[2]Ockham would be unhappy with my account of both material and simple supposition. He holds that a term can exhibit material supposition when it is suppositing for an expression other than itself. Thus, Ockham claims that in the Latin sentence 'Hominem currere est propositio vera', 'hominem currere' is suppositing materially; nonetheless, it is suppositing here not for itself, but for 'Homo currit'. Likewise, he thinks that a term can supposit simply when it supposits for an intention of the soul whose semantical role in the language of the soul is different from the semantical role which the suppositing term plays in overt speech. Thus, 'hominem currere' supposits simply in '*Hominem currere* est propositio mentalis', but it supposits in that proposition not for the intention (*hominem currere*) whose semantical role it shares, but for the intention *Homo currit*. My own view is that Ockham is confused here. Were he to have attended to the distinction between direct and indirect quotation, he would not have assimilated what are clearly quite different uses of language.

[3]Actually, the issue is more complicated than my definition suggests; for the subject of '*Intention* is an intention' is suppositing simply, even though it is suppositing for one of its significata$_1$. Likewise, although the word 'noun' is suppositing for one of its significata$_1$ in ' "Noun" begins with an "n" ', it is suppositing materially in that context. Ockham handles the complexities such examples introduce by saying that where a term supposits personally, it supposits for the object or objects it signifies$_1$ *and is functioning significatively*. We catch the force of this qualification if we note that all the exceptions to the rule that a term suppositing personally supposits for its significata$_1$ are general terms. Some general terms (those signifying$_1$ certain intentions or linguistic expressions) can supposit materially or simply and yet be suppositing for one of their significata$_1$, but when they do they cease to play their standard signi-ficative role and function as singular rather than general terms.

[4]Ockham never explicitly tells us that his initial account of supposition is subject to these limitations, but in subsequent chapters of the section on supposition, he points to deficiencies in the original account and revises it accordingly. I shall attempt to organize Ockham's presentation of his theory by construing his original account and the revisions he points to as a series of different theories of supposition, each more powerful than its predecessor. The final theory in the series will present itself as a general theory capable of handling the supposition of terms in all linguistic contexts.

[5]By the time Ockham wrote the *Summa,* logicians employed the term '*appellatio*' more narrowly to refer to a property possessed exclusively by expressions functioning as predicates. Ockham himself almost never uses the expression.

[6]Although Ockham does not use the term '*ascensus*' in this context, his contemporaries frequently use it in the sense in which it is employed here.

[7]Actually, Ockham's scheme is more complicated than my account suggests. He divides confused and distributive supposition into two kinds—mobile and immobile supposition. It is only in the case of confused and distributive supposition which is mobile that my definition applies. Where a term supposits immobily (e.g., as 'man' supposits in 'Every man except Socrates runs'), the "descent" which the use of the term licenses does not extend across the appellative domain of the suppositing term; one or more elements are excluded from the "descent." Immobile supposition does not play a very significant role in Ockham's theory, so that, in the interests of simplifying the theory, I ignore it, but it should be clear that my framework for explicating the forms of general supposition could be employed in its case.

[8]Ockham interprets 'Every man is this animal or that animal or . . .' as a proposition in which it is affirmed of each man in turn, that he/she is this animal or that animal or . . . In the interest of keeping the complications to a minimum, I do not consider the first part of Ockhams' definition here. The claim is that where a term has merely confused supposition, its embedding proposition is entailed by any proposition which instantiates it with respect to the term with merely confused supposition. Thus, 'Every man is this animal' entails 'Every man is an animal', inasmuch as if the first proposition is true, the second is true as well; but, of course, 'Every man is this animal' can be true only when $\{AD/\text{'man'}\}$ consists of just one element, so that while the entailment holds, the conditions under which it can apply are almost never satisfied.

[9]My account suggests the possibility of a fourth style of general supposition, a style that is conjunctive but not propositionally inclusive. One might argue that this style of supposition is required to handle the kind of referential force exhibited by 'apostles' in 'All the apostles are twelve'. An even more likely candidate would be 'dog' in 'Some man loves every dog.'

[10]Actually, my account of Ockhams' theory deals only with the supposition of terms in propositions that involve a single quantifier. Ockham himself attempted to apply his theory to the case where one or more quantifiers come under the scope of some other quantifier; but although he makes a number of interesting remarks in this context, it would be wrong to think that he has provided anything like a generalized theory to handle propositions exhibiting nested quantifiers.

[11]Although Ockham is not dealing with the formulae of quantification theory, my account of his view suggests certain affinities with the so-called substitutional theory of quantification. Now, there are fairly clear signs of an incipient substitutionalism in Ockham's account, but he sometimes uses language with a referentialist ring to it. We need not, on this account, accuse Ockham of confusion; for since the domains his theory is geared to handle are all finite, the two views would come to much the same thing.

[12]But while the analogy exists, it would be a mistake to represent the analyses Ockham provides by means of the formulae of quantification theory; for in the language of quantification, it is the quantifier, together with the variables it binds, that plays the referring role. But the apparatus of quantification is the logician's way of reconstructing the role of syncategorematic expressions like 'some' and 'every'. To express Ockham's theory in this way, then, would completely misrepresent what he was trying to do, viz., to provide a theory of generality according to which it is categorematic rather than syncategorematic terms that play the referential role in general propositions.

[13]It is tempting to argue that Ockham would have held that the domains in question are infinite, for he surely would have accepted the Aristotelian slogan that the members of a species are infinite in number. My suspicion, however, is that the concept of infinity at work in this slogan bears no affinity to that found in post-Cantorian mathematics. The slogan was generally employed in explaining the view that it is the universal rather than the individual which is the concern of the sciences. The force of the slogan, then, is simply that the individuals falling under the various infimae species are too numerous to constitute, each of them, subjects for scientific research. Neither does the mathematics of Ockham's day employ a notion of infinity that is recognizably like that found in contemporary mathematics. It is only plausible to assume, then, that it never occurred to Ockham that there was any need for a stronger theory of generality than that provided by supposition theory; and in any case, Ockhams account of number-words bears sufficient affinities to constructivist theories of numbers to suggest that he would have grave doubts about the Cantorian infinities.

[14]Since Latin lacks the definite article, Ockham does not consider the case of definite descriptions. The remarks that hold true of demonstratives-cum-general terms will, however, apply in the case of definite descriptions as well.

[15]Where 'A_1' is a demonstrative or a proper name, 'a' may, of course, be just 'A_1'. Ockham himself limits the characterization to demonstratives, but it seems to me that his intentions are better served by my more general characterization.

[16]The passage in question is found in Part II of the *Summa*.

[17]It is easy enough to see why Ockham might have been reluctant to commit himself to this view. Since it effectively denies that the proposition 'Every A is B' has any internal structure in "Every A is B" is necessary', it makes it difficult to explain just how the proposition figures in inferential contexts. From ' "Every A is B" is necessary' and ' "Every B is C" is necessary', we can infer ' "Every A is C" is necessary'; and clearly it is the internal structures of 'Every A is B' and 'Every B is C' that guarantee the inference.

Summa Logicae
PART I: ON TERMS

1: On the Term in General

All those who treat of logic try to show that arguments are composed of porpositions and propositions of terms. Thus, a term is simply a component part of a proposition. When he defines the notion of a term in the first book of the *Prior Analytics*, Aristotle says, "I call that a term into which a proposition is resolved (i.e., the predicate or that of which it is predicated), when it is asserted or denied that something is or is not the case."[1]

Although every term is (or could be) a part of a proposition, not all terms are of the same kind. Thus, to gain a full understanding of the nature of terms one must know some of the divisions that are drawn among them.

As Boethius points out in his Commentary on the first book of the *De Interpretatione*, discourse is of three types—the written, the spoken, and the conceptual (this last existing only in the mind.)[2] In the same way there are three sorts of terms—written, spoken, and conceptual. The written term is a part of a proposition which has been inscribed on something material and is capable of being seen by the bodily eye. The spoken term is a part of a proposition which has been uttered aloud and is capable of being heard with the bodily ear. The conceptual term is an intention or impression of the soul which signifies or consignifies something naturally and is capable of being a part of mental proposition and of suppositing in such a proposition for the thing it signifies. Thus, these conceptual terms and the propositions composed of them are the mental words which, according to St. Augustine in chapter 15 of *De Trinitate*, belong to no language.[3] They reside in the intellect alone and are

[1] 24^b 16-18.
[2] *Patrologia Latina*, J. P. Migne, ed. (Paris, 1847), T. 64, 297 B.
[3] P. L., T. 42. 1047.

incapable of being uttered aloud, although the spoken words which are subordinated to them as signs are uttered aloud.

I say that spoken words are signs subordinated to concepts or intentions of
the soul not because in the strict sense of 'signify' they always signify the concepts of the soul primarily and properly. The point is rather that spoken words
are used to signify the very things that are signified by concepts of the mind,
so that a concept primarily and naturally signifies something and a spoken
word signifies the same thing secondarily. Thus, suppose a spoken word is used
to signify something signified by a particular concept of the mind. If that concept were to change its signification, by that fact alone it would happen that
the spoken word would change its signification, even in the absence of any new
linguistic convention.

This is all that Aristotle means when he says that spoken words are signs of
the impressions of the soul[4] and Boethius means the same thing when he says
that spoken words signify concepts.[5] In general, whenever writers say that all
spoken words signify or serve as signs of impressions, they only mean that
spoken words secondarily signify the things impressions of the soul primarily
signify. Nonetheless, it is true that some spoken words primarily designate impressions of the soul or concepts, but these words secondarily designate other
intentions of the soul as will be shown later.

The same sort of relation I have claimed to hold between spoken words and
impressions or intentions or concepts holds between written words and spoken
words.

Now, there are certain differences among these three kinds of terms. For
one thing the concept or impression of the soul signifies naturally; whereas
the spoken or written term signifies only conventionally. This difference gives
rise to a further difference. We can decide to alter the signification of a spoken
or written term, but no decision or agreement on the part of anyone can have
the effect of altering the signification of a conceptual term.

Nevertheless, to silence hairsplitters it should be pointed out that the word
'sign' has two different senses. In one sense a sign is anything which when apprehended brings something else to mind. Here, a sign need not, as has been
shown elsewhere, enable us to grasp the thing signified for the first time, but
only after we have some sort of habitual knowledge of the thing. In this sense
of 'sign' the spoken word is a natural sign of a thing, the effect is a sign of its
cause, and the barrel-hoop is a sign of wine in the tavern. However, I have not
been using the term 'sign' in this wide sense. In another sense a sign is anything which (1) brings something to mind and can supposit for that thing; (2)
can be added to a sign of this sort in a proposition (e.g., syncategorematic ex-

[4] 16^a 3-7.
[5] P. L., T. 64, 298 A.

pressions, verbs, and other parts of speech lacking a determinate signification); or (3) can be composed of things that are signs of either sort (e.g., propositions). Taking the term 'sign' in this sense the spoken word is not the natural sign of anything.

2: On Three Senses of 'Term'

The word 'term' has three senses. In one sense a term is anything which can be the copula or the extreme (i.e., subject or predicate) of a categorical proposition or some determination of the verb or extreme. In this sense even a proposition can be a term since it can be a part of a proposition. The following, for example, is true: ' "Man is an animal" is a true proposition'. Here, the whole proposition, 'Man is an animal', is the subject and 'true proposition', the predicate. In another sense 'term' is used in contrast with 'proposition', so that every simple expression is called a term. It was in this sense that I used the expression in the preceding chapter.

In a third and still narrower sense 'term' is used to mean that which, when taken significatively, is able to be the subject or the predicate of a proposition. Using the expression in this sense it is incorrect to call verbs, conjunctions, adverbs, prepositions, and interjections terms. Even many names are not terms in this sense. Syncategorematic names are the case in point. Although they may be the extremes of a proposition when construed materially or simply, they cannot be when construed significatively. Thus, the sentence ' "Reads" is a verb' is well formed and true if 'reads' is construed materially; however, if we were to take the expression significatively, the proposition would make no sense. The same is true of the following propositions: ' "Every" is a name', ' "Formerly" is an adverb', ' "If" is a conjunction', ' "From" is a preposition'. It is this sense of 'term' that Aristotle defines in the first book of the *Prior Analytics*.[1]

In this third sense of 'term' not only can one simple expression be a term, but even an expression composed of two simple expressions can be a term. Thus, the combination of an adjective and a noun and even the combination of a participle and an adverb or a preposition and its object can yield an expression that is in this sense correctly called a term, for a compound expression formed in one of these ways can be the subject or the predicate of a proposition. In the

[1] 24^b 16-18.

proposition 'Every white man is a man', neither 'man' nor 'white' is the subject; rather, the compound of the two,'white man', is the subject. The same holds in the case of the proposition 'The one running quickly is a man'; neither 'the one running' nor 'quickly' is the subject; it is the compound expression 'the one running quickly' that serves as subject.

Nor is it only a name in the nominative case that can be a term. Even in one of the oblique cases a name can be a term, for in those cases a name can be the subject or predicate of a proposition. Still, in an oblique case a name cannot be the subject with respect to just any verb. Thus, the Latin sentence 'Hominis videt asinum' is not well formed, although 'Hominis est asinus' is. But the question of which verbs can and cannot take an oblique case as subject is one that belongs to grammar, the role of which is to deal with constructions of words.

3: On the Correspondence between Vocal and Mental Terms

Now that we have exposed the various senses of 'term' we should continue our account of the divisions drawn among simple terms. There are, we have seen, three kinds of simple terms—spoken, written, and conceptual. In all three cases we can subdivide the notion of a term in similar ways. In the case of spoken and written language terms are either names, verbs, or other parts of speech (i.e., pronouns, participles, adverbs, conjunctions, prepositions); likewise, the intentions of the soul are either names, verbs, or other parts of speech (i.e., pronouns, adverbs, conjunctions, prepositions). However, since there is no reason to postulate irrelevant elements among mental terms, one might wonder whether, among intentions, participles constitute a separate part of speech over and above verbs in the way that they do in spoken and written language; for the participle of any verb, with the appropriate form of 'to be', signifies precisely what the corresponding form of that verb by itself signifies. The multiplicity of synonymous expressions in no way enhances the significative power of language; whatever is signified by an expression is signified equally by its synonym. The point of the multiplicity at work in the case of synonymous terms is the embellishment of speech or something of that nature, so that the relevant multiplicity has no place at the conceptual level. But since the distinction which spoken language exhibits between verbs and their participial forms does not enable us to express anything we could not express without the distinction, there is no need to postulate mental participles to correspond to spoken participles. A similar doubt is possible in the case of pronouns.

Mental and spoken names, on the other hand, differ in that although all of the grammatical features of mental names belong to spoken names, the reverse is not true; whereas some grammatical features belong to both mental and spoken names, others are peculiar to spoken and written names (the grammatical features of these two kinds of names being always the same). Case and number belong to mental and spoken names alike. Thus, just as the spoken propositions 'Man is an animal' and 'Man is not the animals' have distinct predicates, one of which is singular and the other, plural, so it is with the corresponding mental propositions which the mind asserts before any word is uttered: the predicate of the one is singular; that of the other, plural. Further, the spoken propositions 'Man is man' and 'Man is not man's' have predicates which differ in case; the same holds true of the corresponding propositions in the mind.

On the other hand, gender and declension are grammatical features peculiar to spoken and written names. These features do not add to the significative power of language. Thus, it sometimes happens that two names are synonymous; and, nevertheless, they are of different genders or belong to different declensions. Consequently, it is not necessary to assign a corresponding multiplicity of grammatical forms to natural signs, for we can eliminate from mental names all of those grammatical features with respect to which spoken names can differ, while remaining synonymous. It is less clear whether the distinction between an adjective and its comparative and superlative forms is limited to conventional signs, but since there would be little profit in pursuing it I shall not deal with the issue. The notion of quality prompts a similar question. I shall consider it in another context.

The foregoing makes it clear that although sometimes the thing signified is such that merely by varying certain grammatical features (e.g., case, number, or degree of comparison), we can alter the truth-value of propositions, this never happens with gender or declension. Admittedly, in the interests of good grammar, we must frequently pay attention to the gender of a name. Thus, whereas the Latin sentence 'Homo est albus' is well-formed, 'Homo est alba' is not, the difference being traceable only to a difference in gender. But good grammar aside the gender and declension of the subject or predicate are irrelevant. On the other hand, to know whether a proposition is true or false one must attend to the number and case of the subject and predicate. Thus, while 'Man is an animal' is true, 'Man is the animals' is false. The same point holds in other cases.

Thus, while spoken and written names have some grammatical features of their own, they share others with mental words. The same is true in the case of verbs. Grammatical features that are common include mood, number, tense, voice, and person. In the case of mood this is clear, for distinct mental propositions correspond to the spoken propositions 'Socrates reads' and 'Would that Socrates read'. This is true also in the case of voice, for we must assign different mental propositions to the spoken propositions 'Socrates loves' and 'Socrates is loved'. Nevertheless, mental verbs exhibit only three voices, for the common and deponent verbs of spoken languages do not effect the significative power of language. Common verbs are equivalent to verbs in both the active and passive voice; whereas, deponents are equivalent to verbs in the middle or active voice; but, then, we need not attribute those grammatical forms to mental verbs. Number, however, is a grammatical feature that mental verbs exhibit, for different mental propositions correspond to the following: 'You are reading' and 'You all are reading'. The same is true in the case of tense, for different mental propositions correspond to the spoken propositions: 'You are reading' and 'You have read'. The point also holds for person, for we must distinguish mental propositions in the case of 'You read' and 'I read'.

That it should be necessary to postulate such things as mental names, adverbs, conjunctions, and prepositions is shown by the fact that to every spoken proposition there corresponds a mental proposition. Just as those parts of the spoken proposition which contribute to the significative power of language are distinct, so also are the corresponding elements in mental propositions. Therefore, since spoken names, verbs, adverbs, conjunctions, and prepositions are essential in generating all the diverse propositions and sentences making up spoken language (for with only spoken names and verbs at our disposal, we would be unable to express all that we can express with the help of the additional parts of speech), distinct elements must likewise be necessary in the generation of mental propositions.

Grammatical features peculiar to spoken and written verbs include conjugation and figure, for sometimes it happens that verbs from different conjugations are synonymous; and similarly, with verbs that differ in figure.

The careful reader will have no difficulty in expanding the foregoing remarks to cover the remaining parts of speech and their grammatical features. Nor should anyone be surprised that I speak of mental names and verbs. Let him first read Boethius' commentary on the *De Interpretatione*; he will find the same thing there.[1] However, when Aristotle defines both the name and the verb in terms of spoken words, he is using the terms 'name' and 'verb' in a narrower sense to cover only the spoken name and the spoken verb.[2]

---

[1]   P.L., T. 64, 407 C.

[2] 16^a 19-20; 16^b 5-7.

4: On Categorematic and Syncategorematic Terms

Both spoken and mental terms are subject to yet another division, for some terms are categorematic while others are syncategorematic. Categorematic terms have a definite and determinate signification. Thus, the term 'man' signifies all men; the term 'animal', all animals; and the term 'whiteness', all whitenesses.

Examples of syncategorematic terms are 'every', 'no', 'some', 'all', 'except', 'so much', and 'insofar as'. None of these expressions has a definite and determinate signification, nor does any of them signify anything distinct from what is signified by categorematic terms. The number system provides a parallel here. 'Zero', taken by itself, does not signify anything, but when combined with some other numeral it makes that numeral signify something new. Likewise, a syncategorematic term does not, properly speaking, signify anything; however, when it is combined with a categorematic expression it makes that categorematic expression signify something or supposit for something in a determinate manner, or it performs some other function with regard to the relevant categorematic term. Thus, the syncategorematic term 'every' does not, by itself, signify any definite thing; but when it is combined with the term 'man', it makes that term stand or supposit confusedly and distributively for all men; when it is combined with the word 'stone', it makes that term stand for all stones; and when it is combined with the term 'whiteness', it makes the expression stand for all whitenesses. Other syncategorematic terms are like 'every'; for although, as I shall show later, the precise function of syncategorematic terms varies, the same general account holds for all.

Someone may object that since the term 'every' is significant, it must signify something. The correct response is that we call the term significant not because it signifies something, but because as I have indicated it can make a term signify something or stand or supposit for something. To use the language of Boethius, 'every' does not signify anything in a determinate or definite way;[1] the same holds true not only in the case of syncategorematic terms, but also in the case of conjunctions and prepositions.

However, the case is different with some adverbs, for they signify determinately the very things that categorematic names signify, although they signify them in a different mode of signification.

---

[1] P.L., T. 64, 552 C.

5: On Concrete and Abstract Names That Are Not Synonyms

Leaving aside the other parts of speech, we shall discuss names. First we shall examine the distinction between abstract and concrete names.

Abstract and concrete names are names which have the same stem but different endings. Thus, in each of the following pairs we have names that begin with the same syllable or sequence of syllables, but which differ in ending: 'just'—'justive', 'brave'—'bravery', 'animal'—'animality'. Always (or at least frequently) the abstract name has more syllables than the concrete. This is clear in the examples just presented. Equally often, the concrete name is an adjective and the abstract name a noun.

Concrete and abstract names can function in many ways. Sometimes the concrete name signifies, connotes, designates, or expresses and also supposits for something, which the abstract name in no way signifies and, consequently never supposits for. Examples are 'just'—'justice', 'white'—'whiteness', etc. 'Just' supposits for men in the proposition 'The just are virtuous'; it would be incorrect to say that it supposits for justice; for although justice is a virtue, it is not virtuous. On the other hand, 'justice' supposits for the quality of a man, not the man himself. It is because of this that it is impossible to predicate this sort of concrete name of its abstract counterpart: the two terms supposit for different things.

Concrete and abstract terms of this sort can function in one of three modes; we can treat these modes along the lines of species under a genus. In the first mode either the abstract expression supposits for some accident or form inhering in a subject and the concrete expression, for the subject of that form or accident, or, vice versa. Examples of concrete and abstract names functioning in this first mode are 'whiteness'—'white'; 'heat'—'hot'; and 'knowing'—'knowledge' (provided we limit ourselves to the knowledge of finite creatures), for in all these examples the abstract name supposits for an accident inhering in a subject and the concrete name for the subject of that accident. The reverse happens with names like 'fire' and 'fiery'. Thus, while 'fire' supposits for a subject, 'fiery', a concrete name, supposits for an accident of fire; for we say that the heat of the fire is fiery, but not that it is fire; and similarly, we say that knowledge is human, but not that it is a man.

In the second mode either the concrete name supposits for a part of a thing and the abstract, for the whole thing, or vice versa. 'Soul' and 'besouled' are examples; for man is besouled, but he is not a soul. Here, 'besouled' supposits for man and 'soul', for a part of man. However, in the propositions 'The soul is human' and 'The soul is not man', 'man', the abstract name, supposits for the whole and 'human', for the soul which is a part of man.

Nonetheless, it should be noticed that sometimes a concrete name can be used in two different senses, so that it can function in both the first and second modes. Thus, the name 'besouled' can supposit for a whole, since we say that man is besouled; and it can also supposit for the subject receiving the soul, since we say that the body, which is the other part of the composite, is besouled. Many other terms which can be used in a number of different senses behave like 'besouled' in this regard.

In the third mode concrete and abstract names supposit for distinct things, neither of which is a subject or part of the other. This can happen in many ways. Thus, the things signified might be related as cause and effect, as when we speak of a project as being human but not a man; or they might be related as sign and thing signified. Thus, we say that the difference of man is an essential difference, not because it is the essence of man, but because it is a sign of some part of man's essence. Another possibility is that the things signified be related as place and thing located in the place. Thus, we call a thing located in England, English. The list could go on. I shall leave the matter to those who are clever with examples.

As with the first two modes (where sometimes a concrete name supposits for a part or a form and the abstract name for the whole or the subject, and sometimes just the reverse happens), so here in the third mode, reversal of function is possible. For sometimes a concrete name supposits for an effect or a thing signified and the abstract name supposits for the cause or the sign; sometimes the reverse happens. Nor is this limited to names pertaining to causality and signification; it holds true across the third mode.

We have noted that one name can, when taken in different senses, be concrete in both the first and second modes. Likewise, a name can be concrete in both the first and third modes—indeed, in all three modes. But, then, the distinction between the three modes is not based on the fact that one is universally denied of the others. It is rather that each mode is particularly denied of the others, and that is all that is needed for the distinction. Likewise, it should not trouble us if it were to turn out that one and the same term were concrete with respect to one expression and abstract with respect to another.

It should be noted that due to the poverty of language, sometimes a concrete name will have no abstract name corresponding to it. The Latin word 'studiosus' lacks an abstract counterpart when it is taken to mean 'virtuous'.

6: On Concrete and Abstract Names
That Are Synonyms

Concrete and abstract names can, however, function in other ways. Sometimes concrete and abstract names are synonymous. To avoid confusion it should be pointed out that the expression 'synonym' has two senses, one narrow; the other, broad. In the narrow sense expressions are synonymous if all those who use them intend to use them to signify one and the same thing. I am not here using the term 'synonym' in this sense. More broadly, expressions are synonymous which simply signify the same thing (so that nothing is in any way signified by one of the terms which is not in the same way signified by the other). In this sense terms are called synonymous even when those using the terms do not believe that they signify the same thing, but rather think that something is signified by one which is not signified by the other. The terms 'God' and 'Godhead' provide an example. These terms are synonymous (in the broad sense) even though some people may think that 'God' signifies a certain whole and 'Godhead', a part of that whole. It is in this second sense that I intend to use the expression 'synonym' in this chapter and many others that follow.

I want to claim, then, that sometimes abstract and concrete names are synonymous, and I think that this is Aristotle's view also. He would agree that in each of the following cases we have synonymous expressions: 'God'–'Godhead', 'man'–'humanity', and 'animal'–'animality'. It is because such expressions are synonymous that language does not incorporate abstract terms to correspond to all concrete names. Thus, whereas writers frequently use the abstract forms 'humanity' and 'animality', they seldom or never use expressions like 'cattle-hood', 'donkeyhood', and 'goathood'. The corresponding concrete forms—cattle','donkey', and 'goat'—are, however, all in general use. Ancient philosophers construed the terms 'cold'–'coldness' and 'heat'–'hotness' as pairs of synonymous names. In the same way they construed 'animal'–'animality' and 'man'–'humanity' as pairs of synonyms. These writers realized that expressions like 'cold'–'coldness' and 'heat'–'hotness' differ in number of syllables and that one term from each pair is concrete and the other abstract; nonetheless, they did not distinguish between the terms with respect to signification. As in the case of all synonymous terms they employed the plurality of names only because they wished to embellish style or something of that nature.

Aristotle and his Commentator maintain that some of the names of substances and the abstract names formed from them are synonymous. Synonymy exists when the abstract term supposits neither for an accident of the substance designated by the concrete term, nor for one of its parts, nor for a whole to which it belongs, nor for something completely distinct from it. According to these philosophers, 'animality' and similar abstract expressions function in this way; for 'animality' does not stand for an accident of an animal, nor for one of an animal's parts, nor for some whole of which animal is itself a part, nor for some extrinsic thing completely distinct from an animal.

Some deny that quantity is a thing distinct from substance and quality. In their view all such abstract terms as belong in the category of quantity or stand for properties of things falling under that category function in the same way. This, of course, does not hold for those who want to construe quantity as an absolute entity totally distinct from substance and quality. But if we adhere to the former view, we must say that 'quantified' and 'quantity' are synonymous; likewise, 'long'—'length', 'wide'—'width', 'deep'—'depth', and so on.

Those who say that figure is nothing different from quantity (or from substance and quality) must treat such abstract names as pertain to figure in the same way; and similarly for abstract expressions relating to the other species of quantity. Thus, they are forced to say that names like 'figure'—'figured', 'straight'—'straightness', 'curved'—'curvature', 'hollow'—'hollowness', and 'convex'—'convexity' are synonymous expressions. However, these philosophers are willing to construe such expressions as synonymous only if neither includes, even in a disguised way, some expression not included in the other.

Further, those who deny that relation is a thing really distinct from absolute entities must likewise hold that concrete and abstract relatives are synonymous names, i.e., expressions like 'father'—'fatherhood', 'similar'—'similarity', 'cause'—'causality', 'risible'—'risibility', 'apt'—'aptitude', 'susceptible'—'susceptibility', and 'double'—'duplicity'.

Nevertheless, one could consistently hold this view about relations while maintaining that concrete and abstract relatives are not synonymous. One could claim that the abstract expression supposits for two things taken together. Thus, one might say that 'similarity' supposits for two things which are similar. But, then, it would be false to say that the similar thing is similarity, although it would be true to say that similar things are similarity. Likewise, those who hold the views about substance, quantity, and figure outlined earlier in the chapter could hold that in one sense no abstract and concrete terms are synonymous. I shall explain this point later. The thing to notice is that they could, then, hold that a proposition in which an abstract name is predicated of its concrete counterpart is always false. But those who hold the view I have outlined and wish to preserve talk about synonymy must grant that, in all cases where abstract and concrete terms are synonymous, predication in either direction is possible.

Thus, those who hold the relevant views about substance have to grant that the following are true propositions: 'A man is humanity', 'An animal is animality'; and, consequently, they are committed to the truth of propositions such as the following: 'Humanity runs', 'Animality is white', etc. Those who hold the relevant views about quantity must concede that propositions like the following are true: 'Substance is quantity', 'Quality is quantity', 'Substance is length', 'Quality is width'; and, as a consequence, they must grant the following propositions: 'Quantity runs', 'Width disputes', 'Width speaks', and so on. Those who hold the views I mentioned about figure must grant that propositions like the following are true: 'Substance is figure', 'Curvature is a substance', 'Figure is white', and 'Figure eats'. Those who hold the views I have outlined about relation must grant that 'Man is a relation' is true, and also that propositions like the following are true: 'Relation is substance', 'Quality is a relation', 'Man is a relation', 'Similarity runs', 'Paternity is fielty', and 'Similarity is duplicity'.

Later I shall show how one can hold the roots of these views without being committed to the truth of such propositions. Similarly, I shall show how one can deny propositions like the following: 'Matter is privation', 'Air is darkness', 'Man is blindness', 'The soul is original sin', 'The soul is ignorance', 'Man is negation', and 'The body of Christ is death', while preserving the view that 'privation', 'shadow', 'blindness' and similar expressions do not designate anything on the part of the thing distinct from what is designated by the subjects of these propositions, i.e., man, matter, etc.

7 : The Correct Account
of Abstract and Concrete Names

Since I have claimed it to be the view of Aristotle and his Commentator that the names 'man' and 'humanity' are synonymous, I shall digress long enough to state the truth of the matter and to indicate whether these terms really are synonymous. According to Aristotle, nothing is signified by the name 'man' that is not in the same way signified by 'humanity' and vice versa. In Aristotle's view every created entity is either matter, form, a composite of matter and form, or an accident; but when we list the various possibilities, it becomes obvious that none of them is designated more by one of these expressions than by the other. Granting this, it is clear that the following proposition is false: 'The intellective soul is humanity'.

Nor will it do any good to split hairs in the way that those do who wish to say that while 'humanity' signifies only the specific nature, 'man' signifies the individual difference, for, as I shall show, this account is not only false but incompatible with Aristotle's view.

We can establish this by a single argument. The argument runs as follows: just as man and humanity are related, so also are Socrates and Socrateity related. (Those I am arguing against frequently speak by forming an abstract expression out of the name 'Socrates' in the same way that one forms an abstract name from the term 'man'). These thinkers hold that 'Socrates' does not signify anything formally or really distinct from what is signified by 'Socrateity' and vice versa; therefore, 'man' does not signify anything different from 'humanity' and vice versa. The assumption is proved as follows: if something is signified by one of the terms 'Socrates' and 'Socrateity', which is not signified by the other, then it would have to be either the specific nature, the matter, the form, the composite of matter and form, or some accident. It is clear that the specific nature is signified equally by neither or both of the two names, and proponents of this view all agree that none of the other items listed above is signified by one of these terms to the exclusion of the other. Nor can they claim that the individual difference which they postulate is signified by either of the terms to the exclusion of the other. For in their view it is Socrates that confers the individual difference upon the specific nature, but the same must be said of Socrateity. Otherwise, Socrateity would not differ in any way from humanity; but, then, given their way of arguing, just as humanity is present in Plato, so also would Socrateity be present in Plato. Thus, there is nothing these thinkers can point to on the part of the thing which is signified by 'Socrates' and not also signified in the same way by 'Socrateity' and vice versa. Consequently, they must grant that the following proposition is true: 'Socrates is Socrateity', from which it follows that Socrates is this humanity exhibiting Socrateity. This, in turn, implies that Socrates is humanity. The inference here is from the less general to the more general on the part of the predicate. But, then, Socrates is humanity; therefore, man is humanity, and if that is true there is nothing signified by the name 'man' which is not also signified by 'humanity' and vice versa.

It follows from all of this that in Aristotle's view nothing is signified by the name 'man' which is not also signified by the name 'humanity' and vice versa. This, at least, is his intended view; therefore, he would either grant that 'Man is humanity' is literally true or he would deny the proposition, but only because one of the two terms incorporates, in a disguised way, some syncategorematic expression not incorporated in the other. I shall say more about this later.

Nevertheless, even though this is Aristotle's intended view, theology shows it to be false; for even if we were to grant that neither of these expressions includes any syncategorematic elements not included in the other, it would still be incorrect to say that 'man' and 'humanity' are synonymous. The fact is that these terms can supposit for distinct things, and one of them can signify or consignify something which the other cannot. The name 'man' truly supposits for the Son of God; and, therefore, it signifies or in some way designates the Son of God; but the name 'humanity' does not supposit for the Son of God, nor does it, any more than the name 'whiteness', signify the Son of God. Thus, whereas, 'The Son of God is man' is true, 'The Son of God is humanity' is false. But not everything designated by one of these terms is designated in the same way by the other, so that they are not synonymous.

One easily can see how it is that these names do not, in all contexts, signify the same thing if he examines their respective nominal definitions. The name 'humanity' signifies a nature composed of body and intellective soul; it connotes nothing about the sustenance of that nature; i.e., whether it is sustained by some subject, such as the Divine Person or not sustained at all. It supposits always for the relevant nature; and, consequently, it can never supposit for the Son of God; for He cannot *be* the relevant nature. The name, 'man', on the other hand, signifies the nature in question, indicating besides that the nature is either a self-subsistent entity (not residing in any other subject) or that it is sustained by some subject. Thus, we can state the nominal definition of 'man' as follows: a man is either a nature composed of body and intellective soul residing in no subject or some subject sustaining a nature composed of body and intellective soul. Take any man and one of the two elements in the description will hold. For it is true that Socrates is a nature composed of body and intellective soul, not sustained by some subject, but the following is false: 'Socrates is a subject sustaining such a nature.' That the latter proposition is false should be clear. Suppose that Socrates is a subject sustaining the relevant nature. For what, then, does the name 'Socrates' supposit? If it supposits for that nature, then the nature sustains itself, which is impossible; for nothing can sustain itself. Further, it is impossible that the name supposit for something distinct from that nature, for then it would have to supposit either for a part of the nature or for some substance distinct from the nature or for a composite of that nature and something else; but each of these suggestions is hopeless, as I shall indicate in what follows.

It will not do to say that 'Socrates' supposits for a composite of the nature and the individual difference and that the composite sustains the nature. As I shall show further on there is no such composite. Besides, even if we grant this point, the explanation does not succeed, for if Socrates sustains the nature, it is necessary that Socrates also sustain some individual nature. But Socrates sustains no individual nature; for the individual nature, in their view, always includes the relevant difference; and, as a consequence, a composite of the nature and the individual difference sustains a composite of the nature and the individual difference, which is absurd.

Nor will it do to say that the subject in 'Socrates sustains human nature' supposits for something composed of a singular nature and a negation of dependence upon some subject; for then Socrates would be a thing composed of both an affirmation and a negation; but this is absurd on two counts. First, no truly subsistent thing can be composed of such things and, second, no composite can sustain the relevant nature—it is not supposed to depend on any subject—and the relevant composite is a subject. The conclusion, then, is that the proposition 'Socrates is a subject sustaining human nature' is literally false. Nevertheless, Socrates is a nature composed of a body and an intellective soul, sustained by nothing; and, as a consequence, he is a man. Still, 'The Son of God is a man' is true, not because the Son of God is such a nature composed of body and intellective soul, but because He is a subject sustaining such a nature and terminating its dependence.

Several conclusions follow from the above remarks. First, even if 'A man is humanity' were to be granted, the proposition 'Every man is humanity', is false. Indeed, the proposition 'Some man is not humanity' is true. Assume for the sake of argument that neither of the names 'man' and 'humanity' includes, in a disguised way, any syncategorematic terms not included in the other. Then, it would be true that a man is humanity since this man (say, Socrates) is humanity, for if we grant the above assumption we cannot claim that the subject and predicate supposit for distinct things. We must say that they supposit for one and the same thing. Consequently, the proposition would be true. But even if we make the relevant assumption, it would still be false to say that every man is humanity; for there would be one exception. If we should say, referring to the Son of God, 'This man is humanity', we would be saying something false. Thus, the subjects of the two true propositions, 'A man is humanity' and 'A man is not humanity' stand or supposit for different things. But should anyone make the above assumption he must, to be consistent, grant that sometimes it is possible to predicate an abstract term of its concrete counterpart and vice versa. Indeed, he should even say that it is possible for an abstract term to be both truly affirmed and truly denied of its concrete counterpart and vice versa; the qualification is that the subject be construed particularly. Such predication is not, however, possible when the subject is taken universally. He ought to grant that in such cases the concrete term supposits for different things. Take for example the proposition 'This humanity is a man'. The proposition is true when we are referring to the humanity of Socrates; however, if the humanity referred to, be that of the Divine Word or some other Divine Person, then the proposition is false. The reason is that the name 'man' always supposits for humanity, except in those cases where the humanity in question is something added to some other thing. Thus, because humanity sometimes is added to another thing and sometimes is not, 'man' sometimes supposits for humanity and sometimes does not. Consequently, the concrete sometimes is predicated of the abstract and sometimes is not and vice versa.

Another conclusion can be derived from the foregoing remarks. Every proposition (composed of a similar concrete and abstract term) in which the verb or a determination of the verb so functions that the things designated by the subject and predicate are said to be distinct is, if taken universally, false. This point holds even if the nature under consideration is very different from the one we have examined. The reason is as follows: concrete and abstract terms of this sort do not supposit for distinct things except in the case of the Divine Person Who sustains the human nature in Christ. This should be clear, for if it were otherwise the term would have to function in one of the following ways: one of the terms supposits for a part of a thing and the other for the whole; the two supposit for two different parts of the same thing; the two names supposit for two totally different substances; or one of the names supposits for a substance and the other for an accident. But each of these is obviously false. The conclusion, then, is that they do not supposit for distinct things except when one of them supposits for a Divine Person. Consequently, any proposition asserting that the entities signified by such names are distinct is false.

As a consequence we must grant that each of the following propositions is literally false: 'Every man possesses humanity', 'Every humanity is in man', 'Every animal has animality', etc. Nothing can possess itself or be in itself, and such propositions do indeed assert that the thing for which the subject supposits has that or is in that for which the predicate supposits. But clearly they are all false since the subject and the predicate supposit for the same thing. Thus, in chapter 16 of the *Monologion,* Anselm indicates that it is not proper to say that the Highest Nature, God, has justice, but rather that the Highest Nature is justice.[1] Likewise, it is not, strictly speaking, correct to say that this man, referring to Socrates, has humanity, but rather that he is humanity.

Nonetheless, when the saints say that God possesses justice, that God possesses wisdom, goodness, and knowledge, and that in God is wisdom, they are, despite the false implications, saying something that is true. In the same way although propositions like 'Man has humanity' and 'Humanity is in Socrates' are literally false, they are, in ordinary contexts, unexceptionable.

It also follows that, strictly speaking, it is false to say that humanity subsists in its proper subject or that humanity depends upon its proper subject or that the proper subject terminates the dependence of the nature. On the contrary, it should be granted that humanity is itself a subject. Thus, unless some syncategorematic element impedes the predication, the proposition 'Humanity is a subject' ought to be granted without qualification. Nevertheless, even if we were to make the relevant assumption about syncategorematic elements, it would still be true that humanity is not a subject when it is added to something else. For when it is so added it immediately ceases to be a subject. The name 'subject' has the connotation of not being added to something else. The nominal definition of that name or any term equivalent to it runs as follows: a subject is a complete thing, one and not many, and sustained by no subject.

[1]   P. L., T. 158, 165 A.

When the two expressions are taken significatively, one can substitute this definition for 'subject' and vice versa. Once this is done it is easy to determine which propositions are true, and which, false.

8: On the Third Mode
of Concrete and Abstract Names

While important in themselves, the questions discussed in the previous chapter have forced us to digress from the central point. We shall return to the main issue and consider another way in which concrete and abstract names can function. In the process we will be able to clarify some points made earlier.

There are abstract names (or some could be introduced into usage) which incorporate, in a disguised way, syncategorematic terms or adverbial qualifications. The result is that each of these abstract names is equivalent in signification to the combination of a concrete name (or some other term) and some syncategorematic term (or other expression or group of expressions). For the speakers of a language can, if they wish, use one locution in place of several. Thus, in place of the complex expression 'every man', I could use 'A'; and in place of the complex expression, 'man alone', I could use 'B', and so on with other expressions.

Now, assume that this sort of account holds for some abstract names. We would have a case where an abstract name and a concrete name neither supposit for nor signify different things, but where predicating one of these terms of the other would yield a false proposition and where terms predicable of one of these terms would not be predicable of the other. Suppose, for example, that the abstract term 'humanity' were to be equivalent in signification to the expression 'man as man' or 'man insofar as he is man'. Then 'Man runs' would be true, but since 'Man insofar as he is man runs' is false, 'Humanity runs' would be false. Or suppose that 'humanity' were equivalent to the expression 'man necessarily . . .' (so that the one expression could be used in place of the other). Then, it would be false that humanity is a man; for it is false to say that man is necessarily a man. No man is necessarily a man, but only contingently. Similarly, it would be false to say 'Humanity is white'; for 'Man is necessarily white' is false.

Following the same general procedure, one could claim for any pair of concrete and abstract names, that while the names neither signify nor supposit for distinct things, first, predicating one of the other yields a false proposition and, second, things predicable of one are not necessarily predicable of the other. Thus, one could claim that although quantity is not a thing distinct from sub-- stance and quality, both of the following propositions are false: 'Substance is quantity' and 'Quality is quantity'. If the name 'quantity' were equivalent in signification to the complex expression 'necessarily quantified while remaining in the nature of things', then while preserving the view (that quantity is not a thing distinct from substance and quality), one could consistently claim that 'Substance is quantity' is false; for the proposition 'Substance is necessarily quantified so long as it remains in the nature of things' is also false. The same sort of account will hold in other contexts, whether the things involved are created or divine.

Thus, using the same technique, one could claim that while the Divine Essence, Intellect, and Will are, in no way, distinct, the proposition 'God understands by His Intellect' is true and the proposition 'God understands by His Will' is false. Likewise, while contending that the soul is not distinguished from the intellect and will, one could hold that the proposition 'The intellect understands' is true and the proposition 'The will understands' is false, and so on with other examples.

I think that the difficulties which arise with regard to such examples are not real, but only verbal or logical. Thus, those who are ignorant of logic uselessly fill innumerable volumes on these issues, inventing difficulties where none exist, thereby abandoning the problems they ought to examine.

Although abstract names are seldom or never employed in everyday speech as equivalent in signification to several expressions, they are frequently used in this way in the writings of saints and philosophers. Thus, in the fifth book of his *Metaphysics,* Avicenna says "Horseness is nothing more than horseness; for by itself it is neither one nor many; nor does it exist in sensible things, nor in the soul."[1] In saying this Avicenna only means that *horse* is not defined as being either one thing or many, nor as existing in the soul or in things outside. None of these notions is contained in the definition of *horse*. Thus, Avicenna was using the term 'horeseness' as equivalent in signification to several expressions, either taken alone or with the mediation of a verb and copula. He clearly did not mean that horseness is some entity which is neither one thing nor many and neither outside the soul nor in the soul. For this is both impossible and absurd. He merely meant that none of these notions is part of the definition of *horse.* That this is what he means is clear enough to one who examines his remarks carefully. Thus, he says, "Since it" (i.e., the universal) "would be man or horse, this intention is something other than an intention like horseness or hu-

---

[1] *Avicennae Metaphysica* (St. Bonaventure, New York: Franciscan Institute Publications, 1948 (a typescript of 1520 edition)), Tract. V, chapter I-A, 134.

manity which exhibits universality, for the definition of horseness is distinct from the definition of universality; nor is universality contained in the definition of horseness; for horseness has its own definition, which does not lack universality."[2] From these and other remarks (which in the interests of brevity I omit), it is perfectly clear he merely means that none of these things is placed in the definition of *horse* or horseness. Thus, in that passage he means to use the name 'horseness' in such a way that it is equivalent in signification to several expressions. Otherwise, the following inference would not be valid: one, many, and similar notions are not placed in the definition of horseness; therefore, horseness is not one thing. The inference, on the contrary, would be invalid in the way that the following inference is invalid: white is not placed in the definition of man; therefore, man is not white.

The foregoing remarks enable us to expose a fallacy in a form of argument which verbally, at least, appears valid. Consider the following: every absolute entity is a substance or quality; quantity is an absolute entity; therefore, quantity is a substance or quality. The general form of argument here is 'Every *B* is *A*; *C* is *B*; therefore, *C* is *A*'. We can expose a fallacy in this form of argument if we properly interpret the relevant terms. Thus, interpret '*B*' as 'man'; '*A*' as 'animal'; and '*C*' as 'the necessarily risible thing'; here, the interpretation is such that for '*C*' we can substitute the whole expression 'the necessarily risible thing' and vice versa. But when we interpret the argument in this way we get a false conclusion from true premises. Thus, 'Every man is an animal; the necessarily risible thing is man; therefore, the necessarily risible thing is animal'. But that this argument is fallacious indicates that the general form, 'Every *B* is *A*; *C* is *B*; therefore, *C* is *A*' is itself fallactious. More generally, attending to this particular use of abstract terms enables us to preserve many seemingly false remarks found in traditional writings.

Not only can an abstract name be equivalent in signification to several expressions; the same thing can happen to concrete names and expressions of other kinds. Thus, those expert in logic hold that the Latin term 'totus' includes the term it distributes, so that when used syncategorematically, it is equivalent to the Latin expression 'quaelibet pars' ('each part'). Thus, the Latin sentence 'Totus Sortes est minor Sorte' is equivalent to the Latin sentence 'Quaelibet pars Sortis est minor Sorte' ('Each part of Socrates is less than Socrates'). Similarly, the Latin word 'quodlibet' incorporates the term it distributes, so that it is equivalent to the phrase 'omne ens' ('each thing'). Otherwise, the Latin sentence 'Quodlibet est homo vel non homo' would make no sense. So it is with many other words. When one utters the Latin word 'curro', the first person pronoun is understood; 'curro', then, is equivalent to 'curro' plus the relevant pronoun. The same holds true of many other expressions; if we do not

[2] *Ibid.*

recognize this fact, we will have great difficulty in grasping the intentions of authors.

Thus, one expression is sometimes equivalent to several. It can also happen that when one expression is added to another, the resulting whole is equivalent to yet another complex expression, nor need these two complex expressions be structurally the same. Sometimes expressions found in the first complex will have a different case, mood, or tense in the second, and sometimes they are simply eliminated. Thus, if the term 'totus' is construed syncategorematically, 'Totus Sortes est minor Sorte' is equivalent to 'Quaelibet pars Sortis est minor Sorte', where 'quaelibet pars' replaces 'totus' and the oblique form 'Sortis' replaces the nominative form 'Sortes'. Some hold that the proposition 'The generation of a form occurs in an instant' is equivalent to the proposition 'No part of a form comes to be before another but all come to be together.' Here, the copula 'is' is eliminated. Likewise, some say that the proposition 'Quantity is an absolute thing' is equivalent to the proposition 'The distance between parts and the extension of parts would be absolute things, were they to continue existing without substance and quality'. If this analysis is correct it is clear that the following inference is invalid: every absolute thing is a substance or a quality; quantity is an absolute thing; therefore, quantity is a substance or a quality.

Should someone say that following this procedure I could put a stop to any syllogism simply by saying that this or that term in the syllogism conceals some syncategorematic term, I would respond as follows: to know whether an inference is valid, one must understand the meanings of the terms and, then, judge accordingly whether the relevant inference is valid. And because, with many terms, it is clear that according to standard usage no such syncategorematic term is concealed, one need merely appeal to the standard rules governing the syllogism to determine whether the syllogism in question is valid. Still, logicians can determine for every inference whether it is valid by analyzing the terms into their nominal definitions; once this is done, the rules will enable him to determine what should be said about the inference.

All abstract privatives and negatives (with many other terms) can be analyzed in terms of the general procedure outlined above, but more of that later. Further, this procedure gives us a basis for denying all such propositions as 'Matter is privation', 'Air is darkness', 'The soul is sin', and so on. It also enables us to preserve propositions like the following: 'God does not create sin' and 'God is not the author of evil'. In the treatise on fallacies I shall explain the source of invalidity in inferences like the following: this is evil; God makes this; therefore, God makes evil.

9: On the Fourth Mode of
Concrete and Abstract Names

We need to discuss one last mode of abstract and concrete terms. Some abstract names are such that they supposit only for many things taken together while their concrete forms can be truly predicated of just one individual taken singly. 'People' and 'popular' provide an example. A man can be popular, but he cannot be a people. Likewise, those who claim that number is not an entity distinct from things enumerated are committed to the view that all abstract and concrete names pertaining to number are expressions like 'people' and 'popular'. In this view one should claim that many men constitute a number and that many animals constitute a number and, more specifically, that the angles of a triangle constitute the number three and the angles of a square, the number four. The same holds true in other cases unless one wishes to follow the procedure of the previous chapter and claim that such predications fail because the relevant expressions are equivalent in signification to several expressions.

Although there may be other modes of abstract and concrete terms, enough has been said about this distinction and about the relevant analysis into several expressions. Thus, no one should blame me if I pass over some of these modes in this work. It is not my intention here to discuss every point and leave nothing for the clever student to examine on his own. My intention is rather to examine cursorily some basic issues to aid those untutored in logic.

10: On Connotative and Absolute Names

We have examined the distinction between concrete and abstract names; now we shall consider another distinction among names, one which the scholastics frequently employ. This is the distinction between names that are purely absolute and names that are connotative. Purely absolute names are those which do not signify something principally and another thing (or the same thing) secondarily. Rather, everything signified by an absolute name is signified primarily. The name 'animal' provides an example. This name signifies cattle, donkeys, men, and other animals; it does not signify one thing primarily and another thing secondarily so that it is necessary for one item to be signified in the nominative case and another in one of the oblique cases, nor does the nominal definition of such a term exhibit any particles or names in different cases. Indeed, strictly speaking, absolute names do not have nominal definitions, for a name with a nominal definition has only one such definition. Where a word has a nominal definition, the meaning of that word cannot be expressed by different sentences, such that terms from one sentence signify things not in any way designated by terms from the other sentences. However, in the case of purely absolute terms the meaning of the name can be expressed by different sentences whose constitutive terms do not signify the same thing. For example, 'angel' is a purely absolute term (provided, of course, the name is taken to signify the substance and not the office of an angel). Now, there is not just one way of expressing the meaning of this name. On the contrary, one person can explicate the meaning of the name by saying, "By 'angel' I mean a substance separated from matter;" but another can say, "An angel is a substance which is both intellectual and incorruptible;" and still another can say, "An angel is a simple substance which does not enter into composition with anything else." Now, each of these explicates the point of the name 'angel' as well as the others; nonetheless, in each sentence there is a term which signifies something which is not signified in the same way by any term from the other two sentences; therefore, none of these is, properly speaking, a nominal definition. So it is generally with purely absolute names; none of them has what, in the strict sense, is called a nominal definition. Examples of such names are the following: 'man', 'animal', 'goat', 'stone', 'tree', 'fire', 'earth', 'water', 'heaven', 'whiteness', 'blackness', 'heat', 'sweetness', 'odor', 'flavor', and so on.

A connotative name, on the other hand, is one that signifies one thing primarily and another thing secondarily. Connotative names have what is, in the strict sense, called a nominal definition. In the nominal definition of a connotative term it is frequently necessary to put one expression in the nominative case and another in one of the oblique cases. The term 'white' provides an example. The term has a nominal definition, one expression of which is in the nominative case and another, in one of the oblique cases. Thus, if someone should ask for the nominal definition of 'white', the answer would be "something informed with whiteness" or "something having whiteness." It is clear that here we have one term in the nominative case and another in an oblique case. Further, sometimes a verb is found in the nominal definition of a connotative name. Thus, if one asks the meaning of 'cause', the correct response is "something upon the existence of which another thing follows" or "something capable of producing something else" or something of that sort.

All the concrete names functioning in the first way outlined in chapter 5 are connotative terms, for all those concrete names signify something in the nominative case and something else in an oblique case; that is, in the nominal definition of those names, an expression signifying one thing is in the nominative case and an expression signifying something else is in one of the oblique cases. This is clear with names like the following: 'just', 'white', 'besouled', 'human', and with other such names as well.

Likewise, all relative names are connotative, because in the definition of a relative name, there are different expressions which signify different things or the same thing in different modes. The name 'similar' provides an example. Should one define 'similar', he would say, "that is similar which has a quality of the same sort as another thing," or something to the same effect.

It is clear, then, that when we take the term in its broadest sense, the name 'connotative' is more general than 'relative'.

Furthermore, those who maintain that quantity is not an entity distinct from substance and quality must claim that all names from the genus of quantity are connotative. Thus, they must say that 'solid' is a connotative term, for in their view a solid is simply a thing whose parts are separated from each other in length, breadth, and depth. In the same way they claim that the nominal definition of 'continuous quantity' is simply 'A thing having its parts lying at a distance from each other'. Thus, to be consistent, they must hold that terms like 'figure', 'curvature', 'straightness', 'length', and 'height' are connotative names. Indeed, those who claim that every entity is either a substance or a quality must hold that all the expressions in the categories other than substance and quality are connotative names. As will be shown later, they must even hold this with respect to some of the names in the genus of quality.

Expressions like 'true', 'good', 'one', 'potency', 'act', 'intellect', 'intelligible', 'will', and 'desirable' must also be construed as connotative names. Thus, the nominal definition of 'intellect' is as follows: 'The intellect is a soul capable of understanding'. Here, the soul is signified in the nominative case and the act of understanding by the rest of the sentence. The name 'intelligible' is also a connotative term; it signifies the intellect in both the nominative case and an oblique case. Thus, the definition goes: 'The intelligible is something which can be apprehended by the intellect'. Here, the intellect is signified both by the term 'something' and the term 'intellect'. The same thing must be said with regards to 'true' and 'good'; 'true' is convertible with 'being'; therefore, it signifies the same thing as 'intelligible'. Similarly, 'good' is convertible with 'being', and it signifies the same thing as the phrase, 'something which, according to right reason, can be willed and loved'.

11: On Names of First and Second Imposition

All divisions we have considered so far apply both to terms which naturally signify and to terms which are merely conventional signs. Now we shall examine some divisions that are drawn only among terms that are conventional signs.

First of all, among names that signify conventionally, some are names of first imposition and others, names of second imposition. Names of second imposition are those which are used to signify conventional signs and all such features as pertain to conventional signs in their function as conventional signs.

The common term 'name of second imposition' has two senses however. In the broad sense names of second imposition are those which signify conventional utterances. An expression which is, in this sense, a term of second imposition may also signify intentions of the soul or natural signs; but it is only as signs of conventional utterances that they are terms of second imposition. In their application in grammar expressions like 'name', 'pronoun', 'verb', 'conjunction', 'case', 'number', 'mood', and 'tense' are all, in the broad sense, terms of second imposition. These names are called names of names; the reason for this is that they are used to signify parts of speech insofar as they are significant. Those names, on the other hand, which are predicated of verbal utterances whether or not they are significant are not called names of second imposition. Thus, although names like 'quality', 'utterance', and 'spoken word' signify conventional signs and are true of them, they also signify verbal utterances which are not significant; consequently, they are not names of second imposition. The expression 'name', however, is a name of second imposition, for the word 'man' was not some other name before it was used to signify; likewise, the expression 'of man' did not have a case before it was used to signify; the same holds true of other such expressions.

In the narrow sense expressions are names of second imposition which, while signifying only conventional signs, can never apply to intentions of the soul, natural signs. Examples are 'figure', 'conjugation', and similar expressions. All other names (i.e., those which are names of second imposition in neither the first nor second sense) are names of first imposition.

However, 'name of first imposition' has two senses. In the broad sense all names which are not names of second imposition are names of first imposition. In this sense syncategorematic signs like 'every', 'no', 'some', and 'all' are names of first imposition. In the narrow sense only those categorematic names which are not names of second imposition are called names of first imposition. In this sense syncategorematic names are not names of first imposition.

Taking the expression 'name of first imposition' in the narrow sense, there are two sorts of names of first imposition; for some are names of first intention, and others are names of second intention. Names of second intention are those employed to signify intentions of the soul or natural signs, some conventional signs, and features accompanying such signs. Examples are 'genus', 'species', 'universal', 'predicable', etc. Each of these names signifies only natural or conventional signs.

But the common term 'name of second intention' has both a broad and a narrow sense. In the broad sense an expression is called a name of second intention if it signifies intentions of the soul, natural signs, whether or not it also signifies conventional signs in their capacity as signs. In this sense names of second intention can be either names of first or second imposition.

12: On Names of First and Second Intention

In the previous chapter I indicated that certain expressions are names of first intention and others, names of second intention. Ignorance of the meanings of these terms is a source of error for many; therefore, we ought to see what names of first and second intention are and how they are distinguished.

First, it should be noted that an intention of the soul is something in the soul capable of signifying something else. Earlier we indicated how the signs of writing are secondary with respect to spoken signs. Among conventional signs spoken words are primary. In the same way spoken signs are subordinated to the intentions of the soul. Whereas the former are secondary, the latter are primary. It is only for this reason that Aristotle says that spoken words are signs of the impressions of the soul.[1] Now, that thing existing in the soul which is the sign of a thing and an element out of which a mental proposition is composed (in the same way as a spoken proposition is composed of spoken words) is called by different names. Sometimes it is called an intention of the soul; sometimes an impression of the soul; and sometimes the similitude of the thing. Boethius, in his commentary on the *De Interpretatione,* calls it an intellect.[2] He does not, of course, mean that a mental proposition is composed of intellects in the sense of intellectual souls. He only means that a mental proposition is composed of those intellective things which are signs in the soul signifying

[1] 16^a 3-7.
[2] P.L., T. 64, 298 A.

other things. Thus, whenever anyone utters a spoken proposition, he forms beforehand a mental proposition. This proposition is internal and it belongs to
no particular spoken language. But it also happens that people frequently
form internal propositions which, because of the defect of their language,
they do not know how to express externally. The parts of such mental propositions are called concepts, intentions, likenesses, and "intellects".

But with what items in the soul are we to identify such signs? There are a variety of opinions here. Some say a concept is something made or fashioned by
the soul. Others say it is a certain quality distinct from the act of the understanding which exists in the soul as in a subject. Others say that it is simply the act of
understanding. This last view gains support from the principle that one ought
not postulate many items when he can get by with fewer. Moreover, all the theoretical advantages that derive from postulating entities distinct from acts of
understanding can be had without making such a distinction, for an act of understanding can signify something and can supposit for something just as well
as any sign. Therefore, there is no point in postulating anything over and above
the act of understanding. But I shall have more to say about these different
views later on. For the moment, we shall simply say that an intention is something in the soul which is either a sign naturally signifying something else (for
which it can supposit) or a potential element in a mental proposition.

But there are two kinds of intentions. One kind is called a first intention.
This is an intention which signifies something that is not itself an intention of
the soul, although it may signify an intention along with this. One example is
the intention of the soul predicable of all men; another is the intention that is
predicable of all whitenesses, blacknesses, etc.

But the expression 'first intention' can be understood in two senses. In the
broad sense an intentional sign in the soul is a first intention if it does not signify only intentions or signs. In this broad sense first intentions include not
only intentions which so signify that they can supposit in a proposition for
their significata, but also intentions which, like syncategorematic intentions,
are only signs in an extended sense. In this sense mental verbs, mental syncategorematic expressions, mental conjunctions, and similar terms are first intentions. In the narrow sense only those mental names that are capable of suppositing for their significata are called first intentions.

A second intention, on the other hand, is an intention of the soul which is
a sign of first intentions. Examples are *genus, species,* and the like. One intention common to all men is predicated of all men when we say, "This man is a
man; that man is a man; . . ." (and so on for all individual men). In the same way,
we predicate an intention common to intentions signifying things when we say,
"This species is a species; that species is a species; . . ." (and so on). Again, when
we say "*Stone* is a genus," "*Animal* is a genus," and "*Color* is a genus," we predicate one intention of another just as we predicate one name of different names

when we say that 'man' is a name, 'donkey' is a name, and 'whiteness' is a name. Now, just as names of second imposition conventionally signify names of first imposition, a second intention naturally signifies a first intention. And just as a name of first imposition signifies something other than names, first intentions signify things that are not themselves intentions.

Still, one could claim that in a strict sense, a second intention is an intention which signifies exclusively first intentions; whereas, in a broad sense a second intention can also be an intention signifying both intentions and conventional signs (if, indeed, there are any such intentions).

13: On Univocal and Equivocal Terms

The next point to consider is the division of conventionally significant terms into those that are equivocal and those that are univocal. In the *Categories*, Aristotle examines denominative terms with equivocal and univocal terms;[1] but since we have already said a good deal about denominatives in preceding chapters, we shall discuss only univocal and equivocal terms.

First, it should be noted that only words—conventional signs—can be univocal or equivocal. Properly speaking, the distinction does not apply to intentions or concepts.

A word is equivocal if, in signifying different things, it is a sign subordinated to several rather than one concept or intention of the soul. This is what Aristotle means when he says that one and the same name applies, but that the account of substance corresponding to the name is different.[2] By "account of substnace," he means a concept or intention of the soul including the mental description and definition as well as the simple concept. He wants to say that while these differ, there is just one name. A clear example of equivocality is found in the case of a word belonging to different languages, for in one language the expression is used to signify things signified by one concept; whereas, in the other it is used to signify things signified by some other concept. Thus, the expression is subordinated in signification to several different concepts or impressions of the soul.

There are, however, two types of equivocality. In the first case a term is equivocal by chance. Here a term is subordinated to several concepts, but it

[1] 1[a] 1-16.
[2] *Ibid.*

would be subordinated to one of these concepts even if it were not subordinated to the other(s); and similarly, it could signify one thing even if it did not signify the other(s). An example is the name 'Socrates', which is assigned to several men. But equivocality can also be intentional. Here, a word is first assigned to one thing or several things and is, thus, subordinated to one concept. But, afterwards, because the things signified by the term are similar to or bear some other relation to other things, the term is used to signify something new. Its new use, however, is not merely accidental. If it had not been assigned to items of the first sort it would not be used in the second case. An example is the term 'man'. In the first instance, this term is used to signify all rational animals, all those things which are subsumed under the concept *rational animal*. But afterwards, those using the term see a similarity between men and their images in pictures. Thus, they use the term 'man' to signify the pictorial representations of men but notice they would not use the term 'man' to signify or stand for the representations of men unless they had first used the word in the case of real men. For this reason we say that 'man' is equivocal by intention.

Every expression that is subordinated to just one concept is called univocal, whether the term signifies several different things or not. But properly speaking a term is not called univocal unless it signifies or could signify indifferently each of several different things. The term is univocal because all of the several things it signifies are also signified by one concept. Thus, a univocal term is a sign subordinated in signification to one natural sign which is an intention or concept of the soul.

The distinction between univocal and equivocal terms does not apply merely to names but also to verbs and other parts of speech. Indeed, a term can be equivocal by the very fact that it can function as different parts of speech, i.e., as both a name and a verb, a name and a particle, a name and an adverb, etc.

It is important to notice that the division of terms into equivocal and univocal is not simply a division into opposites. Thus, the following proposition is not always false: 'Some equivocal term is univocal'. Indeed, in some contexts it is true; for one and the same word is truly equivocal and univocal, but not with respect to the same people. In the same way one person can be both a father and a son, but not with respect to the same individual. Likewise, the same thing can be both similar and dissimilar, but not with respect to the same thing. Thus, if a term belongs to different languages, it is clear that it can be univocal in each of the languages. Thus, the man who speaks only one of the languages does not want to make any distinction when the term appears in a proposition, but the term is equivocal to the man who knows both languages; and consequently, those who know both languages frequently would have to distinguish propositions in which the relevant term appears. The same term is univocal to one and equivocal to the other.

The foregoing makes clear that a univocal term is not one that has a single definition. Many univocal terms have nothing that could properly be called a definition. Thus, when Aristotle says that univocal terms are those to which the name is common, but the account of substance is the same, he is taking the term 'account' for the intention of the soul to which, as primary sign, the relevant word is subordinated.[3]

But it should be noted that 'univocal' has two senses. In a broad sense every word or conventional sign that corresponds to a single concept is univocal. In a narrower sense we call a term univocal only if it is predicable of certain things or of the pronouns designating those things in the first mode of perseity. We call the term univocal with respect to those things.

For the present, we can content ourselves with distinguishing two senses of 'denominative term'. In the narrow sense a term is denominative if, first, it begins with the same sound as an abstract term but has a different ending and, second, it signifies some accident. Thus, 'brave' is denominative with respect to 'bravery' and 'just' is denominative with respect to 'justice'. In a broad sense a term is said to be denominative if it has the same stem as an abstract term but a different ending. In this sense it is irrelevant whether the term signifies an accident. Thus, 'souled' is denominative with respect to 'soul'.

For the present, this suffices as an account of the various divisions among terms. Later we shall add some points that have been omitted.

14: On the Universal

It is not enough for the logician to have a merely general knowledge of terms; he needs a deep understanding of the concept of a term. Therefore, after discussing some general divisions among terms we should examine in detail the various headings under these divisions.

First, we should deal with terms of second intention and afterwards with terms of first intention. I have said that 'universal', 'genus', and 'species' are examples of terms of second intention. We must discuss those terms of second intention which are called the five universals, but first we should consider the common term 'universal'. It is predicated of every universal and is opposed to the notion of a particular.

First, it should be noted that the term 'particular' has two senses. In the first sense a particular is that which is one and not many. Those who hold that

[3] *Ibid.*

a universal is a certain quality residing in the mind which is predicable of many (not suppositing for itself, of course, but for the many of which it is predicated) must grant that, in this sense of the word, every universal is a particular. Just as a word, even if convention makes it common, is a particular, the intention of the soul signifying many is numerically one thing a particular; for although it signifies many things it is nonetheless one thing and not many.

In another sense of the word we use 'particular' to mean that which is one and not many and which cannot function as a sign of many. Taking 'particular' in this sense no universal is a particular, since every universal is capable of signifying many and of being predicated of many. Thus, if we take the term 'universal' to mean that which is not one in number, as many do, then, I want to say that nothing is a universal. One could, of course, abuse the expression and say that a population constitutes a single universal because it is not one but many. But that would be puerile.

Therefore, it ought to be said that every universal is one particular thing and that it is not a universal except in its signification, in its signifying many things. This is what Avicenna means to say in his commentary on the fifth book of the *Metaphysics.* He says, "One form in the intellect is related to many things, and in this respect it is a universal; for it is an intention of the intellect which has an invariant relationship to anything you choose." He then continues, "Although this form is a universal in its relationship to individuals, it is a particular in its relationship to the particular soul in which it resides; for it is just one form among many in the intellect."[1] He means to say that a universal is an intention of a particular soul. Insofar as it can be predicated of many things not for itself but for these many, it is said to be a universal; but insofar as it is a particular form actually existing in the intellect, it is said to be a particular. Thus 'particular' is predicated of a universal in the first sense but not in the second. In the same way we say that the sun is a universal cause and, nevertheless, that it is really and truly a particular or individual cause. For the sun is said to be a universal cause because it is the cause of many things (i.e., every object that is generable and corruptible), but it is said to be a particular cause because it is one cause and not many. In the same way the intention of the soul is said to be a universal because it is a sign predicable of many things, but it is said to be a particular because it is one thing and not many.

But it should be noted that there are two kinds of universals. Some things are universal by nature; that is, by nature they are signs predicable of many in the same way that the smoke is by nature a sign of fire; weeping, a sign of grief; and laughter, a sign of internal joy. The intention of the soul, of course, is a universal by nature. Thus, no substance outside the soul, nor any accident outside the soul is a universal of this sort. It is of this kind of universal that I shall speak in the following chapters.

[1] *Avicennae Metaphysica,* Tract. V, chapter 1-E, 140-141.

Other things are universals by convention. Thus, a spoken word, which is numerically one quality, is a universal; it is a sign conventionally appointed for the signification of many things. Thus, since the word is said to be common, it can be called a universal. But notice it is not by nature, but only by convention, that this label applies.

15: That the Universal Is Not a Thing Outside the Mind

But it is not enough just to state one's position; one must defend it by philosophical arguments. Therefore, I shall set forth some arguments for my view, and then corroborate it by an appeal to the authorities.

That no universal is a substance existing outside the mind can be proved in a number of ways:

No universal is a particular substance, numerically one; for if this were the case, then it would follow that Socrates is a universal; for there is no good reason why one substance should be a universal rather than another. Therefore no particular substance is a universal; every substance is numerically one and a particular..For every substance is either one thing and not many or it is many things. Now, if a substance is one thing and not many, then it is numerically one; for that is what we mean by 'numerically one'. But if, on the other hand, some substance is several things, it is either several particular things or several universal things. If the first alternative is chosen, then it follows that some substance would be several particular substances; and consequently that some substance would be several men. But although the universal would be distinguished from a single particular, it would not be distinguished from several particulars. If, however, some substance were to be several universal entities, I take one of those universal entities and ask, "Is it many things or is it one and not many?" If the second is the case then it follows that the thing is particular. If the first is the case then I ask, "Is it several particular things or several universal things?" Thus, either an infinite regress will follow or it will be granted that no substance is a universal in a way that would be incompatible with its also being a particular. From this it follows that no substance is a universal.

Again, if some universal were to be one substance existing in particular substances, yet distinct from them, it would follow that it could exist without them; for everything that is naturally prior to something else can, by God's power, exist without that thing; but the consequence is absurd.

Again, if the view in question were true, no individual would be able to be created. Something of the individual would pre-exist it, for the whole individual would not take its existence from nothing if the universal which is in it were already in something else. For the same reason it would follow that God could not annihilate an individual substance without destroying the other individuals of the same kind. If He were to annihilate some individual, he would destroy the whole which is essentially that individual and, consequently, He would destroy the universal which is in that thing and in others of the same essence. Consequently, other things of the same essence would not remain, for they could not continue to exist without the universal which constitutes a part of them.

Again, such a universal could not be construed as something completely extrinsic to the essence of an individual; therefore, it would belong to the essence of the individual; and, consequently, an individual would be composed of universals, so that the individual would not be any more a particular than a universal.

Again, it follows that something of the essence of Christ would be miserable and damned, since that common nature really existing in Christ would be damned in the damned individual; for surely that essence is also in Judas. But this is absurd.

Many other arguments could be brought forth, but in the interests of brevity, I shall dispense with them. Instead, I shall corroborate my account by an appeal to authorities.

First, in the seventh book of the *Metaphysics*, Aristotle is treating the question of whether a universal is a substance. He shows that no universal is a substance. Thus, he says, "it is impossible that substance be something that can be predicated universally."[1]

Again, in the tenth book of the *Metaphysics*, he says, "Thus, if, as we argued in the discussions on substance and being, no universal can be a substance, it is not possible that a universal be a substance in the sense of a one over and against the many."[2]

From these remarks it is clear that, in Aristotle's view, although universals can supposit for substances, no universal is a substance.

Again, the Commentator in his forty-fourth comment on the seventh book of the *Metaphysics* says, "In the individual, the only substance is the particular form and matter out of which the individual is composed."[3]

Again, in the forty-fifth comment, he says, "Let us say, therefore, that it is

[1] 1038^b 8-9.
[2] 1053^b 17-19.
[3] *Aristotelis Opera Cum Averrois Commentariis* (Frankfurt: Minerva, 1962 (a photostat of the 1562-1574 edition)), vol. 8, 197, recto, B.

impossible that one of those things we call universals be the substance of anything, although they do express the substances of things."[4]

And, again, in the forty-seventh comment, "It is impossible that they (universals) be parts of substances existing of and by themselves."[5]

Again, in the second comment on the eighth book of the *Metaphysics*, he says, "No universal is either a substance or a genus."[6]

Again, in the sixth comment on the tenth book, he says, "Since universals are not substances, it is clear that the common notion of being is not a substance existing outside the mind."[7]

Using these and many other authorities, the general point emerges: no universal is a substance regardless of the viewpoint from which we consider the matter. Thus, the viewpoint from which we consider the matter is irrelevant to the question of whether something is a substance. Nevertheless, the meaning of a term is relevant to the question of whether the expression 'substance' can be predicated of the term. Thus, if the term 'dog' in the proposition 'The dog is an animal' is used to stand for the barking animal, the proposition is true; but if it is used for the celestial body which goes by that name, the proposition is false. But it is impossible that one and the same thing should be a substance from one viewpoint and not a substance from another.

Therefore, it ought to be granted that no universal is a substance regardless of how it is considered. On the contrary, every universal is an intention of the mind which, on the most probable account, is identical with the act of understanding. Thus, it is said that the act of understanding by which I grasp men is a natural sign of men in the same way that weeping is a natural sign of grief. It is a natural sign such that it can stand for men in mental propositions in the same way that a spoken word can stand for things in spoken propositions.

That the universal is an intention of the soul is clearly expressed by Avicenna in the fifth book of the *Metaphysics*, in which he comments, "I say, therefore, that there are three senses of 'universal'. For we say that something is a universal if (like 'man') it is actually predicated of many things; and we also call an intention a universal if it could be predicated of many." Then follows the remark, "An intention is also called a universal if there is nothing inconceivable in its being predicated of many."[8]

From these remarks it is clear that the universal is an intention of the soul capable of being predicated of many. The claim can be corroborated by argument. For every one agrees that a universal is something predicable of many, but only an intention of the soul or a conventional sign is predicated. No

[4] *Ibid.*, 198, verso, B.
[5] *Ibid.*, 198, recto, B.
[6] *Ibid.*, 210, recto, B.
[7] *Ibid.*, 256, verso, A-B.
[8] *Avicennae Metaphysica,* Tract. V, chapter 1-E, 140.

substance is ever predicated of anything. Therefore, only an intention of the soul or a conventional sign is a universal; but I am not here using the term 'universal' for conventional signs, but only for signs that are universals by nature. That substance is not capable of functioning as predicate is clear; for if it were, it would follow that a proposition would be composed of particular substances; and, consequently, the subject would be in Rome and the predicate in England which is absurd.

Furthermore, propositions occur only in the mind, in speech, or in writing; therefore, their parts can exist only in the mind, in speech, and in writing. Particular substances, however, cannot themselves exist in the mind, in speech, or in writing. Thus, no proposition can be composed of particular substances. Propositions are, however, composed of universals; therefore, universals cannot conceivably be substances.

16: Against Scotus' Account of the Universal

It may be clear to many that a universal is not a substance outside the mind which exists in, but is distinct from, particulars. Nevertheless, some want to claim that the universal is, in some way, outside the soul and in particulars; and while they do not want to say that a universal is really distinct from particulars, they say that it is formally distinct from particulars. Thus, they say that in Socrates there is human nature which is contracted to Socrates by an individual difference which is not really, but only formally, distinct from that nature. Thus, while there are not two things, one is not formally the other.

I do not find this view tenable:

First, in creatures there can never be any distinction outside the mind unless there are distinct things; if, therefore, there is any distinction between the nature and the difference, it is necessary that they really be distinct things. I prove my premise by the following syllogism: the nature is not formally distinct from itself; this individual difference is formally distinct from this nature; therefore, this individual difference is not this nature.

Again, the same entity is not both common and proper, but in their view the individual difference is proper and the universal is common; therefore, no universal is identical with an individual difference.

Again, opposites cannot be attributed to one and the same created thing, but *common* and *proper* are opposites; therefore, the same thing is not both common and proper. Nevertheless, that conclusion would follow if an individual difference and a common nature were the same thing.

Again, if a common nature were the same thing as an individual difference, there would be as many common natures as there are individual differences; and, consequently, none of those natures would be common, but each would be peculiar to the difference with which it is identical.

Again, whenever one thing is distinct from another it is distinguished from that thing either of and by itself or by something intrinsic to itself. Now, the humanity of Socrates is something different from the humanity of Plato; therefore, they are distinguished of and by themselves and not by differences that are added to them.

Again, according to Aristotle things differing in species also differ in number, but the nature of a man and the nature of a donkey differ in species of and by themselves; therefore, they are numerically distinguished of and by themselves; therefore, each of them is numerically one of and by itself.

Again, that which cannot belong to many cannot be predicated of many; but such a nature, if it really is the same thing as the individual difference, cannot belong to many since it cannot belong to any other particular. Thus, it cannot be predicable of many; but, then, it cannot be a universal.

Again, take an individual difference and the nature which it contracts. Either the difference between these two things is greater or less than the difference between two particulars. It is not greater because they do not differ really; particulars, however, do differ really. But neither is it less because then they would admit of one and the same definition, since two particulars, can admit of the same definition. Consequently, if one of them is, by itself, one in number, the other will also be.

Again, either the nature is the individual difference or it is not. If it is the difference I argue as follows: this individual difference is proper and not common; this individual difference is this nature; therefore this nature is proper and not common, but that is what I set out to prove. Likewise, I argue as follows: the individual difference is not formally distinct from the individual difference; the individual difference is the nature; therefore, the nature is not formally distinct from the individual difference. But if it be said that the individual difference is not the nature, my point has been proved; for it follows that if the individual difference is not the nature, the individual difference is not really the nature; for from the opposite of the consequent follows the opposite of the antecedent. Thus, if it is true that the individual difference really is the nature, then the individual difference is the nature. The inference is valid, for from a determinable taken with its determination (where the determination does not detract from or diminish the determinable) one can infer the determinable taken by itself; but 'really' does not express a determination that detracts or diminishes. Therefore, it follows that if the individual difference is really the nature, the individual difference is the nature.

Therefore, one should grant that in created things there is no such thing as a formal distinction. All things which are distinct in creatures are really distinct and, therefore, different things. In regard to creatures modes of argument like the following ought never be denied: this is A; this is B; therefore, B is A; and this is not A; this is B; therefore, B is not A. Likewise, one ought never deny that, as regards creatures, there are distinct things where contradictory notions hold. The only exception would be the case where contradictory notions hold true because of some syncategorematic element or similar determination, but in the same present case this is not so.

Therefore, we ought to say with the philosophers that in a particular substance there is nothing substantial except the particular form, the particular matter, or the composite of the two. And, therefore, no one ought to think that in Socrates there is a humanity or a human nature which is distinct from Socrates and to which there is added an individual difference which contracts that nature. The only thing in Socrates which can be construed as substantial is this particular matter, this particular form, or the composite of the two. And, therefore, every essence and quiddity and whatever belongs to substance, if it is really outside the soul, is just matter, form, or the composite of these or, following the doctrine of the Peripatetics, a separated and immaterial substance.

17: Responses to Objections

The ability of a doctrine to handle objections is a sign of its truth. Consequently, I shall outline some objections against the foregoing and show how they can be met. Many men of no small authority hold that the universal is, in some sense, an entity outside the soul and belonging to the essence of particular substances. They bring forth arguments and authorities to show this:

(1) It is claimed that when things both really agree and really differ, there is something by which they agree and something else by which they differ. But Socrates and Plato really agree and really differ; therefore, they must agree and differ with respect to different things. They agree with respect to humanity, matter, and form; therefore, they each include an entity over and above these things, an entity in terms of which they are distinguished. These additional entities are called individual differences.

(2) Again, Socrates and Plato agree more than Socrates and a donkey; therefore, there is something in which Plato and Socrates agree but something in which Socrates and the donkey do not agree. However, Socrates and Plato do not agree in anything that is numerically one. Therefore, that in which they agree is not a particular; it must be something common.

(3) Again, in the tenth book of the *Metaphysics*, Aristotle says that in every genus there is some one thing that is first and the measure of all other things in that genus.[1] But no particular can be the measure of all other particulars in the same genus, for no particular can be the measure of all individuals of the same species; therefore, there is something over and above particulars.

(4) Again, every common notion belongs to the essence of what is subsumed under it; therefore, a universal belongs to the essence of substance. But non-substantiality is not a part of the essence of any substance; therefore, some universal must be a substance.

(5) Again, if no universal were a substance, then all universals would be accidents and, consequently, all the categories would be accidents. Thus, the category of substance would itself be an accident. Consequently, some accident would be more general than substance. Indeed, it would follow that one and the same thing would be more general than itself; for if universals are accidents, they must be placed in the genus of quality; and, consequently, the category of quality would be common to all the universals. Thus, it would be common to the universal which is itself the category of quality.

Other arguments and innumerable authorities are adduced in behalf of this view, but in the interests of brevity I shall not consider them now. I shall, however, refer to them in a number of places later in the book. To the objections raised I respond as follows:

Response to (1) To the first objection I grant that Socrates and Plato both really agree and really differ; they agree specifically and differ numerically. But I want to claim that it is in terms of the same thing that they agree specifically and differ numerically; and here I do not differ from those who distinguish between the common nature and the individual difference, for they are forced to say that it is in terms of the same thing that the individual difference is both really the same as and formally different from the nature. One might object here that the same thing cannot be the cause both of agreement and of the difference which is its opposite. While the claim is true, it is beside the point; for specific identity and numerical difference are not intrinsically opposed. It ought to be granted, therefore, that Socrates agrees specifically with Plato and differs numerically from him by one and the same thing.

Response to (2) In the same way the second argument fails. For it does not follow that if Socrates and Plato agree more than Socrates and the donkey, there is some one thing with respect to which they agree more. But it is sufficient they

[1] 1053^b 24-30.

agree more of and by themselves. Thus, I say that Socrates agrees more with
Plato in virtue of his intellective soul; and, similarly, that he agrees with Plato
more than with the donkey with respect to his whole being. Thus, if we are to
be accurate we should not say that Socrates and Plato agree in some one thing
which is their essence; we should say rather that they agree in several things, for
they agree in their forms and in themselves taken as wholes.

Of course, if by contradiction there was one nature in both of them, they
would agree in that too; but one might as well say that if by contradiction God
were frivolous, He would rule the world badly.

Response to (3) With regard to the third point one should say that although
an individual may not be the measure of all the individuals of the same genus
or the same lowest level species, nonetheless, one and the same individual can
be the measure of individuals from another genus or of many individuals from
the same species. This is all that is needed to preserve Aristotle's view.

Response to (4) The response to the fourth objection is that, properly speaking, no universal belongs to the essence of any substance, for every universal is
an intention of the soul or a conventional sign and nothing of either sort can
belong to the essence of substance. Consequently, no genus nor any species
nor any other universal belongs to the essence of any substance. But, strictly
speaking, it should be said that a universal expresses or indicates the nature of
a substance; that is, it expresses the nature which is a substance. The Commentator makes this point in the seventh book of the *Metaphysics,* when he notes
that although it is impossible that any universal belong to the essence of anything, universals do express the essence of things.[2] Thus, all authorities who
say that universals belong to the essence of substance or are in substance or are
parts of substances should be interpreted as saying only that universals indicate,
express, designate, and signify the essences of things.

But one might object along the following lines: common names like 'man'
and 'animal' signify substantial entities but not particular entities. The items
they signify are substantial; but if they were particular substances, the term
'man', for example, would signify all men and clearly it does not.

In response to this objection I want to claim that common names signify
only particulars. Thus, the name 'man' does not signify anything other than the
thing which is a particular man. Consequently, the only substantial entity for
which it can supposit is a particular man. Indeed, it ought to be granted that the
name 'man' signifies indifferently all particular men, but it does not follow that
the term 'man' is equivocal. The reason is that although it signifies several individuals equally, it signifies them all by one convention; and in signifying them
it is subordinated to only one concept and not several. Thus, it can be predicated of them univocally.

Response to (5) With respect to the last objection it should be noted that

[2] *Aristotelis Opera,* 198, verso, B.

those who hold that intentions of the soul are qualities of the mind have to claim that all universals are accidents; nevertheless, not all universals are signs of accidents. On the contrary some are signs of substances only; they constitute the category of substance. Other universals constitute the other categories. Therefore, it should be granted that the category of substance is an accident, although it signifies substances and not accidents; and, consequently, it should be granted that some accident (i.e., the accident which is a sign only of substances) is, of itself, more general than substance. But this is not more perplexing than the claim that some word is a name of many substances.

But does not this imply that one and the same thing is more general than itself?

I think not, for in order that one thing be more general than another a distinction between them is required. Thus, although all universals are qualities, one can deny that all universals are per se less general than the common term 'quality'. The general term 'quality' is a quality; but this is not a case where one term is more or less general than another, for we are dealing here with just one term.

One might also object that since no one term is predicable of different categories, 'quality' cannot be common to different categories. But here we must ask whether the categories are being taken significatively or not. When the categories are not taken significatively, one and the same thing can be predicated of different categories. Thus, the propositon ' "Substance" is a quality' is true if the subject supposits materially or simply for an intention. In the same way ' "Quantity" is a quality' is true if 'quantity' does not stand significatively. It is in this way that the same thing is predicated of different categories. In the same way the proposition ' "Substance" is a word' and ' "Quality" is a word' are both true provided the subjects are suppositing materially and not significatively.

Likewise, one might object that the notion of *spiritual quality* is more general than any category, for it is predicated of several different categories and no one category is predicated of all the categories. The correct response here is that the notion *spiritual quality* is not predicated of all the categories when these are taken significatively, but only when they are taken as signs. Thus, it does not follow that the notion of *spiritual quality* is more general than any category; for one term is more general than another if, when both are taken significatively, the first is predicated of more items than the second.

A similar difficulty arises with the name 'expression', for this name is one subsumed under the notion 'name'. 'Expression' is a name and not every name is the name 'expression'. Nonetheless, the name 'expression' is somehow more general than all names, more general even than the term 'name'; for every name is an expression, but not every expression is a name. Thus, it seems that the same thing is both more general and less general than some other thing. The difficulty is removed when we note that the argument just presented is conclusive only if the relevant common terms are suppositing uniformly in all the propositions in which they appear. Careful consideration shows that they are not.

Nevertheless, one could use the term 'less general' in a different way. He could argue that one term is less general than another if the second is predicated of the first (along with others) when the first is suppositing in some way or other. Thus, it might be that the more general term cannot be predicated of its inferior when the inferior is suppositing in a different way, so that it would not be predicated of that inferior when it supposits in all ways. In this new sense one could hold that the same thing is both more and less general than some other thing, but in the revised usage 'less general' and 'more general' cease to function as opposites. They are simply different notions.

18: On the Five Universals in General

Now that we have shown what a universal is we ought to determine how many species of universals there are. There are five species, and this can be shown in the following way. Every universal is predicated of many either *in quid* or not *in quid*. If it is predicated *in quid*, then it can be used as an answer to the question 'What is it?' There are two possible cases here. In the first case the many things of which the universal is predicated are all alike so that they agree essentially, although it can happen that one of them is composed of several such similar things: here we have a lowest level species. In the second case not all the things of which the universal is predicated agree in the aforesaid way, but among them there are things which are dissimilar both as wholes and in their parts. *Animal* is an example. *Animal* is predicated of both *man* and *donkey*, but the similarity in substance between two men is greater than that obtaining between a man and a donkey. The same is true in the case of *color*. This term is predicable of both whiteness and blackness, but neither this blackness nor one of its parts agrees as much with this whiteness or one of its parts as one bit of whiteness agrees with another. For this reason the intention predicable of whiteness and blackness is not a lowest level species but a genus. But *whiteness* is a lowest level species with respect to all whitenesses. Admittedly, it sometimes happens that one whiteness agrees more with a second whiteness than with a third. Thus, equally intense whitenesses seem to agree more than two whitenesses of different intensities. Nevertheless, given two such whitenesses, one always agrees with some part of the other as much as any two whitenesses agree with each other. For this reason, *whiteness* is a lowest level species and not a genus with respect to whitenesses.

Nevertheless, it should be noted that both 'genus' and 'species' have two senses, one broad and the other narrow. In the narrow sense we call something a genus if it can be used to answer the question 'What is —?' where the relevant object is referred to by a pronoun. Thus, one could answer the question 'What is this?' (where 'this' refers to Socrates) by saying that he is an animal, that he is a man, and so on with other genera. The same point holds of species. But in the broad sense something is said to be a genus or species which can be used to answer the question 'What is—?' where the question incorporates some connotative form which is not absolute. Thus, *colored* seems to answer the question 'What is the white?' However, a what-question whose referential device is a demonstrative pronoun can never be answered by *colored;* for no matter what we take to be the referent of 'this' in 'What is this?' one could never correctly answer that question with *colored.* If in asking the question one is referring to the subject of whiteness, then it is clear that the question is not correctly answered in that way. If the referent is whiteness, it is likewise clear that one cannot respond by saying "Colored;" for whiteness is not itself colored. If the referent is an aggregate, then again the response "Colored" is inadequate; for as I shall show later, no aggregate is colored. Finally, if the referent be the term 'white', the response is incorrect; for no term is colored. Thus, since one can correctly respond to the question, 'What is the white?' by saying 'Colored", *colored* can be called a genus in the broad sense of the term. Nevertheless, since *colored* cannot be used as an answer to a what-question whose referential device is the demonstrative pronoun, it is not a genus in the narrow sense of 'genus'. The same sort of account holds in the case of species. This distinction is necessary since without it we cannot handle many of the texts of Aristotle and other writers. Using this distinction we can explicate the various rules that hold apropos of genus and species. Many of these must be understood to hold of things that are species and genera in the first sense. Such rules do not apply in the case of what we call genera and species in the broad sense, and this will become clearer as we go on.

But if a universal is not predicated *in quid,* it can express one part of a thing and not another while expressing nothing extrinsic to the thing. In this case we have a difference. If *rational,* for example, is the difference of man, it expresses a part of man, such as the form, but not, for example, the matter. On the other hand, a universal can express something which is not a part of the thing. In that case it is predicable either necessarily or contingently. If contingently we call it an accident, if necessarily we call it a property.

But it should be noted that sometimes the extrinsic thing designated can be a proposition, the truth of which is required if existence is to be predicated of a thing. Thus, those who say that quantity is not something distinct from substance and quality claim that the name 'quantity' designates that the proposition 'Anything of which this term is predicated has its parts distant from each other' is true.

It should also be noted that in many views the same thing can, in the broad sense of the term, be a genus with respect to one thing and a property or an accident with respect to others. Thus, with respect to some things *quantity* is a genus, viz., body, line, surface, etc. Nevertheless, in the view which claims that quantity is not something distinct from substance and quality, quantity is either an accident or a property with respect to substance and quality. But this is impossible when we take the term 'genus' in the strict sense. The same point holds in the case of species.

One might object that both *being* and *one* are universals but not genera, or one might say that the common notion *universal* is a universal and, nevertheless, that it is neither a genus nor species. In response, the following points should be made:

First, one can say that the relevant division concerns only universals that are not predicated of all things. *Being,* however, is predicated of all things and *one* is either an accident or a property.

Second, it should be said that the common term *universal* is a genus and therefore, when 'genus' is predicated of a species it stands not for itself but for the species.

19: On the Individual

Next we shall examine each of the five universals in some detail, but first we shall examine the notion of an individual, the notion of that which is contained under every universal. It should be noted that among logicians the following names are convertible: 'particular', 'individual', 'suppositum', but among theologians 'individual' and 'suppositum' are not convertible. The reason is that while only a substance can be a suppositum, an accident can be an individual. In this chapter, however, we shall use the expressions in the way that logicians do.

In logic the term 'particular' has three senses. In the first sense that is said to be a particular which is numerically one and not many. In this sense every universal is a particular. In another sense a particular is a thing outside the mind that is one and not many and not a sign of anything. In this sense every substance is a particular. In the third sense a particular is a sign proper to just one thing; it is also called a discrete term. Thus, Porphyry says that a particular is that which is predicated of one thing.[1] But this definition does not make any sense if it is construed as a definition of something existing outside the mind, e.g., Socrates or Plato or something of that nature. Such things are not predicated either of one or of many. The definition must be understood as an account of a certain kind of sign, a sign which is proper to one thing and predicated of one thing. Put in another way, 'particular' is not predicated of anything which can supposit for several things in one and the same proposition.

But even taking the term 'particular' in this sense, it can be used in three ways. First, proper names like 'Socrates' and 'Plato' are particulars. Second, demonstrative pronouns are particulars. Thus, 'this' when used to refer to Socrates in 'This is a man' is a particular. Finally, the demonstrative pronoun, taken with some common term (e.g., 'this man' and 'this animal') is a particular. And just as one can distinguish senses of 'particular' one can distinguish senses of the expressions 'singular' and 'suppositum'.

When I was a student I learned a doctrine that has been passed on to us from the ancient philosophers. According to that doctrine the suppositum of a common term can be either per se or per accidens. Thus, the per se supposita of the term 'white' are 'this white' and 'that white', but the per accidens supposita are 'Socrates', 'Plato', and 'that donkey'. No sense can be made of this distinction unless we use the term 'suppositum' to stand for particulars, in the sense of signs of things. Using the term 'suppositum' for something that is not a sign of things, it is impossible that a term have per se and per accidens supposita. But taking 'suppositum' in another way, i.e., for a term proper to one thing, then something is called a suppositum of a term because that term can be predicated of it (not for itself but for its significatum). The per se supposita of a general term are all those complex expressions formed by a demonstrative pronoun and the general term in question; whereas proper names and demonstrative pronouns are said to be the supposita per accidens of that term. Phrased in this way, the distinction between per se and per accidens supposita is important; for it is impossible for one of a pair of contraries to be truly predicated of a per se suppositum of the other contrary. Thus, the following is impossible: this white thing is black. But of a per accidens suppositum of one contrary, the other contrary can be predicated, although not during the period in which it is the suppositum. Thus, if 'Socrates' is now a suppositum of 'white', it still is possible

[1] *Isagoge,* chapter II. See *The Organon of Aristotle,* trans. O. F. Owen, (London: Bohn, 1853) vol. 2, 617.

that Socrates be black because the same thing can be the per accidens suppositum of two contraries, although not simultaneously, but only successively.

20: On Genus

Next we should speak of the five universals. Following Porphyry we shall
first discuss the notion of a genus.

Both Aristotle and Porphyry define the notion of a genus in the following
way: A genus is that which is predicated *in quid* of many things differing in
species.[1]

It should be noted that in this definition a genus is not something outside
the mind belonging to the essence of those things of which it is predicated. It
is rather a certain intention of the mind predicable of many, standing not for
itself, but for the thing which it signifies. Similarly, when I utter the proposition 'Man is an animal' one word is predicated of another word, but the word
we predicate does not stand for a word. We do not intend to use the word for
itself but for the thing which it signifies; thus it is predicated of a thing. In the
same way the mental intention that is a genus does not stand for itself when
predicated but for the thing it signifies. Therefore when a genus is predicated
of a species, it is not asserted that the subject is the predicate, nor that the
predicate belongs to the subject in real existence. It is asserted, rather, that
what is designated by the subject is the very thing that is designated by the predicate. But the intention *genus* is not predicated of things outside the mind. Such
things cannot be subjects for that intention. On the contrary it is predicated
of the signs of such things; nevertheless, the genus does not belong to the essence
of those things, for no intention of the soul can belong to the essence of any
external thing.

It follows, therefore, that the genus is not a part of the species; and, further,
that the genus does not designate a part of the species. On the contrary the
genus designates the whole thing, and in the strict sense of 'to designate' it
does not designate matter more than form or vice versa. However, using the
word in a loose sense, one can say that the genus sometimes designates the matter and not the form; but this is only to say that in every object signified by such
a genus the matter has the same definition as the genus, but the form does not.

But even so, not every genus (even speaking in this loose sense) signifies the

[1] 102[a] 31-32; *Isagoge,* chapter II (p. 611, Owen).

matter of a thing, because there are genera which are common to simple objects lacking any composition of matter and form. *Color*, for example, is common to colors, but colors are not composed of matter and form. Thus, when the philosophical authorities say that the genus is a part of a thing or that it is the matter of a thing or something of the like, they ought to be glossed to read that the genus is said to be a part of a thing or the material element of a thing because it is, so to speak, the material element in the definition or the description of the thing. In natural things the matter is presupposed by the form and the form comes to it. Similarly if something is to be defined, one first posits the genus; the essential or accidental differences are added afterwards. Thus, the genus is a part of the definition, and it is first in definition in the way in which matter is first in the composite thing. For this (and for no other) reason writers say that the genus is the matter and a part of a thing.

One might want to say that the genus is a part of the definition; but since the definition is really the same as the thing defined, the genus is a part of the thing defined. The response is that, properly speaking, it is false to say that the definition is really the same as the thing defined. What is true is that the definition and the definitum signify the same thing and that is all that the authors mean here.

It should be noted also that the genus is predicated of both species and particulars. And here we must be aware that things are different as we focus on the loose and strict senses of 'genus'. In the strict sense every genus requires distinct and dissimilar things for which the terms of which it is predicated supposit. But when we take the term 'genus' in a broad sense this is not so. Indeed, it is sufficient that the things of which the intention *genus* is predicated and which supposit for other things merely be common notions which exclude each other. Thus, if it were the case that the only substantial entities were men, the intentions *multitude* and *number* could, in this loose sense, be construed as genera. For *many* and *multitude* could be predicated of the common notions *two*, *three*, *four*, etc., none of which is predicated of the others. But many authoritative texts are not to be construed as using the notion of a genus in this loose sense.

21: On Species

Philosophers define the notion of a species in a similar way. They say that a species is something predicated *in quid* of many things which differ numerically.

First it ought to be noted that like genera species are intentions of the soul. Consequently they do not belong to the essence of individuals, although they are predicable of individuals.

The difference between a species and its genus is not the kind of difference which separates a whole from its parts; for properly speaking, the genus is not a part of the species, nor is the species a part of the genus. They differ rather in that the species is common to fewer items than its genus so that the genus is the sign of more things and the species of fewer. Thus, the name *animal* signifies more things than the name *man*, for the former signifies all the animals; whereas, the latter signifies only men. This point holds true of genera and species generally. It is in this sense that the species is the subjective part of a genus; it signifies fewer things. Thus, even the word 'man' can be said to be a part of the word 'animal', that is, 'man' signifies fewer things than 'animal'. This is the correct way to use the term 'subjective part'.

The genus when predicated of the species does not stand for itself but for the things which it signifies. Similarly, the species when predicated of many individuals stands not for itself but for the individuals in question. The species is not many; it is predicated of many. Neither is the species really in the particular, for then it would be a part of the individual. But this is impossible, for the species is neither matter nor form; and, further, there are individuals which do not have parts. Consequently, the species cannot be part of an individual. It is on the contrary a sign of the particular; it signifies all the particulars subsumed under it.

But it should be noted that of the intentions which are genera and species, some are highest level genera, others are subalternate genera and species, and still others are lowest level species.

A highest level genus is a genus which does not have any genera above it; that is, a highest level genus is something which when taken universally does not have some other genus predicable of both itself and some other genus. However, according to one view, it is possible to predicate some other genus of a highest level genus. Thus, some say that this is true: substance is a quantity, but since they deny that 'Every substance is a quantity' is true, they can consistently hold that substance is a highest level genus. They could also say that a highest genus is that of which, universally taken, no other genus is predicated *in quid*. Thus although they would agree that substance is a quantity, they would deny that quantity is predicated *in quid* of substance universally taken.

But the lowest level species is an intention not having a species under it; that is, a lowest level species is not predicated *in quid* of any common notion, although it may be predicated *in quid* of many particulars. Those universals that fall between the highest level genera and the lowest level species are called subalternate genera and species.

22: On the Comparison of Species and Genus

Now that we have seen what genera and species are we ought to compare these intentions to bring out their common and peculiar features.

They differ in that while the genus is predicated of the species, the species is not predicated of the genus. This should not be understood to mean that the species is in no way predicated of the genus. That would be wrong; for since the genus is predicated of the species, the species is in turn predicated of the genus. From 'Man is an animal', for example, we can derive by conversion, 'An animal is a man'. If the genus is predicated of the species, it follows necessarily that the species is predicated of the genus. This point should be understood along the following lines: when a genus actually contains under it different individuals from different species, the genus is truly predicated of the species taken universally; but the species is not predicated of the genus taken universally, although it is truly predicated of the genus when the genus is taken particularly. Thus, it is true that every man is an animal, but it is false that every animal is a man.

Suppose, however, that there were no animals except man. In addition to the truth of both the indefinite proposition 'An animal is a man' and the particular proposition 'Some animal is a man', the universal proposition 'Every animal is a man' would also be true (as well as 'Every man is an animal'). Thus, the species can be predicated of the genus taken not only particularly but universally, but this possibility does not exist in the case where the genus incorporates specifically different particulars.

It should be noted that although the genus is predicated of the species, such predication is not always necessary. Thus, the following proposition is not necessary: 'Man is an animal', for if there were no men the proposition would be false. In the same way 'Some composite of body and intellective soul is an animal' would be false because of the false implication. Although it is contingent that man is an animal, the conditional proposition 'If a man is, then an animal is' is necessary.

Another difference is that the genus contains the species but the species does not contain the genus. This should be understood to mean that while the genus is capable of being predicated of more things—that is what 'contains' means here—than the species, the species cannot be predicated of more things than its genus.

Also, a genus is naturally prior to its species. This should not be understood to mean that the intention which is a genus is by nature prior to the intention which is its species. For it can surely happen that the intention which is a species can be in the soul without the intention which is its genus; the reverse can also happen. Thus, when someone forms the proposition 'Socrates is a man', it is not necessary that he have in his mind all of the intentions which are genera vis-a-vis Socrates. When they have said that the genus is by nature prior to its species, writers have only meant that the genus is more general than its species. Thus, although existence is predicated of a genus, it does not necessarily follow that it is predicated of all the species under the genus. It is possible that existence be truly denied of some species when it is truly predicated of the relevant genus. The reverse, however, is not possible. And this is only to say that inferences like the following are valid: a man is; therefore, an animal is and a stone is; therefore, a substance is. The reverse of these inferences however are not valid.

A further point of divergence is that if the relevant genera are destroyed, the species are also destroyed. This should not be understood in the sense of 'real destruction' so that if the genus is corrupted it is necessary that its species also be corrupted, but not conversely, for that is simply false. For even if the generic intention *animal,* which is predicable of both men and donkeys, were to cease to exist in my soul (thus to be corrupted), it is not necessary that the intention *man*, which is its species, also cease to exist in my soul. The aforesaid point should be understood in terms of logical destruction. Thus, an inference moving from the negation of a genus to the negation of a species is valid. The following, for example, is valid: Animal is not; therefore, man is not. The converse, however, is not a valid inference. Similarly, it follows that if *A* is not an animal, *A* is not a man; the reverse, however, does not follow. Likewise, from 'No animal runs', we can infer that no man runs but not the reverse.

There are many other points of difference separating genera and species. Since I have spoken of these elsewhere and since an understanding of them can be derived from what I have said here and from what I shall say further on, I shall not pursue the matter.

Genera and species agree in that both are predicable of many. Theology confirms this point, for although there is just one sun, divine power could produce many. Likewise, even if there is just one angel of a given species, God could, if He wished, produce many angels of one and the same species. This is true in spite of the fact that the Philosopher would deny it.

Genera and species also agree in that both are prior to that of which they are predicated. This should not be understood to mean that a genus is naturally prior to its species and the species in turn to its particulars. That is false, for a particular can exist even if there are no souls; whereas, species and genera require a soul for their existence. They are said to be prior in that while the inference from an individual to its species and genus is valid, the reverse form of inference is not valid.

A third point of agreement is that genera and species constitue wholes. The term 'whole' here should be understood to mean 'more common'.

23: On Difference

The third species of universal is difference. For the sake of clarity it should be noted, as Porphyry points out, that the term 'difference' is used in three senses.[1] One of these is broad, one narrow, the third still narrower.

In the very broad sense a difference is anything which is predicated of something, although not *in quid*, and denied of something else. In this sense the term 'difference' covers not only what is most properly called difference but also property and accident. Thus, the term is common to three different species of universals: difference, property, and accident.

In the narrow sense a difference is what is proper to one thing and cannot belong to another, or as Porphyry says a difference (in the narrow sense) is what belongs to a thing and cannot successively belong and fail to belong to that thing without the thing's ceasing to exist. In this sense 'difference' covers the inseparable accident of which I shall speak later.

In the narrower sense 'difference' refers to what is called the specific difference.

One can, however, divide the notion of difference in another way. Although this new division is not incompatible with the first, it yields four senses in which something can be a difference: a strict sense, a broad sense, a broader sense, and a broadest sense.

In the narrowest sense a difference is what is predicated of something in the first mode of perseity, but which does not signify anything extrinsic to the thing for which it supposits and of which it is predicated. In this sense, 'difference' refers to one of the five universals and designates the topic to be considered in this chapter.

In a broader sense a difference is what is necessarily predicated of something, but which cannot belong to all things. In this sense it can be said that *risible* is a difference of man, because the proposition 'Man is risible' is necessary.

In a still broader sense a difference is what is predicated of something but cannot, as a matter of natural fact, be affirmed and denied of that thing with-

[1] *Ibid.*, chapter III (p. 618, Owen).

out the thing ceasing to exist. In this sense an inseparable accident is a difference.

Finally, in the broadest sense a difference is anything which is predicated of one thing, but not of all things; and in this sense even a separable accident is said to be a difference. Thus, if Socrates is white and Plato black, it can be said that *white* is a difference of Socrates; for while Socrates is white Plato is not.

Leaving aside for the present the last three elements in this division, let us concentrate on the first. It should be understood that a difference is not something belonging to the essence of a thing; it is an intention of the soul predicable of the things contained under it, but not *in quid*. Such an intention is said to be a difference because, although not predicable *in quid*, it can function as the middle term in an argument in which we conclude that the thing of which it is the difference is different from some other thing. Thus, *rational* is the middle term for deriving the negative proposition that man is not a donkey or something else different from man. Consider the following argument: Every man is rational; no donkey is rational; therefore, no donkey is a man. Thus, it should not be thought that the difference is something intrinsic to a species by which one species is distinguished from another; for then the difference would not be a universal, but would be matter, form, or the whole composed of matter and form. On the contrary the difference is a predicable proper to one species, but not another. It is called the essential difference not because it belongs to the essence of a thing, but because it expresses part of the essence of a thing and nothing extrinsic to the thing.

The difference, as I am now using the term, always expresses a part of the thing. Some differences express the material part while others express the formal. Thus, the difference of man, *rational*, expresses man's intellective soul in the way that *white* expresses whiteness and *besouled* the soul. But the difference *material* expresses matter in the same way that *besouled* expresses the soul. Consequently, we must reject the view of those recent writers who say the difference is taken only from the form and not the matter; the difference can be taken from either the matter or the form. Although one difference is taken from the matter and another from the form, every difference when placed in a definition functions as form; for as the form comes to the matter and presupposes it, so in definition the difference always comes to the genus. First we assign the genus and second the difference. The point holds regardless of whether the difference is taken from the matter or the form. Thus, *body* is defined as a substance having matter. We posit the genus *'substance'* first and then the difference *having matter*. The difference in question, however, is taken from and principally designates the matter.

From the foregoing, it follows that no species which is common to simple entities (i.e., those lacking composition in terms of matter and form) has an essential difference, for an entity of that sort has no parts. It can, however, have accidental differences.

It also follows that no species which is common to simple things, whether it belongs in the category of substance or some other category, is definable by what can properly be called a definition. A species of this sort can, of course, be defined in terms of definition by addition. Therefore all the authorities who say, for example, that every genus is divided by its differences or that species have a constitutive difference can be interpreted in one of two ways. Either they are speaking only of genera and species which actually have essential differences. Thus, when they say that every genus is divided by its differences they mean that every genus which has such differences is divided by them. Or they are using the term 'difference' to cover both essential and accidental differences—in my scheme the first and third kinds of differences.

It should be pointed out that when asserted such propositions as 'The difference is that by which the species goes beyond the genus'; 'The difference is constitutive of the species'; 'The difference divides the genus into its species'; 'The difference is that by which particulars differ'; and 'The difference is a part of the species', do not mean that the difference is some real entity present in the species. Rather, the difference is a predicable which is proper to something and which belongs in the definition of that thing. 'The species goes beyond the genus by its difference' means that the difference belongs in the definition of the species, but not in the definition of the genus. Similarly, 'The difference is constitutive of the species' means that the difference completes the definition of the species. In the same way, 'The difference is that by which particulars differ' means that the difference is proper in predication to one thing and not another and that it can function as a middle term for concluding that one thing is to be denied of another. 'The difference is part of the species' means that the difference expresses a part of the thing which is signified by the species or is a part of the definition which signifies the same thing as the species. Thus when Porphyry says that differences are potentially in the genus, he means that the difference is not predicated of the genus taken universally but particularly.[1]

Therefore, the difference is an intention of the soul which expresses a determinate part of a thing and which is predicable *in quale* of the same things that the species with which it is convertible is predicable *in quid*. That the difference is an intention of the soul is clear from the fact that it is a universal. Every universal, I have shown, is an intention of the soul, unless one also wants to call conventional signs universals; but I am not now speaking of universals which are conventional; only of those which are universal by nature.

That the difference expresses a part of the thing is clear. The difference must signify something on the part of the thing. It does not signify the whole thing

[1] *Ibid.* (p. 621, Owen).

because then it would be indistinguishable from the species. It signifies either a part of the thing or something extrinsic to it. But it does not signify anything extrinsic; otherwise, it would be a property or an accident. The only remaining possibility is that it signify a part of the thing. The difference then always expresses a part of the thing in the way that *white* expresses whiteness. Consequently the difference always is (or ought to be) concrete in form, and corresponding to it (in the way that *whiteness* corresponds to *white*), there should be an abstract term which directly signifies the relevant part of the thing. Thus, the abstract term should always supposit for a part and the concrete term for the whole composed of that part and some other part.

It is clear that the difference is predicated *in quale*, for by the difference one does not respond to the question 'What is it?' but to the question 'How is it qualified?' For if it should be asked 'How is man qualified?' an appropriate response would be that he is rational or material. Thus, the differentia is predicated *in quale*. It is predicated of the same items as the species because it is convertible with the species. Thus, one should not claim that *soul* is the difference of *body*, but rather *besouled*. Similarly it is not *reason* that is the difference of man, but *rational*.

24: On Property

Next we shall examine the notion of property. The term 'property' has four senses. In one sense we say that a property is something that belongs to one species or one genus but which, nevertheless, need not belong to all things subsumed under that species or genus. The common term *grammatical* is said to be a property of man because it belongs only to men. It does not, however, belong to every man; for not every man is grammatical. Similarly, *to move by progressive motion* is said to be proper to animal since it does not belong to anything but animals, nevertheless, it does not belong to every animal.

In a second sense a property is something which belongs to every particular of some particular species, but not only to that species. One might say that *biped* is a property of man.

In a third sense a property is one which belongs to some species taken universally, but not at all times. It belongs to a particular at one time, but not at another. Thus, if every man were to turn grey in his old age, then *to turn grey* in this sense would be a property of man.

In the fourth sense a property is anything which belongs to some common notion taken universally, to no other notion, and to all of the items subsumed under the notion, with the consequence that the property is convertible with that common notion and necessarily predicable of the notion for as long as existence can be predicated of it. It is in this sense that the notion of a property is said to be one of the five universals. The other three senses are included under the notion of accident. Thus, *risible* is a property of man; for it belongs to every man, only to men, and always to men. God could not create a man without making him risible for the man would truly be able to laugh. There would not be anything contradictory in the man's laughing. He would be risible, for that is what we mean by 'risible'. *Risible*, then, is a property of man. *Laughing* however, is not a property of man; it is an accident. The two predicables *laughing* and *risible* are not one and the same. They differ in that one is affirmed of something of which the other is denied.

Included in this fourth sense of 'property' are such passions as belong not only to more general notions but also to their logical inferiors. Every property is the property of something, but it is not the property of just anything. Thus, a passion of a genus is predicated of the species, but it is not the property of the species.

It should be noted that a property is not something really inhering in that of which it is the property; for then it would not be a universal, nor belong to something universally taken, nor be predicated of many.

A property, then, does not inhere in the subject whose property it is said to be. It need not even designate an absolute thing inhering in that which is designated by the subject. Sometimes it designates a thing distinct from and extrinsic to the entity designated by the subject. Sometimes it designates this thing affirmatively and sometimes negatively. Properties designating affirmatively an extrinsic entity are *heat-producing, creative,* and the like. Thus, *heat-producing* does not designate a thing inhering in that which is heat-producing; it designates on the contrary something which can be produced by it. (Here, I am speaking of the first subject of *heat-producing.*)

Likewise, *creative* does not designate a thing inhering in God; it designates something that can be produced by God. Negative properties are *immortal, incorruptible, immaterial,* etc.

Nevertheless, some properties designate things inhering in or capable of inhering in that which is designated by the subject; the following passions are of this sort: *alterable, capable of being heated, beautifiable, capable of becoming white.*

Secondly, it should be noted that every affirmative proposition which is not equivalent to a negative proposition and in which a property is predicated is equivalent to a proposition expressing possibility. If the relevant proposition were not equivalent to a proposition expressing possibility, then the proposition could, by divine power, be false while the proposition ascribing existence to the relevant subject were true. Propositions like the following are contingent: 'Substance is quantified', 'Every fire is hot', and 'Man laughs'; whereas, propositions like 'Every man is susceptible of discipline', 'Every body is mobile', and 'Every man can laugh' are necessary. They cannot, that is, be false while the proposition ascribing existence to the subject in question is true; but this is to say that they are equivalent to modal propositions expressing possibility. Thus, 'Every man is risible' is equivalent to 'Every man can laugh'. In the second proposition the subject is taken for that which is. (In that way a childish objection is blocked.)

The reason why the first set of porpositions is contingent (why, that is, they can be false while the corresponding existential propositions are true) is that God can create an object without also creating an entity distinct from it. At least He can do this where the first is prior and the second posterior.

In way of summary it should be said that a property as we have been using the term (where a property is a universal distinct from other universals) is an intention predicable of some species *in quale* and convertible with it. It connotes affirmatively or negatively something extrinsic to the thing which is designated by the subject. It is not, however, necessary that the extrinsic thing be some entity outside the mind and actually existing in the nature of things. It can be something which is by nature predicable, or it can be a proposition existing or capable of existing in the mind. The same point holds with regards to passions (i.e., universals predicated of a subject in the second mode of perseity); they are not things inhering in an entity outside the mind. In that case a passion could not be predicable of something, nor could it be the predicate of a conclusion in a demonstration; and both of these points hold true of passions. A passion, we must grant, is an intention of the soul.

25: On Accident

The fifth species of universal is accident. Philosophers define it as follows: an accident is what can be present in or fail to be present in a subject without the corruption of that subject.

To see the point of this definition it should be noted that 'accident' has four senses. In one sense an accident is something really inhering in a substance in the way in which heat really inheres in the fire and whiteness in the wall. Taking 'accident' in this sense the previous definition comes out true, for no accident is so present in a subject that God could not remove it from the subject without corrupting that subject. Taking 'accident' in this sense (for something outside the mind) we do not have the fifth species of universal. The accident which is the fifth species of universal is predicable of many; but no accident outside the mind, except a word or a conventional sign of some other sort, can be predicable of many.

In another sense an accident is anything which can be predicated contingently of something in such a way that while the proposition ascribing existence to the relevant subject remains true, the accident can either be or not be predicated of that subject. Using 'accident' in this very general sense there is nothing wrong with saying that God has some accident. Indeed, Anselm attributes this sort of accident to God as is clear in chapter 24 of the *Monologion*.[1] Nevertheless, as Anselm indicates in the same chapter, God is not susceptible of the kind of accident that really inheres in a subject. The accident one can attribute to God is simply a predicable which holds contingently of something. The definition quoted above fits this second kind of accident when we construe 'to be present in or to fail to be present in' to refer not to real inherence, but rather to inherence by way of predication. Thus the definition is construed to mean that an accident is something that can either be predicated or not predicated of a subject without the corruption of that subject.

In the third sense an accident is a predicable; it is predicated contingently and is capable of being successively affirmed and denied of something either as a result of a change in that which is designated by its subject or as a result of a change in some other thing. According to Anselm, many relations are accidents in this sense. They can come or leave (i.e., be affirmed or denied) merely as a result of a change in the thing designated by the subject or as a result of a change in something else.

In the fourth sense an accident is a predicable. It does not designate some absolute thing inhering in the subject. It is capable of being predicated contingently of something, but it can come to be predicated of a subject only as a result of a change in the thing designated by that subject. Thus, those who hold that quantity is not a thing distinct from substance and quality say that quantity is an accident, for it cannot be successively affirmed and denied of a subject except by a local change in that which is designated by the subject. They would say that something is now of greater quantity than it was before simply because its parts now lie at a greater distance from each other than they did before, and they claim this can occur only by means of a local motion in the parts of the thing concerned.

We should note that although nothing is an accident unless it can be removed by divine power from a substance with the substance persisting in existence, the

[1] P. L., T. 158, 178C-179B.

Philosopher would deny this. He would say that there are many accidents in the heavenly bodies which can in no way be taken away from them.

Further, accidents are either separable or inseparable. A separable accident is one which can as a matter of natural fact be removed from its subject without the destruction of that subject; whereas, an inseparable accident is one that cannot. It could, however, be so removed by divine power.

Inseparable accidents differ from properties in that although an inseparable accident cannot as a matter of natural fact be taken away from the subjects whose inseparable accident it is, it could be taken away from some other subject without the destruction of that subject. Thus, although the blackness of the crow cannot as a matter of natural fact be taken away from the crow, blackness can be taken away from Socrates without his destruction. A property, on the other hand, cannot be taken away from anything. A property is no more separable from one of its subjects than from another; anything having it is destroyed by its removal.

In summarizing some points made about universals it should be noted that every universal is an intention of the soul which signifies many things and which can supposit for the many things it signifies. One intention is predicated of an intention distinct from it, not for itself, but for the things it signifies. Therefore, those propositions, in which one intention is predicated of another, do not assert that one intention is another, but rather that what is designated by one intention is what is designated by another. Universals of this sort are not things outside the mind. They do not belong to the essence of things outside the mind, nor are they parts of those things. They are entities in the soul different from each other and from things outside the mind. Some are signs of things outside and others are signs of those very signs. Thus, the name 'universal' is common to all universals; and, consequently, it is a sign of all the universals other than itself. It ought to be granted then that the universal which is predicable of the five universals, standing not for itself but for other universals, is the genus of universals in just the way an expression predicable of all expressions is a name and not a verb, particle, conjunction, or any other part of speech.

These remarks about the universals are sufficient. Those who want a more detailed knowledge about universals and their properties can read my commentary on Porphyry,[2] where I have treated this material at greater length. The points I have omitted here can be found there.

----

[2] See *Expositio In Librum Porphyrii De Predicabilibus,* edited by Ernest A. Moody, St. Bonaventure, New York: Franciscan Institute, 1965.

26: On Definition

Besides the foregoing terms of second intention, many other terms of second intention and second imposition are in common use. Students can be hindered by an ignorance of these terms; therefore, to instruct the novice I shall examine some of the relevant terms.

Some terms that logicians use are common to all universals; others are proper only to some universals. Again some apply to universals only when they are taken together; whereas others apply to one universal with respect to another. Terms which apply to several universals taken together include 'definition' and 'description'.

But 'definition' has two senses. In one sense of the word we speak of essential definitions (definitions expressing what a thing is) and, in another sense we speak of nominal definitions (definitions expressing what a word means).

'Essential definition' has two senses. In the broad sense it covers not only strict but descriptive definition. In the narrow sense, however, a definition is a complex expression signifying the whole nature of a thing without indicating anything extrinsic to the object defined. This can happen in two ways. Sometimes the complex expression will include expressions in one or more of the oblique cases; these constituent expressions will signify essential parts of the thing. Thus, if we define man as a substance composed of body and intellective soul, the oblique forms 'body' and 'intellective soul' express parts of man. A definition of this sort is called a natural definition.

In another form of essential definition no expression is in an oblique case; both genus and difference are in the nominative case. Here the difference expresses a part of the thing defined, but only in the way in which 'white' expresses whiteness. 'White' expresses whiteness, but it does not supposit for whiteness; it supposits, rather, for the subject of whiteness. Similarly, although differences express parts of the things they define, they do not supposit for those parts but for the whole composed of those parts. When we define man as rational animal or animated, sensing, and rational substance, the terms 'animated', 'sensing', and 'rational' supposit for man because man is rational, animated, and sensing. Nevertheless, these terms designate a part of man. Their abstract counterparts also designate a part of man but not in the same manner. A definition of this sort is called a metaphysical definition because the metaphysician defines man in this way.

Besides these two forms of definition, no other is possible except perhaps that form of definition where the parts express more and the whole, the same.

Thus, it is wrong to claim that man, for example, has a logical, natural and metaphysical definition; for the logician, since he does not treat of men (indeed, he does not treat of things that are not signs at all), has no reason to define man. His task is rather to teach how the different sciences treating of man are to define man. Therefore the logician ought not assign any definition of man. He may, of course, use examples, but then his examples ought to include only natural and metaphysical definitions.

Just as it is wrong to divide definitions into the natural, metaphysical, and logical, it is wrong to speak of three men—the natural, the metaphysical, and the logical. Similarly, although one can say that because of the diversity of their constituent expressions, definitions are to be divided into the natural and metaphysical, it is absurd to say that there is a natural man and a metaphysical man. Such a claim must mean either that there is some truly substantial thing outside the soul that is natural man and some other substance that is metaphysical man or that there is some concept of the mind or some word that is natural man and some other concept or word that is metaphysical man. The first alternative can be rejected; for how are these men, both of which are substances, to be distinguished? Either one is a part of the other, or they are wholes which are distinct, or something is a part of both (but not everything that is a part of one is a part of the other). The first and second options clearly are not possible. Nor is the third alternative a viable option; for since natural man is composed only of matter and form, it would be necessary that either his matter or his form not be a part of metaphysical man and then either metaphysical man or natural man would be either exclusively matter or exclusively form; but both possibilities are absurd.

Nor will it do to say that since the metaphysician and the natural philosopher consider man in different ways, man considered by the metaphysician is different from man considered by the natural philosopher. Although it is true that each considers man differently, it does not follow that there would be one man, metaphysical man, and another, natural man. What follows on the contrary, is only that there are diverse considerations of one and the same man. Suppose that Socrates sees Plato clearly while Sortes sees him obscurely. The seeing is different but Plato who is seen is not something different in the two cases. Similarly, the metaphysical and natural considerations of man are different, but the man who is considered is the same. There are not then two different things—natural man and metaphysical man. Nor can it be said that there is a different concept or word in the two cases. The concept is identical either with the definition, a part of the definition, or with something else that is predicated of man; but whichever of these options we take, it is clear that the desired conclusion is not achieved.

It should be clear then that definitions can be different where the thing defined is the same. Although these two definitions differ, they signify the same thing; and whatever is signified by one or by a part of one is signified by the other or by a part of the other. Nonetheless, the parts will differ in mode of signification, since the corresponding parts of the metaphysical and natural definitions will be in different cases.

It should be noted that when, significatively taken, a definition is predicated of something, the corresponding definitum, significatively taken, is also predicated of that thing and vice versa. Further, a proposition composed of a definition and a definitum that is hypothetical, possible, or the equivalent of either of these is a necessary proposition. The following, for example, are both necessary: 'If man is, rational animal is' (and vice versa); and 'Every man can be a rational animal' (where the subject stands for what can be). Nevertheless, no such affirmative proposition which is merely *de inesse* or *de presenti* is ever necessary. Thus, the simple propositions 'Man is a rational animal' and 'Man is a substance composed of body and intellective soul' are not necessary. The reason is that if there were no men, the propositions would be false. Aristotle, however, who claims that propositions like 'Man is an animal' and 'Donkey is an animal' are necessary, would disagree here.

From the aforesaid it is clear that a definition is not identical with the definitum. According to everyone, a definition is a complex expression either mental, vocal, or written; but it cannot be the same as any simple expression. Nevertheless, a definition signifies the same thing as its definitum, and this is what is meant by those who say that the definition and the definitum are really the same thing; they mean that the two signify the same thing.

It should be noted that if we take 'definition' in the strict sense, the only thing that can be expressed by a definition is substance; and if we use the word 'definitum' to mean the term convertible with a definition, only names can be definita. Verbs and other parts of speech cannot.

But a definition in the broader sense, a nominal definition, is an expression explicitly indicating what is designated by an expression. Someone who wants to teach another individual what is meant by the name 'white' says something like "Something having whiteness." Not only names of which 'exists' is predicable are susceptible of this sort of definition, but also expressions of which such predication is impossible. Thus,'vacuum', 'non-entity', 'impossibility', 'infinity', and 'goat-stag' have definitions; that is, there are expressions corresponding to these names which signify the same thing as the names in question. It follows that in this sense of 'definition', it is sometimes impossible, using the verb 'to be' to predicate a definition of its definitum; and this impossibility exists even where both definitions and definitum are significatively taken. 'Chimaera is an animal composed of a goat and a cow', for example, is not true; it carries the false implication that something actually is composed of a goat and a cow. Nevertheless, the proposition in which the terms supposit materially (' "Chimaera" and "animal composed of goat and cow" signify the same thing') is true. People generally understand the first proposition to mean the second, but strictly speaking they are different. In the first book of the *Constructions,* Priscian indicates that one word is frequently used for another;[1] it also frequently happens that one complex expression is used in place of another. Nevertheless, the conditional proposition formed from such a definitum and definition is true. 'If anything is an chimaera, it is composed of goat and cow' is true.

Not only names but other parts of speech such as verbs and conjunctions are capable of being defined by this form of definition. Adverbs like 'where', 'when', and 'how many', for example, can be defined. In such cases the definition cannot be predicated of the definitum when both are taken significatively. But when the terms are being taken materially, an expression like 'signifies the same as' (which is employed with terms taken materially) can be used to connect them, or some other expression can be predicated of the definitum taken materially. Thus, one can say, " 'Where' is an interrogative adverb of place" or " 'When' is an interrogative adverb of time" and so on.

27: On Description

A description is a complex expression composed of accidents and properties. Thus, Damascene says in his *Logic* (chapter 14), "A description is composed of accidents, i.e., properties and accidents. For example, 'Man is a risible thing, who walks erect and has broad nails'. All of the elements of this description are accidents. Because of this it is said that a description conceals or fails to make manifest the substantial existence of the subject; it focuses only on the consequences of that substantial existence."[1]

It is clear then that nothing included in a description is predicated of the description *in quid* or in the first mode of perseity; it is in this that description differs from definition.

The foregoing passage indicates also that the term 'accident' is used not only for an object actually inhering in something else but also for that which is predicated contingently of something. According to Damascene a description is composed of accidents of some subject. A description, however, is composed

[1] *Institutiones Grammaticae,* ed., Krehl (Leipzig, 1820), vol. 2, 89.

[1] *St. John Damascene's Dialectica,* an edition of Robert Grosseteste's version, Owen A. Colligan ed. (St. Bonaventure, New York: Franciscan Institute Publications, 1953), chapter 14, 28-33.

only of things predicable of a subject; therefore, Damascene must be calling things predicable of a descriptum accidents; and these can only be concepts, spoken words, or written words.

It follows that a description and its descriptum are not always convertible; for since accidents are only contingently predicable of something, it is possible that the descriptum be predicated of a subject but not the description. But this is always due to some imperfection in that of which the descriptum is predicated. Thus, man can be described as follows: man is a biped having two hands; and, of course, one could enlarge on this description by adding features that belong only to man. But even when that is done it is still possible that there be an object of which the description is false, but the descriptum true—a man, for example, who lacks hands. The reason for this is that the individual involved is not perfect.

Nevertheless, 'description' can be used in two senses, one broad and the other narrow. The doctor uses the term in the broad sense. In the narrow sense a description is composed only of properties so that a description and its descriptum are always convertible.

28: On Descriptive Definition

A descriptive definition is one composed of both substantial and accidental items. To use the example Damascene cites in the book referred to, 'Man is a rational animal, walking erectly, and having broad nails'. Thus, some complex expressions are composed of things predicable in the first mode of perseity (definitions); others are composed of things that are not predicable in the first mode of perseity (descriptions); and still others are composed of both; these we call descriptive definitions. But, of course, since each definition, description, and descriptive definition is an expression, none is really identical with the definitum or descriptum; they do, however, signify the same thing.

29: On Definitum

Next we shall consider the notions of definitum and descriptum. 'Definitum' has two senses. In the first sense a definitum is that whose parts or essence is expressed by a definition; in this sense, it is particular substances that are defined. Thus the definition 'rational animal' is a definition of all men because the essence of all men is designated by that definition. The definition designates essence of nothing except particular men, for the only things that are rational animals are individuals like this man and that man. Using 'definitum' in this sense it should be granted that the particular substance is defined.

'Definitum' is used in another way for that which is convertible with the definition and of which the definition is truly predicated. In this sense the definitum is an expression which is convertible with the definition and which signifies exactly the same thing as the definition. Using 'definitum' in this sense singular things are not defined. Only the species is defined, for it is only the species and not the particular which is convertible with the definition; no particular is.

Employing this distinction we have the tools for glossing the texts of Aristotle and his commentator, for some of these texts say that definition is of singulars while others say that species are the things defined.

The same sort of distinction should be drawn in the case of 'descriptum'. That term can be used for an expression of which the description is first and foremost predicated, standing for the thing described and not for itself; or it can be used for the thing designated by the name and the relevant description.

30: On Subject

We have discussed terms which, like 'definition' and 'description' are not applied to universals taken singly. As we noted no one universal by itself is a definition or a description; every definition or description is composed of several universals. Next we shall consider terms like 'subject', 'predicate', etc., that apply in the case of every universal.

First, as Damascene says in chapter 8 of his *Logic,* " 'Subject' is used in two senses; there is the subject with respect to existence and the subject with respect to predication. As regards existence, we say that a substance is subject for its accidents; for they can exist only in substance; without substance they cannot exist. The subject of predication, on the other hand, is the particular."[1]

From these remarks we can see that something is called a subject because it really underlies something that inheres in it and is actually present in it. Used

[1] *Ibid.,* chapter 8, 21-26.

in this way the term 'subject' has two senses. In the strict sense we call something a subject with respect to the accidents which really inhere in it and without which it can continue to exist. In the broad sense something is a subject simply because it underlies something else. Here, the object which a subject underlies need not be an accident; it can be the substantial form which informs the subject in question. In the broad sense even matter is said to be a subject with respect to substantial forms.

In another sense a subject is that part of a proposition which precedes the copula and of which something else is predicated. In the proposition 'Man is an animal', 'man' is the subject because 'animal' is predicated of 'man'.

But even here we must distinguish, for in one sense a subject is that which can be the subject in any proposition, true or false. In this sense any universal can be a subject with respect to any other. This comes out in propositions like 'Every animal is a donkey' and 'Every whiteness is a crow'. In another sense a subject is anything that is the subject of a true proposition where there is direct predication. In this sense, 'man' is subject with respect to 'animal', but not vice versa. In a third sense we use the term 'subject' more strictly for that which is the subject of the conclusion of a demonstration, which is or can be known by what, in the strict sense, is called science. Using 'subject' in this sense there are as many subjects in the totality of the sciences as there are conclusions having distinct subjects. Thus there are many subjects in logic as well as in metaphysics and natural philosophy. But in the strictest sense a subject is that which is first in some order of priority among those things that are called subjects in the sense just ellucidated. And sometimes the most general among such subjects is called the subject, sometimes the most perfect, and so on with respect to the various orders of priority.

The common trait exhibited by the things we call subject in these different senses is that each is a subject as regards predication.

31: On Predicate

A subject we have said is that part of a propositon preceding the copula. In similar fashion we can say that the predicate is that part of a proposition which follows the copula. Nevertheless, some want to say that the predicate is the copula together with what follows it; but since that controversy depends on features peculiar to conventional expressions, I shall ignore it for the present.

Whether we construe the predicate as including the copula, the term 'predicate' is used in a variety of senses. In one sense anything is a predicate which is the extreme of a proposition and not its subject; in this sense anything can be a predicate because anything can be the predicate of a true or false proposition.

In another sense we call that a predicate which is predicated in a true proposition where we have direct predication. In this sense 'animal' is a predicate with respect to 'man' but not with respect to 'stone'.

In a third sense a predicate is that which is predicated, by direct predication, of some subject of which there can be science in the strict sense. It is in this sense that the philosopher uses 'predicate' in the first book of the *Topics* where he distinguishes the four predicates—genus, definition, property, and accident; under the genus he also includes difference.[1] He does not mention species here because although the species is predicated of the individual, the individual cannot be the subject of a proposition grasped by what in the strict sense is called science. It is for this reason that he does not list species here.

The verb connecting the predicate with the subject is called the copula.

32: On Inherence and Being In

We say that predicates are predicated of their subjects; but we also say that predicates are in, belong to, and inhere in their subjects. Such locutions should not be understood to imply that predicates really inhere in their subjects in the way that whiteness inheres in the wall. On the contrary these locutions are synonymous with 'predicated of'. They should not be taken in any other way. Thus, all the accidents which constitute the nine categories can be said to be in substance as in a subject, but not because they really inhere in substance; the notion is, rather, that of inherence by way of true predication. Some who say that quantity is an accident which is in substance want to deny that quantity actually inheres in substance; they mean on the contrary that it is contingently predicated of substance so that it is possible for substances to exist when the proposition 'Substance is a quantity', is false.

Similarly, other expressions like 'come to', 'leave', 'present in', and 'absent from' are frequently used in place of 'predicated of'. The venerable Anselm in his

[1] 101^b 37-102^b 26.

Monologion says, "While some of those things (e.g., colors) that are said to be accidents can come to or leave the thing participating in them only with some change in that thing, others (e.g., certain relations) can be present in or absent from that of which they are predicated without any change in that thing."[1] Anselm is using the terms 'come to', 'leave', 'present in', and 'absent from' in place of 'predicated of'; likewise, logicians frequently use 'participate in' for 'to be a subject of'.

33: On Signification

Logicians use the term 'signify' in a number of ways. First, a sign is said to signify something when it supposits for or is capable of suppositing for that thing in such a way that the name can, with the verb 'to be' intervening, be predicated of a pronoun referring to that thing. Thus 'white' signifies Socrates, for 'He is white' is true where 'he' refers to Socrates. Likewise, 'rational' signifies man, for 'He is rational' is true where 'he' refers to man, and so on with many other concrete terms.

In another sense we say that a sign signifies something when it is capable of suppositing for that thing in a true past, present, or future proposition or in a true modal proposition. Thus 'white' not only signifies what is now white but also what can be white; for if we take the subject of the proposition 'What is white can run' for what can be, then it supposits for those things that can be white.

If we take 'signify' and the related term 'significatum' in the first sense, then it frequently happens that a word and the concept corresponding to it cease to signify some object which they previously signified as a result of a change in that object. But when we use these terms in the second sense neither a word nor its concept ceases to signify an object merely as a consequence of some change in the external object.

In another sense we say that a thing is signified by a word or concept which is taken from the expression or concept signifying that thing in the first mode, or when the thing is that on the basis of which the word or concept is imposed. Thus, since 'whiteness' signifies whiteness, we say that 'white' signifies whiteness. 'White', however, does not supposit for whiteness. In the same way 'rational', if it really is the difference of man, signifies man's intellective soul.

[1] P.L., T. 158, 178C.

In the broadest sense of all we say that a term signifies provided it is a sign which is capable of being a part of a proposition or a whole proposition and designates something, whether primarily or secondarily, whether in the nominative or one of the oblique cases, whether by actually expressing or merely connoting something, whether by signifying affirmatively or merely negatively. In this sense we say that the name 'blind' signifies sight because it does so negatively, similarly, that 'immaterial' signifies matter negatively and that both 'nothing' and 'non-being' signify being but in a negative way. Anselm discusses this mode of signifying in *On the Fall of the Devil.*[1]

Therefore, in some sense of 'signify' every universal can be said to signify. In chapter 8 of *Logic*, Damascene says, "The universal is what signifies many, for example, 'man' and 'animal'."[2] Every universal signifies many in the first or second way since every universal is predicated of many either in a *de inesse* present tense proposition or in a past, present, or future proposition or in a modal proposition. Clearly then those are wrong who say that the word 'man' does not signify all men. According to the aforementioned authority the universal term 'man' signifies many things; but since it does not signify many things which are not men, it must signify many men. This point must be granted; for nothing is signified by 'man' except men, and not one man more than another.

Therefore every universal signifies many things. Genera and species, since they can be predicated of a pronoun referring to some object, do not signify many except in the first or second sense. But of the remaining universals many signify in the first or second sense only; whereas others signify in the third or fourth senses as well. Thus every universal that is not a genus or species, while signifying many things in the nominative case, also signifies something else in one of the oblique cases. This is clear with 'rational', 'risible', and 'white', and similarly of course with other universals.

34: On Division

A universal not only signifies many but is divided into many. 'To be divided', however, has a number of senses. For something is said to be divided when by a real partition of the whole one part is physically separated from another. In

[1] *Ibid.,* T. 158, 339B-341C.
[2] *Dialectica,* chapter 8, 27-28.

this sense we say that the carpenter divides wood, the mason divides stone, and the blacksmith, iron.

But in another sense we speak of dividing something in such a way that no part of the thing is actually separated from another part. This sort of division applies to items under which many things are subsumed. In this sense I might divide the word 'dog' into its significata, saying that one kind of dog is a barking dog and another is a celestial body, and so on. I do not in this case separate one part of the word from another. Rather, I take the many to which the word is common, and I separate them under different common notions. It is in this sense that logicians speak of division. "There are," Damascene says in chapter 12 of *Logic*,[1] "eight ways of dividing things. (1) A genus can be divided into its species, as *animal* is divided into *rational* and *irrational*. (2) A species is divided into its individuals, as *man* is divided into Peter and Paul and the other inidividuals who are men. (3) A whole is divided into its parts, either into similar parts or dissimilar parts. We have a division into similar parts when the parts are each called by the name of the whole and have the same definition as the whole. Thus we might divide flesh into many fleshes: each element in the division is called flesh and has the definition of flesh. Division into dissimilar parts occurs when the parts have neither the same name nor definition as the whole. Thus we can divide Socrates into his head, his hands, and his feet: none of these has the same name or the same definition as Socrates. (4) We can also divide an equivocal word into its various significata and this can happen in two ways, either as a whole or as a part." After providing some examples Damascene continues, "(5) We can divide a substance into its accidents, as when we say that some men are white and some black. (6) We can also divide an accident into its substances, as when we say that some white things have souls and some do not; and (7) We can divide an accident into its accidents, as when we say that some cold things are dry and some wet. Finally, (8) We can divide something into those things that derive from it or we can divide something into those things from which it derives. Thus in the first case we say that the medical art gives rise to medical books and to medical instruments, and in the second that health derives from healthy foods and healthy water."

It should be noted that in the aforesaid modes of division we take one thing, and without physically dividing or separating one part from another, we generate many things. Nevertheless, in some modes of division that which is divided designates something which can really be divided into items which are designated by the dividentia. The third and fourth modes of division are examples. In other modes this is not so. When we say that some men are white and some black, we are not dividing a whole into its real parts; those parts are, however, actually separated from each other.

It should be noted also that when we speak of a substance as being divided

[1] *Ibid.,* chapter 12, 17-44.

into its accidents, an accident into its substances or an accident into its accidents, the term 'accident' is used to mean that which is contingently predicated of something, viz., that actual existent which is designated by the subject. And it is clear that frequently in the authorities 'accident' is not used for some accidental thing really inhering in substance, but for 'what can be contingently predicated of substance'. If the aforesaid author had taken 'accident' for something really inhering in a subject, he should have said that man is divided into whiteness and blackness and not into white men and black men and, similarly, in the other cases.

35: On Whole

The word 'whole' has a number of senses. In one sense we say that a whole is something incorporating many parts without which it cannot exist in nature. It is impossible that a man exists without his body and rational soul, that air exists without the relevant matter and form, and that wood exists without this or that part. In all these cases the part belongs to the essence of the whole and not vice versa.

In another sense we call something a whole which is common to many. In this sense a genus is a whole with respect to its species, and a species is said to be a whole with respect to its individuals. Here, a whole is something common. It is in this sense that logicians frequently use the term.

But for every sense of the term 'whole' there is a corresponding sense of the term 'part'. Thus, some parts belong to the essence of the whole while others are said to be parts only because they are less general than that of which they are said to be parts. Finally, we call those things subjective parts which belong to the essence of the whole no more than the whole belongs to their essence; and as that kind of part can exist without its whole, so also can the corresponding whole exist without its parts.

Although the words 'part' and 'whole' have a number of other senses, these will suffice for the present.

36: On Opposition

Next we shall consider opposition. It should be noted that the term 'opposite' signifies not only things (both those that are in the soul and those outside) but also signs of things. But things outside the soul, things that are not signs, can only be opposed as contraries; or, according to one view, they can also be opposed as relatives. The point is clear. For when objects are opposed there are only two possibilities. Either the opposed objects are both absolute things. Then the only form of opposition that can possibly obtain is that of contrariety. This is clear from induction (or they can also be opposed as relatives; then they cannot be opposed except as relatives and contraries). Or one of the objects is an absolute thing and the other a relative thing. But in this case the objects are not really opposed. Thus, when absolute forms are so related that they cannot simultaneously but only successively be present in the same subject, they are opposed as contraries. Nevertheless, as I shall show later, this form of contrariety is subject to degrees. If we speak of that form of opposition which obtains between signs (concepts, spoken words, and written words), then, according to the Peripatetics the term 'opposite' is predicated of both complex and simple terms.

There are three ways in which complex terms can be opposed. Some are contradictories. Here we have two propositions with the same subject and the same predicate, one of which is affirmative and the other negative. This characterization, however, is incomplete, for one of the propositions must be universal and the other particular or indefinite, or both must be singular. For example, the following propositions are opposed as contradictories: 'Every man is an animal' and 'Some man is not an animal'. Likewise, the following: 'Every man is an animal' and 'A man is not an animal'. In this last case we have contradictories because an indefinite proposition, when its subject is taken significatively, is always convertible with the corresponding particular proposition. Thus the universal contradicts both the particular and the indefinite. Likewise the following propositions are contradictories: 'No man is an animal' and 'Some man is an animal' / 'A man is an animal'. The following also contradict each other: 'Socrates is an animal' and 'Socrates is not an animal'.

Some propositions are opposed as contraries: the universal affirmative and the universal negative. This obtains when the subjects are taken significatively; otherwise it is not necessary. The following propositions are not opposed as contraries: ' "Every man" is a general term combined with the sign of universality' and ' "No man" is a general term combined with the sign of universality.'

There is no name for the third form of opposition between complex terms. Propositions that are neither contradictories nor contraries are such that either they imply contradictories or one implies the contradictory of the other. Since the relevant implications hold, propositions of this sort cannot be simultaneously true. Thus, the following propositions are opposed: 'No animal runs' and 'Some man runs'. Since they do not have the same subject, they are neither contraries nor contradictories. They are opposed, rather, because 'Some man runs' entails the contradictory of 'No animal runs'; for it follows that since some man runs some animal runs.

From the foregoing it is clear that propositions which are related as subalterns and subcontraries are not opposed; they can be simultaneously true.

Among simple terms there are four forms of opposition. Some simple terms are contraries. These are simple terms which signify whatever they signify affirmatively and positively rather than negatively (that is there are no negative terms nor any expressions equivalent to such in the definitions expressing the meaning of the terms) and which, in addition, cannot be affirmed of one and the same thing simultaneously but only successively. Expressions are also contraries which cannot be truly predicated of the same thing either simultaneously or successively provided that they signify things which cannot be present in the same thing simultaneously. Examples of the first kind of contrariety are 'white' and 'black'. These terms signify nothing negatively; nevertheless, taken significatively they cannot be affirmed of the same thing simultaneously, although they can be affirmed successively. Nevertheless, as will be indicated later there are degrees in this kind of opposition. Examples of the second kind of contrariety are 'whiteness' and 'blackness'. These terms signify the kind of things outlined, and the terms themselves cannot either simultaneously or successively be affirmed of the same object while suppositing for that object. As with the first form of contrariety, there can be degrees here.

But some simple terms are opposed as positive and privative. Here the terms are such that one of them signifies whatever it signifies positively and the other, while signifying something positively, signifies negatively what its opposite signifies affirmatively. This comes out in the definition expressing the meaning of the term, for in that definition a negative expression precedes the positive term opposed to it. 'Sight' and 'blindness' are so related, for 'sight' signifies affirmatively whatever it signifies. In the definition expressing its meaning there is no negative term. 'Blindness' or 'blind', on the other hand, signify something affirmatively and something negatively; for 'blind' is defined thus: a blind person is one who does not have the sight which he is apt to have. Here an expression precedes the negative term; its significatum is affirmatively designated by 'blind'. An expression also follows the sign of negation; its significatum is negatively signified by 'blind'. Some one might say that because of the clause which follows, the very same thing is affirmatively designated; but my point still stands; for in any event that thing is designated negatively. Nor is there anything problematical in the fact that a thing is designated both affirmatively and negatively by one and the same term. It is like a point we earlier made: one and the same thing can be signified by the same term in both the nominative and oblique cases.

St. Anselm suggests this distinction between signifying something affirmatively and negatively in chapter 11 of *The Fall of the Devil.* "It is clear that the expression 'nothing' does not, in its signification, differ from the expression 'non-something'. Further, it is obvious that the term 'non-something' has the effect, by its signification, of removing cognitively everything, whether external or internal, which is something and of retaining cognitively nothing, whether internal or external, which is something. But the removal of something can in no way be signified except by the signification of that whose removal is signified. No one understands what 'non-man' signifies except by understanding what man is. Therefore it is necessary that the expression 'non-something', by removing that which is something, signify something." Anselm continues, "It signifies something by removing that notion, not by affirming it." He also says, "Thus, there is nothing repugnant in the joint supposition that evil is nothing and that the term 'evil' is significant. It could signify negatively, thereby affirming nothing."[1]

From these and other remarks which Anselm makes in the same treatise it is clear that some simple terms signify by removing, negating, or denying something and that others signify by affirming or positing something.

It follows that privation is not something inhering in an object outside the mind and that it is not in any way distinct from that which is positive. Blindness does not, on the part of the thing, inhere in the eye. As Anselm says in an earlier passage, "Many things are expressed by a form of language that does not correspond to the facts. Thus, 'to fear' is grammatically in the active voice; in actual fact it is something passive. Similarly, according to the form of speech blindness is said to be something; in actual fact it is not anything at all. Just as we say that an object has sight and that sight is in the object, we say that an object has blindness and that blindness is in it. Actually, blindness is not something; it is, rather, a non-something. To have blindness is not to have something. On the contrary it is the lack of that which is something, for blindness is nothing but sightlessness or the absence of sight in that in which sight ought to be. But sightlessness or the absence of sight is not something existing where sight ought to be rather than where it ought not be. Just because sight ought to be in the eye, it does not follow that blindness is in the eye rather than, say, in the stone where sight ought not be."[2]

It is clear, then, on the basis of this authority that blindness is not something

[1] P.L., 339B-340A.
[2] *Ibid.,* 340C-341A.

existing, on the part of the thing, in the eye and, consequently, that it does not exist anywhere on the part of the thing. Thus, those things which are outside the soul are not opposed as positive and privative. Rather, the signs of things, one of which signifies affirmatively and the other negatively, are opposed by means of privation.

Opposition in terms of relatives obtains among names which cannot be affirmed of the same thing with respect to the same thing. This holds true whether things outside the soul are opposed as relatives or not. It is not, however, because I deny that relations are things outside the mind that I speak of names as relatives. One could use the term apropos of things as well as names of things. But that some names are relatives is clear from the work of the grammarians for whom the relative name constitutes one species of name.

Simple terms are opposed as contradictories when one of them affirmatively signifies some thing or things and the other negatively signifies the same thing or things without signifying anything affirmatively. 'Man' signifies all men affirmatively and 'non-man' signifies those very same men negatively while affirmatively signifying nothing in any determinate or definite way. I add the final qualification to meet the objection of the quibbler who would say that 'non-man' signifies a donkey on the basis that it can supposit for a donkey in the proposition 'A donkey is a non-man'.

It should be noted that all opposites are in themselves really positive and absolute things and that when they supposit for themselves, the expression 'real thing' can be predicated of them. Thus, if the subject in the proposition ' "Non being" is a being' supposits for itself, the proposition is true; for that subject really is a being. It is a subject and therefore a part of a proposition, and no proposition is composed of non-beings.

One might object here that if propositions of this form be allowed to stand, then one of a pair of opposites can be predicated of the other. The response here is simply that there is nothing problematical in one opposite being predicated of the other provided that the second is not suppositing significatively but only simply or materially. Such propositions as ' "Non-expression" is an expression', ' "Non-simple" is simple', and ' "Non-part" is a part' are true. Similarly, the proposition ' "Non-word" is a word' is true; for if the subject is suppositing for itself, it is certain that it is a word; what I utter when I say 'non-word' is surely a word.

For the present this is enough on opposition. The many points I have omitted here I have considered in my commentary on the *Categories*.[3]

---

[3] See *Expositio Aurea super Artem Veterem,* ed., Marcus de Benevento (Bologna, 1496).

37: On Passion

We have yet to consider a term which logicians frequently employ in dealing with demonstration, that is, 'passion'. It should be noted that although this term can be used in a variety of senses, as I have indicated in my commentary on the *Categories,* nevertheless, as logicians usually use the term a passion is not something outside the mind inhering in that whose passion it is said to be. On the contrary a passion is something mental, spoken, or written that is predicable in the second mode of perseity of the subject whose passion it is said to be. Actually, only what is mental and not what is spoken or written is a passion in the strict and proper sense; but in a secondary, extended sense, we call both spoken and written words passions, as when we say that in the spoken proposition 'Every man is risible' a passion is predicated of its subject.

It is clear that a passion is not something outside the soul, something over and above a predicable sign. According to philosophers a passion is predicated in the second mode of perseity of its subject, but only that which is a concept, a spoken word, or a written word can function as predicate. Propositions are composed only of these things and not of objects outside the soul. Thus passions cannot be objects outside the soul.

Again, being has passions; but clearly they cannot inhere in that general notion; therefore. . . .

Again, according to philosophers every passion is the passion of some universal; but nothing extrinsic to the soul inheres first and foremost in some universal; therefore. . . .

Again, we predicate of God the passions proper to Him; but nothing can be said to inhere in God; therefore, passions are not the kinds of things that inhere in their subjects.

It should be said then that a passion is simply something predicable in the second mode of perseity of its subject; and since every such thing is a part of a proposition, we must conclude that a passion is not the sort of thing that exists outside the soul. It follows that it is not impossible for a subject to exist in nature without its passion and, similarly, that it is not impossible for a passion to exist without its subject. Thus, when writers say that the subject cannot exist without its passion, we should understand them to mean that a passion cannot be truly denied of its subject, provided that 'exists' is truly predicated of that subject. Thus, the proposition 'God is not creative' is impossible, even though God can exist and once did when the predicate in question was not an actual existent.

It should further be noted that a passion always supposits for the same thing as its subject, although it may signify in some way something different from that subject, either in the nominative or in one of the oblique cases or affirmatively or negatively. Thus, some passions are called positive and others negative.

It should be clear from the foregoing how one can be a passion of being and really distinct from that general notion being whose passion it is while signifying the same thing as being; for as the definition expressing the meaning of the name indicates, it signifies in a manner different from being. It holds universally that a subject and its passion are really different things, although they supposit for the same thing and although predicating one of the other yields a necessary proposition.

38: On Being

Having dealt with terms of second intention and second imposition we shall turn our attention to those terms of first intention that are called the categories. But first we shall consider some expressions that are common to all things, both signs and things that are not signs. 'Being' and 'one' are terms of this sort.

It should first be noted that the term 'being' has two senses. In one sense the term is used to correspond to one concept that is common to all things and is predicable *in quid* of everything in the way in which a transcendental is capable of being predicated *in quid*.

One can prove that there is one common concept predicable of everything in the following way: if there is no one such common concept, then there are different concepts for different things. Let us suppose that there are two such concepts, A and B. Following out this supposition, I can show that some concept more general than A and B is predicable of an object, C. Just as we can form the verbal propositions 'C is B', 'C is A', and 'C is something,' we can form three corresponding mental propositions. Two of these are dubious and one is certain; for someone can doubt which of the first two is true, while knowing that the third is true. If this is granted, I argue as follows: two of the propositions are dubious and one is certain. The three propositions all have the same subject; therefore, they have different predicates. Were it not so, one and the same proposition would be both certain and dubious; for in the present case the first two are dubious. But if they have

different predicates, the predicate in '*C* is something' is not the predicate
in either '*C* is *B*' or '*C* is *A*'. It is, we can conclude, a different predicate.
But it is clear that the relevant predicate is neither less general nor convertible with either *A* or *B*. It must therefore be more general. But this is
what we set out to prove—that some concept of the mind, different from
those that are logically subordinated to it, is common to everything. That
must be granted. Just as one word is capable of being truly predicated of
everything, there is some one concept of the mind that can be truly predicated of every object or of every pronoun referring to an object.

But while there is one concept common to everything, the term 'being' is
equivocal because it is not predicated of the items logically subordinated
to it according to just one concept; several different concepts correspond to
the term as I have indicated in my commentary on Porphyry.[1]

Further, it should be noted that, as the Philosopher says in the fifth
book of the *Metaphysics,* "Being is said both essentially and accidentally."[2]
In drawing this distinction the Philosopher should not be understood to mean
that some things are beings *per se* and others, beings *per accidens.* What he
is doing on the contrary is pointing to the different ways in which one thing
can be predicated of another through the mediation of 'to be'. This is clear
from the examples he uses. As he notes, we say that the musical is *per accidens* just, that the musical is *per accidens* a man, and that the musical is
per accidens a builder. It should be clear from these examples that he is
only distinguishing the different ways of predicating one thing of another,
viz., *per accidens* and *per se.* It is clear that there are not two kinds of being,
the *per se* and the *per accidens.* Everything is either a substance or an accident, but both substances and accidents are beings *per se.* This point holds
even though we have *per se* and *per accidens* predication.

Similarly, being is divided into being in potency and being in act. This
should not be understood to mean that there are two kinds of beings, those
which do not exist in nature but could and those which actually exist in
nature. By dividing being into potency and act in the fifth book of the
Metaphysics, Aristotle means to show that the term 'being' is predicated of
some things by means of *de inesse* propositions and not by means of propositions equivalent to propositions of possibility.[3] Thus 'Socrates is a being'
and 'Whiteness is a being'. Of other things, Aristotle wants to say, 'being' is
predicated only by means of a proposition of possibility or by a proposition
equivalent to such. Thus 'The Anti-Christ can be' and 'The Anti-Christ is a
being in potency'. He wants to say that being like knowledge and sleep, can

[1] *Expositio,* Chapter III, 39-99.
[2] 1017^a 7.
[3] 1017^a 35-1017^b 1.

be predicated both potentially and actually. But note: things do not sleep
or have knowledge except actually.

We will talk about the other divisions in being elsewhere.. In the interests
of brevity these remarks will suffice for the present.

39: On One

One is a passion of being since it is predicated of being in the second
mode of perseity; for although 'being' signifies what 'one' signifies, it does
not signify this in the same way. Whatever 'being' signifies, it signifies positively and affirmatively rather than negatively. 'One', on the other hand,
signifies all of the things signified by 'being' in both an affirmative and
negative way. This is clear from the definition expressing the meaning of the
word.

'One' has several senses; for as the philosopher indicates in the fifth Book
of the *Metaphysics*, some things are said to be one essentially and others accidentally.[1] This should be understood to mean that the name 'one' is predicated of some things *per se* (i.e., in such a way that the proposition in which
'one' is predicated is a *per se* proposition) and that it is predicated of other
things *per accidens* (i.e., in such a way that the proposition in which 'one' is
predicated is a *per accidens* proposition). Thus the proposition 'Coriscus and
the musical man are one' is *per accidens,* as is the proposition 'The just man
and the musical man are one'. Nonetheless, the following propositions 'The
just man and the musical man are *per se* one' and 'Coriscus and the musical
man are *per se* one' are true. If one should run up against propositions like
'The musical man and the white man are *per accidens* one' and 'The musical
man is *per accidens* one with Coriscus', he should construe them to mean
'The proposition "The musical man and the white man are one" is *per accidens*' and 'The proposition "The musical man is one with Coriscus" is *per
accidens*'. Later I will show how these propositions can be distinguished.

That is essentially one which is not said to be one *per accidens* but *per
se*; although the Philosopher posits many forms of *per se* unity in the fifth
book of the *Metaphysics,* we need only consider the three forms of *per se*
unity that logicians frequently employ.

Some things are said to be numerically one; that is, of terms which supposit for one and the same thing; the expression 'numerically one' is truly
predicable. Examples are 'That man and Socrates are numerically one' and

[1] 1015^{b} 16.

'Marcus and Tullius are numerically one'. Thus when Aristotle says in the fifth book of the *Metaphysics*, that "Things are numerically one which are one in matter," he only means that things are said to be numerically one when they are not distinct either in their matter or in their form.[2]

Further, those things are said to be specifically one for which there is one and the same species. Thus, things specifically one are always either numerically many or numerically one. As Aristotle says in the first book of the *Topics*, "Things are specifically the same which, while being many," (supply here, if they are not numerically one) "are contained under the same species."[3]

Finally, those things are generically one which are contained in the same genus. Things that are generically one are either both specifically and numerically many or they are specifically one. Aristotle says, "Things that are numerically one are always specifically one; but things that are specifically one are not, all of them, numerically one. Likewise, things specifically one are always generically one, but things that are generically one are not all specifically one."[4]

From these remarks it follows that nothing is specifically one unless it is either numerically one or many. Consequently, it is impossible that there be a nature that is specifically one and neither numerically one nor many. Similarly, it is impossible that there be a nature that is generically one without being either specifically one or many. Therefore, it should be said that many individuals are specifically one and that one individual is specifically the same as another individual. Likewise, many individuals of different species are generically one, and an individual of one species is generically one with another individual of another species. Socrates and the donkey are generically one, that is, there is one genus capable of being predicated of both. Similarly, Socrates and Plato are specifically one; they are contained under one species. Put in another way Socrates and Plato are such that we can abstract from them one species common to both.

To the objection that Socrates and Plato are not really one, one should reply that they are really one provided that the term 'one' is being used in the appropriate sense—to mean one in species; for Socrates and Plato really are things such that one species can be abstracted from them. Thus, it should be granted that there is a form of unity less restrictive than numerical unity. Nonetheless, each of those things are one in a sense in which it is impossible that they are one with anything that is in any way distinct from them.

[2] 1016^b 32.
[3] 103^a 13.
[4] 1016^b 36-1017^a 2.

Next we should consider the notions logically subordinated to being, the ten categories. It should be noted that the name 'category', like the name 'genus', is a name of second intention, although the expressions of which it is predicated are simple terms of first intention.

Nevertheless, 'category' has two senses. In one sense it is used to signify the whole series of terms ordered according to greater and lesser generality. In the other sense the word is used for the first and most general term in each such series. In the second sense of 'category', every category is a simple term of first intention inasmuch as it signifies things which are not signs. However, employing the word in the first sense, one can say that in some of the categories there are simple terms of both first and second intention. Put otherwise, some of the categories are composed of both first and second intentions. Thus, in the view which construes intentions or concepts as qualities existing subjectively in the mind, the general term 'genus', for example, belongs in the category of quality; for in that view every genus is a quality. Now, 'genus' is a name of second intention, but the common term 'color' is an expression of first intention. The same point holds in many other cases.

One might object to the above by denying that a first intention can be more general than a second intention.

Similarly one might argue that a first intention cannot be predicated of a second intention, or vice versa.

Finally one might object that a being of the reason is not capable of being in a category of the real; but since a second intention is a being of the reason, it cannot be in a category of the real.

In response to the first objection it should be noted that one first intention is more general than any second intention; for *being* is a first intention, yet it is more general than any notion of second intention. Every second intention is a being, but not vice versa.

In response to the second objection it should be said that no first intention is predicated of a second intention when both are suppositing for themselves; for then it would have to be granted that some second intention is identical with some first intention, and that, of course, is false. Nonetheless, a first intention, suppositing not for itself but for a second intention, can be predicated of a second intention. Thus, the proposition 'The genus of substance is a quality' is true; nonetheless, the predicate 'quality' truly applies because it stands not for itself but for the second intention which is a genus. Similarly, in the spoken proposition 'A name is a quality', a name of first imposition is predicated of a name of second imposition. It does not, however, supposit for itself, but for the name of second imposition of which it is predicated. While the relevant proposition is true, no name of second imposition is identical with a name of first imposition.

In response to the third objection, it should be noted that the expression 'to be in a category' has two senses. In the first sense an object is in a category when the first term in that category, significatively taken, can be predicated of the pronoun referring to that object. In this sense nothing is in the genus of substance except particular substances, for nothing is a substance except particular substances. In this sense of the phrase all the universals designating only substances fall under the category of quality, for all universals are qualities.

In the other sense something is in a category where it is the sort of thing which, significatively taken, can have as its predicate the first term in that category, significatively taken. In this sense universals are in the category of substance; for 'substance', significatively taken, is predicable of some universals, significatively taken. Thus, 'Every man is a substance'; 'Every animal is a substance'; 'Every stone is a substance'; etc. In this sense other universals fall under the category of quality, and so on with the remaining categories. But then the relevant proposition ('No being of the reason is capable of being in a category of the real') is false whether 'to be in a category' is taken in the first or second sense.

Nevertheless, it should be pointed out that in the view that construes intentions, concepts, and passions of the soul as qualities of the mind, the concept is not said to be a being of the reason because it is not a real thing existing in the nature of things, but rather because it exists only in the reason and is an object that the mind uses for some purpose or other. Thus all propositions, inferences, and mental terms are beings of the reason. Nonetheless, they really exist in nature and are beings more perfect and more real than any corporeal qualities. Therefore, when the Commentator and the Philosopher divide being into real being and being of the reason, or being in the soul and being outside the soul, and afterwards divide real being into the ten categories, they are not dividing the notion into opposites in the way in which we divide animal, say, into the rational and the irrational. On the contrary, this is a division of a word into its meanings in the way that Aristotle, in the first book of the *Prior Analytics,* divides the contingent into the contingent-necessary, the contingent by chance, and the possible in general. One of these three notions is predicable of the others, for the following are true: 'The contingent-necessary is possible' and 'The contingent by chance is possible'. In the same way the relevant division of being is not incompatible with the truth of the proposition 'A being of the reason is a real being', provided that we construe 'real being' to be suppositing for something which is a real quality existing in nature. If, however, 'real external being' is taken

to mean 'that which is not in the soul', then the division of being into the
ten categories is not a division of a general notion into its logical inferiors.
On the contrary it is to be construed along the following lines: some real
being outside the soul is designated by this category and some by that, and
so on. Or it would be like the following: every real being outside the soul
is in some category or other. But while we may interpret the categories in
this way, we must grant that many things which are not objects outside
the mind are subsumed under the categories.

41: On the Distinction of the Categories

The next thing to be considered is the number of the categories. All writers
agree that there are ten categories; nevertheless, it seems to me that many recent writers are in disagreement with the ancients on the question of the
structure of the categories. For many writers say that in every category there
are terms ordered according to greater and lesser generality in such a way that
the more general is predicated in the nominative case and in the first mode of
perseity of every item less general than it by a predication of the form 'Every
A is B'. To preserve such forms of predication in the case of adverbs, they invent abstract names. From 'where', which is an adverb, they form an abstract
term like 'whereness'; and from 'when' the name 'wheness'; and similarly in
the case of other such terms.

But the ancients, it seems to me, did not postulate this sort of structure in
each category. They used the name 'category' and terms like 'genus' and 'species' more broadly than many recent writers. When the ancient writers said that
the more general is always predicable of the less general and that every category has under it species, they were extending the use of the term 'predicate'
in such a way that it applies to verbs. They were using the term as we do when
we say that 'walks' is predicated of 'man' in 'Man walks' and when we speak of
the predicates in the propositions 'He is wearing shoes' and 'He is armed'.
They also extended the notion of predication to include the predication of
adverbs and prepositions along with their objects, just as we do in propositions
like 'This is today', 'That was yesterday', 'He is at home', and 'He is in the city'.
In each category we can find some of the relevant predications, but it is not
necessary that there always be proper predication involving only terms in the
nominative case. Thus, not every series of terms is so ordered that the more

general can be predicated of the less general in the strict sense of 'predicate'; some series can be said to be ordered in this way only when we take the term 'predicate' in the broader sense.

Since the view of the ancients seems more plausible to me, I shall try to outline that view in what follows.

The truth of the view can be shown if we look at the way Aristotle ennumerates the categories. He says "Expressions which involve no combination signify substance or quality or quantity or relation or where or when or to be situated or to wear or to do or to suffer."[1] Afterwards, by way of example, he says, "Where, as 'in this place'; when, as 'yesterday'; to be situated, as 'sits' and 'lies'; to wear, as 'wearing shoes' and 'armed'; to do, as 'to cut' and 'to burn'; and to suffer, as 'to be cut' and 'to be burnt'."[2] He makes the same point again in the chapter on doing and suffering.

Likewise, in chapter 32 of his *Logic*, Damascene says "It is necessary to know that there are ten categories, that is, ten most general genera under which every simple term is subsumed. The categories are: substance, as 'stone'; quantity, as 'two' and 'three'; relation, as 'father' and 'son'; quality, as 'white' and 'black'; where, which incorporates terms which express place, as 'in Tyre' and 'in Damascene'; when, which incorporates terms expressing time, as 'yesterday' and 'tomorrow'; to wear, as 'to put on clothes'; to be situated, as 'to stand' and 'to sit'; to do, as 'to burn'; and to suffer, as 'to be burnt'."[3]

These passages from these two writers, one a saint and the other a philosopher, are sufficient to show that neither construes the categories as anything other than certain simple terms containing under them different words or intentions of the soul, of which, nonetheless, they are not always predicable by proper predication in the nominative case.

To see this one should note that in the view of the ancients the items in the categories are just certain simple terms, out of which affirmations and negations (i.e. affirmative and negative propositions) are capable of being composed. To bring this out Aristotle comments, "None of these terms by themselves involves an affirmation. It is, on the contrary, by combining these terms with each other that affirmations are produced."[4] Damascene says that under the ten categories "is subsumed every simple term,"[5] that is, every categorical word which is neither an affirmation nor a negation. Both writers intend that the terms subsumed under the categories are simple terms out of which propositions can be composed. This holds for simple

[1] 1^b 25-26.
[2] 1^b 26-2^a 3.
[3] *Dialectica*, chapter 32, 7-14.
[4] 2^a 4-6.
[5] *Dialectica*, chapter 32, 8-9.

terms of both the mental and the vocal sort; nevertheless, mental terms are prior as I shall show later.

As the Commentator indicates in the seventh book of the *Metaphysics*, the distinction among the categories is taken from the distinction among interrogatives appropriate to substance or an individual substance.[6] The different questions which can be asked about a substance can be answered by different simple terms, and a simple term falls under a category accordingly as it can be used to answer this or that question about substance. Thus, all such simple terms as can be used to answer the question 'What is it?' (asked of some individual substance) fall under the category of substance. Expres-sions like 'man', 'animal', 'stone', 'body', 'earth', 'fire', 'sun', and 'moon' are examples. Those which are used to answer the question 'Of what quality is it?' (asked of some substance) fall in the genus of quality. Examples are 'white', 'warm', 'knowing', 'square', 'long', and 'wide'. Those, on the other hand, which can be used to answer the question 'How much?' (again, as posed of a substance) are contained in the genus of quantity such as 'two cubits', 'three cubits', etc. But those which can be used to answer the question 'Of whom?' or some similar question (for here we have no one general interrogative word) are in the category of relation. Those which can be used to answer the question 'Where?' are in the category of where. However, one cannot answer this question except by means of adverbs and prepositions with their objects. Thus, if it is asked, "Where is Socrates?", the appropriate response is "Here" or "There" or "In Tyre" or "In Damascus" or "At sea" or "On land." All of these simple terms (I call them such since none of them such since none of them involves an affirmation or a negation) are in the category of where. Likewise, one can respond to the question 'When?' only by means of adverbs and prepositions with their objects. Thus, if it is asked, "When was Socrates?", one should respond by saying, "Yesterday" or "On such an such a day." It is precisely such terms which belong in the genus of when. Likewise, to the question raised by asking "What does Soc-rates do?", one can respond by way of verbs saying, "Warms" or "Walks". Such parts of speech, then, belong in the category of action. The same sort of account holds for the remaining categories, although there are not general interrogatives appropriate to all the categories because of the poverty of our language.

It follows from this account that concrete terms like 'white', 'black', 'warm', and 'bitter' fall more directly under the category of quality than their abstract forms. It is for this reason that the Philosopher, when giving examples in the *Categories*, says "Quality as 'white'." Nevertheless, if we take the category of quality as something which universally excludes substance, then only abstract forms belong in the category, not the concrete.

[6] *Aristotelis Opera*, 164, recto, B.

This is what I meant when I said that the abstract terms are in the category per se and the concrete forms by reduction. But in this issue the difficulty is more verbal than real, so I shall not dwell on it. It is sufficient to know that every simple term which can be used to answer a question raised about a substance is in a category. It makes no difference whether it is an adverb, verb, name, or preposition with its object. But some simple terms are not in any category. Thus, conjunctions and syncategorematic terms are not subsumed under any category; for by terms like 'if', 'and', 'every', and 'no', one cannot respond to any of the questions which can be raised about a substance. However, should it turn out that some of these terms can, in some way, be used to respond to a definite question, although not to all of the questions, then those terms can be subsumed under the categories.

42: On Substance

Although we have hardly exhausted the general remarks that can be made about the categories, we shall now examine each of the particular categories in detail. First, we shall consider substance.

It should first be noted that 'substance' has many senses. In one sense substance is said to be anything that is distinct from other things. Writers use the word 'substance' in this sense when they speak of the substance of whiteness, the substance of color, etc.

In a stricter sense substance is anything which is not an accident inhering in something else. In this sense both matter and form as well as the whole composed of these are called substances.

In the strictest sense substance is that which is neither an accident inhering in another thing nor an essential part of something else, although it can combine with an accident. It is in this sense that substance is said to be a summum genus, and according to Aristotle it is divided into first and second substance.

But this should not be construed as the sort of division where the term divided can be predicated of the items dividing it, nor is the term divided predicable of the pronouns referring to the items dividing it. For when the reference is to a second substance, the proposition 'This is a substance' is false. Thus, the proposition 'No second substance is a substance' is true, and we can prove this by employing points established earlier. Earlier we established that no universal is a substance; but every second substance is a universal, since according to Aristotle second substances are either genera or species; therefore, no second substance is a substance.

Again, according to the teaching of Aristotle whatever is universally denied of everything immediately contained under some common term is universally denied of the common term itself, but 'second substance' is denied of everything immediately contained under 'substance'; therefore it is universally denied of substance. Thus, 'No substance is a second substance' is true, so, we can conclude, no second substance is a substance. My assumption is clear, for this is true: 'No corporeal substance is a second substance', as is the proposition, 'No incorporeal substance is a second substance'. We can show that the first of these is true (the same technique could be applied in the case of the second) by repeating the basic pattern of argument; for it is true that no besouled body is a second substance and, similarly, that no souless body is a second substance. We can show that the first of these is true (the same technique could be applied in the case of the second) by repeating the same basic pattern of argument; for it is true that no besouled body capable of perception is a second substance and, similarly, that no besouled body incapable of perception is a second substance. We can show that the first of these is true (the same technique could be applied in the case of the second) by again repeating the basic pattern of argument; for it is true that no besouled body which is capable of perception and rational is a second substance and, similarly, that no besouled body capable of perception, but who is irrational is a second substance. Clearly, the first of these is true; for it is convertible with the true proposition 'No man is a second substance'; and this last proposition is clearly true since each of the singular propositions supporting it is true. We are forced, then, to grant the Aristotelian view that no substance is a second substance. Therefore, when one refers to a second substance less general than 'substance' itself, the proposition 'This is a substance' is false.

It should be said that the division is a division of a common name into less common names. It is equivalent to the following division: of names signifying or designating substances outside the mind, some are names proper to just one substance (these names are first substances) and others are names common to many substances (these names are called second substances). Names which are second substances are further divided; some are genera and others are species. Nonetheless, all second substances are really just qualities. Thus, all those common names that are called second substances are in the category of quality at least in one sense of 'to be in a category', for the term 'quality' is always predicable of the pronoun referring to a second substance. However, in another sense all second substances are in the category of substance, since 'substance' is always predicable of them when they are taken significatively. Thus, in the propositions 'Man is an animal' and 'Man is a substance', 'man' supposits not for itself but for what it signifies. For if it were to supposit for itself, *'Man* is a substance' would be false and *'Man* is a quality' would be true. Likewise, if the word 'man' supposits for itself, the propositions *'Man* is a substance' is false and the proposition *'Man* is a word and a quality' is true. Second substances, then, are simply certain names and qualities signifying just substances. It is for this reason and no other that they are said to be in the category of substance.

It is clear that this account is in agreement with the remarks of the authors, for in the *Categories* the Philosopher says that "every substance seems to signify what is a this-something; of first substances it is indubitably true that they signify what is a this-something."[1] From this passage it is clear that Aristotle holds that first substances signify what is a this-something, but particular substances existing outside the mind do not signify what is a this-something. They are on the contrary things that are signified; therefore, Aristotle is here calling the names of particular substances existing outside the mind first substances. But then *a fortiori*, he must call the relevant names second substances.

Again several times in his commentary on the *Categories*, Boethius indicates that in that treatise the Philosopher is dealing with words and that, consequently, he calls words themselves first and second substances.[2]

Likewise, Aristotle says that first and second substances are in the category of substance, and in the same treatise he stipulates that the only items falling under the categories are the simple terms out of which propositions are composed.[3] Propositions, however, are not composed of substances existing outside the mind; therefore. . . .

Again, Damascene stipulates that only names are to be subsumed under the category of substance.[4]

Therefore, it is not at all incompatible with the remarks of the authors to say that Aristotle calls the common names of substances second substances, nor does Aristotle's own remark that "species are substances more than genera" present any difficulty here.[5] By remarks of this sort Aristotle only means that we can provide a more appropriate answer to the question "What is it?" (asked of some substance) by stating the species rather than the genus. Thus, although a proposition like 'Species are substances more than genera' is, literally taken, false, the point the Philosopher intended to make by the proposition is true.

To sum up: the division in question is a division among names; some are proper and some are common. Proper names are said to be first substances and common names second substances.

Nevertheless, it should be noted that the Philosopher uses the term 'first

[1] 3^b 10-11.
[2] *Patrologiae*, T. 64, 161 C-D.
[3] 1^b 25.
[4] *Dialectica*, chapter 32, 8-9.
[5] 2^b 7.

substance' equivocally in the *Categories*. For sometimes he uses it for the names of substances existing outside the soul as when he says, "First substance signifies what is a this-something";[6] but in other contexts he uses it for the substances themselves that exist outside the soul as when he says, "Substance is that which properly, principally. . . ."[7] Thus, when the Philosopher says "All other things are either said of the principal substances or are in them as subjects,"[8] he is not using the term 'subject' for things which really underly other things, but for the subjects of propositions. As Damascene says in chapter 8 of his *Logic*, " 'Subject' is used in two senses; there is the subject with respect to existence; in this sense the singular substance existing outside the soul is the subject for accidents. There is also the subject with respect to predication; in this sense the particular is the subject with respect to that which is more universal than it."[9] The Philosopher uses the term in the second sense when he says that second substances are said of a subject. Thus, first substances are not subjects really underlying second substances; they are subjects only by way of predication.

It is clear from this that the Philosopher sometimes calls names and signs of substances existing outside the soul first substances; for he says that second substances are said of first substances as subjects, but this could only be by way of predication. Thus, first substance is the subject in predication and second substance its predicate; but no proposition is composed of substances outside the soul; therefore, that first substance which is the subject of a proposition with respect to second substance is not a substance existing outside the soul. Thus, when Aristotle says that if first substances were destroyed it would be impossible for any of the other things to remain, he is not talking of real destruction and real existence.[10] He means, rather, destruction by way of a negative proposition. Thus, he is saying that when 'to be' is not predicated of anything contained under a common term, it is truly denied of the common term itself as well as of the properties and accidents proper to that common term. He only means then that inferences such as the following are valid: 'This man is not; that man is not; that . . . (and so for all individual men); therefore no man is; therefore, nothing is risible, therefore, nothing is grammatical; therefore, there is no grammar; therefore, there is no logic'. If he meant real destruction, what he says would be false; for although there were no stones, the genus *stone* could still exist; for it would still be possible for someone to form the propositions 'No man is a stone' and 'No stone is a donkey'; but neither of these could be formed unless the relevant parts of

[6] 3[b] 10.
[7] 2[a] 11.
[8] 2[a] 33-34.
[9] *Dialectica,* chapter 8, 21-28.
[10] 2[b] 4-6.

the proposition were there beforehand. But that is just to say that the genus *stone* would exist. Of course given the present assumption, it could not be affirmatively predicated of anything in a proposition that is both *de inesse* and in the present tense.

43: On the Properties of Substance

Now that we have seen which terms are to be placed in the categorical hierarchy of substance, we shall examine some of the properties of substance. In the *Categories,* Aristotle mentions a property he claims is common to all substances, both first and second substances—that substance is not in a subject.[1] If this property is understood to apply to substances existing outside the mind Aristotle's point is clear, for none of them is present in a subject. If, on the other hand, the property is taken to hold of first and second substances (things which are names of substances existing outside the mind) then the proposition 'Substance is not in a subject' should be understood in terms of the following proposition, a case of an act signified, ' "To be in a subject" is predicated of no proper or common name of substance taken significatively; "to be in a subject" is denied of every such name significatively taken'. Thus, every proposition like the following is true, 'Man is not in a subject', 'Animal is not in a subject', 'Socrates is not in a subject'. Nevertheless, if such terms were suppositing for themselves and not their significata, it would be true to say that they are in a subject; for they are really just parts of propositions and consequently concepts of the mind or spoken or written words.

But Aristotle himself seems opposed to this account, for he grants that second substances are said of subjects and denies that they are in a subject; but if we take 'second substances' uniformly, then one of these two properties does not apply.

The response is that the Philosopher is not employing the term in just one way; nor is there any requirement that he do so. Frequently it is useful, in the interests of brevity, to employ one and the same term in different ways. Thus, Aristotle only means that the common names of substances are predicated of subjects; nevertheless, of these same names, suppositing as they do in the relevant effected acts, one cannot truly predicate 'to be in a subject'.

[1] 3ª 6-7.

Thus, 'Socrates is an animal' is true; and of 'animal', suppositing as it does in 'Socrates is an animal', one cannot truly predicate 'to be in a subject'; for if 'animal' supposits in that way, 'Animal is in a subject' is false.

Another property of substance—one that belongs to all second substances—is that of being predicated univocally. This property does not belong only to second substances; it belongs to differences as well. It is not, however, a property of first substances.

It should be noted that, properly speaking, nothing is predicated univocally except that which is common to many, nothing except that which signifies many or is capable of signifying many. And, therefore, since first substances are each proper to just one individual and do not signify many, they are not predicated univocally. Second substances, however, signify many things. The name 'man' does not signify primarily one nature common to all men, as many mistakenly think; it signifies on the contrary all particular men primarily as we earlier showed by an appeal to Damascene. Whoever it was that first instituted the use of the term 'man' saw some particular man and coined the term to signify that man and every substance like him. It was not necessary that the common nature occur to the person instituting the use of the term for the simple reason that there is no such common nature. But even though it signifies indifferently many men, 'man' is not equivocal, for in signifying indifferently many men it is a sign subordinated to just one concept and not many.

A third property ascribed to substance consists in the fact that first substance signifies a this-something and second substance a such-like. Since signifying either a this-something or a such-like does not belong to substances existing outside the mind, but only to the signs of such substances, it is clear that the signs, both proper and common, of substances existing outside the mind are called first and second substances. The point must be granted.

Nonetheless, it should be noted that to signify a this-something is simply to signify one thing and not many things; whereas, to signify a such-like is to be capable of signifying many. Therefore, when Aristotle says that second substances signify such-like,[2] he does not mean that second substances signify a quality or something really present in an individual; for this is simply false. That is clear from my previous remarks. He only means that second substances signify many and not just one. This can be proved by examining the relevant passages in the *Categories*. My commentary on the *Categories* makes this clear.

The fourth property of substance is that of having no contrary. It should be noted that there are two very different forms of contrariety. Contrariety can be a property of terms. Thus, we say that 'white' and 'black' are contraries since it is impossible that the two terms 'white' and 'black', while

[2] 3^b 12-23.

standing for the same thing, be truly predicable of that thing simultaneously. Contrariety can also be a property of things. Here, the term has three senses— a strict sense, a broad sense, and a broadest sense. In the strict sense things are said to be contraries which, in a given subject, work towards expelling each other and which, when naturally replacing each other in a subject, do so by stages. In this sense no substance is contrary to any other. In the broad sense things are said to be contraries which, while working towards expelling each other in a subject, do not replace each other in their first subject by stages. In this sense substantial forms are contrary since they expel each other in one and the same matter. In the broadest sense those things are contraries which are composed of things that are contrary in the broad sense. Thus, air and fire are said to be contraries since they are composed of substantial forms that are contrary in the broad sense. Nothing substantial is contrary in the first sense; but in the second and third sense, substances are opposed as contraries. In the *Categories,* the Philosopher speaks of contraries in the first sense;[3] in other places, he speaks of contraries in the other senses.

The fifth property of substance is that of not admitting more and less. This should be understood to mean that no common term in the genus of substance is ever predicated of numerically one substance first with the adverb 'more' and later with the adverb 'less'. Thus, it is not possible that the following two propositions, or others like them, be successively true: 'Socrates is more man now than he was before (or more animal now than before)' and 'Socrates is less man (or less animal) now than he was before'. Thus, of no term suppositing for substance can   predicates like the following be truly predicated: 'This is more man (or more animal) now than it was before' or 'This is less man (or less animal) now than it was before'. It is, however, possible to say of numerically one substance "This is more white now than it was before."

The sixth property of substance is that substance, while remaining numerically one and the same thing, can successively admit contraries. Thus, numerically one and the same man can be first black and afterwards white. But this property belongs to substance and to no other being, as Aristotle notes in the *Categories.* He says, "But it seems most proper to substance that, while remaining numerically one and the same thing, it should be susceptible of contraries. For among the other things, there is no one of them which is not a substance and which, while remaining numerically one and the same, is susceptible of contraries. Thus, a color while remaining numerically one thing is not both white and black; nor is an action while one and the same thing both good and evil. The same thing holds for other things which are not substances. But substance while numerically one and the same can admit con-

[3] 3[b] 24.

traries. Thus a man while numerically one and the same thing can be first black, later white; first warm, later cold; first evil, later good. This sort of characteristic is found in no other kind of thing."[4] It is clear from this passage that, according to Aristotle, to admit contraries is a property of substance alone. It is then impossible, in his view, for anything distinct from substance to admit contraries.

We can infer from this that Aristotle maintained two views. First, we can infer that, for Aristotle, quantity is not an accident distinct from substance both really inhering in substance and really serving as a subject of corporeal qualities. This is a view held by many recent writers who say that quantity is an accident existing in substance and the subject of qualities. For if this view were true, it would necessarily follow that something other than substance, while remaining numerically one and the same thing, could admit contraries by undergoing a change; for if this view were true, quantity would first receive one quality and later a quality contrary to it. In fact, quantity would admit contraries more immediately than and before substance since on that view substance is not the immediate subject of contrary qualities, but only the mediate subject. It does not, as a consequence, admit contrary qualities except by the mediation of quantity.

Likewise, we can infer that for Aristotle no accident is the subject of any other, at least not of accidents which have contraries. For if it were, something other than substance could admit contraries successively.

It follows then that it is incompatible with Aristotle's view to hold that the intellect and will are accidents of the intellective soul in which intellections, volitions, and other such acts and habits are first and foremost received. In the same way the sense powers are not for Aristotle certain accidents in which other accidents reside. We can conclude that he would reject the view that relations are entities really distinct from substances, subjectively existing in entities (quantity and quality) that inhere in substance.

Thus, Aristotle's intended view is that every accident exists immediately in substance so that nothing which plays the role of subject mediates the relaton between a substance and any of its accidents. To clarify his view by meeting difficulties, Aristotle poses himself a problem about statements and opinions. These are not substances; nevertheless, they appear to admit of contraries; for one and the same statement is first true and afterwards false. In resolving this difficulty Aristotle says, "But although a statement may admit contraries, it differs in the way in which it admits them, for those things which are substances admit contraries as a result of a change in themselves. Thus, that which was warm becomes cold through a change; it has entered a new state. Similarly, that which is white was black, and the good man was formerly depraved. The same holds true in other cases; it is by

[4] 4ᵃ 10-21.

undergoing a change that substances are capable of admitting contraries. Statements and opinions, however, remain completely unchanged. It is because of a change in things that a statement admits contraries. Thus, a statement to the effect that this or that person is sitting remains unchanged in itself; but because the facts change, the statement is at one time true and at another false. The same holds true in the case of opinions. Thus, it is a feature peculiar to substances that by undergoing a change, they can admit contraries."[5]

It should be clear, then, that for Aristotle only substances can undergo a change from one of a pair of contraries to the other. But this would be false if quantity were the immediate subject of qualities and, nevertheless, really different from substance. Therefore, the fact that a statement is once true and later false is not due to the fact that the statement itself undergoes a change and thereby first exhibits truth and later falsity. It is due, rather, to a change, at least a local change, on the part of some substance.

To clarify Aristotle's resolution of the difficulty it should be noted that the name 'contrary' as well as the verb 'to admit' can be taken in different senses. We have already noted that the name 'contrary' is equivocal, and for the present we can focus on two senses of 'contrary'. In one sense contraries are things outside the mind. Thus, we speak of whiteness and blackness as contraries; but in another sense it is terms that are contraries, as when we say that the terms 'white' and 'black' are contraries. Thus, we say that contraries can hold true of one and the same thing, taken particularly, e.g., 'Man is white' and 'Man is black'; but it can only be with respect to terms that this is the case. However, there are two senses, one strict and one broad, in which terms can be contraries. In the strict sense terms are contrary because they signify contrary things; and in the broad sense terms are contrary which, while suppositing for the same thing, cannot be truly predicated of the same thing simultaneously, but only successively.

'To admit', on the other hand, has two senses—one thing can admit another either through real inherence or through predication.

Taking 'to admit' in the first sense speech cannot in any way, admit of contraries. However, if we use the expression 'contrary' in the broad sense in which terms can be contraries and employ the term 'admit' in the second sense, speech can admit of contraries. That is, speech does not receive contraries in the form of accidents inhering in a subject. Nevertheless, contraries can be successively predicated of speech, not of course contraries which work towards expelling each other from a subject but terms which cannot, while suppositing for the same thing, be truly predicated of the same thing simultaneously, but only successively. Substance, on the other hand, receives by way of inherence contraries in the form of accidents in a subject.

[5] 4^a 28-4^b 3.

Aristotle adds this point, commenting, "If anyone should reject this view and claim that opinions and statements can admit of contraries" (supply; by way of real inherence), "he would be wrong" because speech does not really receive contraries at all. He continues, "For statements and opinions can admit contraries," (that is, statements and opinions can admit contraries by way of predication) "not because they themselves admit of some contrary" (supply, through real inherence) "but because of a change in some other thing. It is because things either are or are not such and such that a statement is said to be true or false and not because the statement can admit contraries. In short, nothing can change either opinions or statements."[6] Aristotle means to grant that the contraries 'true' and 'false' successively hold true of a statement, while that statement remains numerically one thing. Thus, 'You sit,' is first true and afterwards false; nevertheless, he would want to say that the statement does not really receive contraries just because it was once true and later false. Nothing has really changed on the part of the statement. Its being once true and now false is due to the fact that while it now signifies things other than as they are, it formerly signified things as they actually were. Thus, it now signifies that you are sitting, but since you are not sitting, it is false. Earlier it was true because you were indeed sitting just as the statement signified. Nevertheless, the statement receives nothing in itself, nor is it changed in any way. It is for this reason that Aristotle adds, "Thus, since no change occurs in them, they cannot admit of contraries."[7]

In the process of making his point Aristotle makes it clear that the truth and falsity of propositions are not qualities of propositions which actually inhere in propositions. If they were it would follow that a proposition which is at one time true and at another time false would really admit contraries. It would also follow that in the case where something is first moving and afterwards at rest, a new quality would come to exist in the soul of the person who forms the proposition, 'This thing is moving' and another quality would be lost. It would even follow that some written proposition would be changed by the mere fact that a fly moves. But these things are all false and absurd.

Furthermore, obvious heresies would result in theology; for if the truth and falsity of propositions were qualities of propositions in the way that whiteness and blackness are qualities of bodies, then whenever some truth exists, 'This truth exists' is true. It is like the situation where some whiteness exists and the proposition 'This whiteness exists' is true. The same point holds for falsity. Now, I take the falsity of the proposition 'God creates something from nothing'. On the opinion in question this is a quality of the

[6] 4^b 3-11.
[7] 4^b 11-12.

proposition actually inhering in that proposition and, consequently, an object distinct from God. Now either that thing can be created by God or it cannot. If it cannot, it is something different from God which God cannot create, but that contradicts the Gospel passage, "All things were made by Him and without Him nothing was made." If it can be created from nothing by Him, then suppose it actually exists. On the present supposition, the proposition 'This falsehood is created from nothing by God' comes out true. But the following is a valid inference: 'This falsehood is created from nothing by God; therefore, something is created from nothing by God'. But, then, 'Something is created from nothing by God' will be true and not false. But the falsity of this proposition does not exist so that God does not create it from nothing. It is clear that falsity is not the relevant sort of quality of propositions.

What then are truth and falsehood? Like Aristotle I hold that truth and falsity are not really distinct from the true or the false proposition. Thus, if the abstract terms 'truth' and 'falsity' do not incorporate any syncategorematic terms or expressions equivalent to such, one must grant the following propositions: 'Truth is a true proposition' and 'Falsity is a false proposition'.

But does the preceding argument not also work against my construction of truth and falsity? The answer is no, for if it is assumed that the following propositions are true: 'Truth is a true proposition' and 'Falsity is a false proposition', it follows that the following is false: 'Wherever this falsity exists, this is true, "This falsity exists" '. Therefore, it must be granted that the falsity of the proposition 'God creates something from nothing' can be created by God from nothing. Nevertheless, it can be held that the proposition 'This falsehood is created by God' is impossible. In the same way, while 'The white can be black' is true, 'The white is black' is impossible. The reason my view can hold this and the preceding view cannot is that in my view 'truth' and 'falsity' are not absolute names but connotative names. In the former view, however, they must be construed as absolute names like 'whiteness' and 'blackness' and 'cold' and 'heat'. I agree with Aristotle's view that except for substance, nothing can admit contrary qualities by way of inherence. Thus, at the end of the chapter on substance he says, "Thus, it is peculiar to substance that while being numerically one and the same, it can, because of a change on its own part, admit contraries. Concerning substance, these remarks suffice."[8]

[8] 4^b 17-19.

44: On Quantity Against the Moderns

Next we shall consider the category of quantity. It should be noted first that the common term *quantity* is an intention of the soul containing under it other intentions ordered according to greater and lesser universality. Recent writers frequently hold that every quantity is a being really and totally distinct from both substance and quality. They maintain that continuous quantity is an accident lying between a substance and its qualities, that it is subjectively in substance while being the subject of qualities. Likewise, they hold that discrete quantity is a thing really distinct from substance; they hold the same view as regards place and time. Their position ought to be examined closely.

I want to show first that this account runs counter to Aristotle; second, I want to present some arguments against the view; third, I shall outline an opposing view which seems to me Aristotelian, regardless of whether it is true or false, orthodox or heretical.

In the preceding chapter I showed that this account is incompatible with Aristotle. I showed that, for Aristotle, no accident really distinct from substance can admit contraries by itself undergoing a change; but if quantity were an accident and the subject of quality, it is clear that it would change in receiving qualities. By undergoing change, then, it would receive contraries. But this is incompatible with Aristotle's account.

Again, as is clear in the fourth book of the *Physics*, Aristotle holds that air can be condensed without changing in either all or some of its qualities.[1] Thus, when air is condensed it is not necessary that it lose some of the qualities or at least not all of the qualities it had before. On the basis of this I argue: when air is condensed, either the whole quantity that was there before remains or it does not. If it does, then the same quantity is now less than before only in this—that the parts of the quantity lie closer to each other than they did before; but since the parts of substance, in exactly the same way, lie closer now than they did before, quantity seems to be a superfluous entity. But if the whole quantity which was first present does not remain, then some part is lost; but an accident is always corrupted when its immediate subject is corrupted. It follows then that not every quality remains, and that is incompatible with Aristotle's view.

Again, Aristotle holds that every accident is in some first subject in such a way that if the accident has parts, one part of the accident is in one part of the subject and another part of the accident is in another part of the subject. Thus, the whole whiteness is in the whole body and a part of the white-

[1] 217^a 27-34.

ness is in a part of the body. If on the other hand an accident is indivisible, then it is in some first indivisible subject. On the basis of this I argue that, for Aristotle, the point is not something different from the line; that the line is nothing different from the surface; that the surface is not different from the solid and; finally, that the solid is not distinct from substance and quality.

That it follows from the preceding principle that the point is not something different from the line, I prove as follows: if the point is an absolute accident distinct from substance, then it is in some first subject. The point is either in a substance or in a line. It is not in a substance, for then it would be in a divisible or indivisible substance. It is impossible that it be in a divisible subject since a part of the point would be in a part of substance, and the point would be a divisible accident which everyone denies. It is also impossible that the point be in an indivisible substance; for according to Aristotle the genus of substance incorporates only matter, form, and the composite of these and Aristotle construes all of these as divisible. Thus, the point is not an indivisible accident existing subjectively and immediately in some substance as its first subject. Nor is its first subject the line or a part of the line; for the line and every part of the line are divisible and, consequently, cannot be the first subject of an indivisible accident. Thus, it is clear that in Aristotle's view a point is not an indivisible accident, but by the same line of reasoning the line is not an accident that is indivisible in breadth and really distinct from surface. Likewise, surface is not an accident indivisible as regards depth and really distinct from the solid. And Aristotle no more holds that the quantity known as the solid is really to be distinguished from substance than that the line and the surface are to be distinguished from the solid.

It seems that for Aristotle continuous quantity is not an absolute thing really and totally distinct from the solid. Therefore, I intend to present some arguments against the widespread view of recent writers. I also intend to indicate some theological difficulties in the view. Whether these theological considerations are decisive, they carry as much weight as such considerations can.

First, I argue as follows: God can conserve in existence any prior absolute thing without a change in its place while destroying that which is posterior to it. On the general view a piece of wood is a substance having parts one of which lies beneath a part of the quantity inhering in the whole and another of which lies beneath another part of that quantity. Further, on that view the substantial object is by nature prior to the quantity inhering in it; therefore, God could, without changing the location of the substance, conserve it in existence while destroying the quantity. If this is possible let us suppose it to happen. Either the substance has one part spatially separated from another or it does not. If it does it is quantified without quantity in which case quantity is superfluous. If it does not, then since its parts were previously

separated from each other spatially, the substance has undergone a change
in place; but this is incompatible with the hypothesis.

Again, anything which by itself and its intrinsic parts is present to something quantified in such a way that the whole is present to the whole and
the parts are present to the parts, is by itself and its intrinsic parts something
whose parts lie at a distance from each other. But anything of that sort is
by itself and its intrinsic parts a quantified object. Now material substance
by itself and its parts is present to something quantified—the quantity which
informs it (I am assuming here that there is such a thing). But by itself and
its parts it really has one part spatially separated from another part; therefore, by itself and its parts it is quantified.

Again, that quantity is not an accident which lies between a substance
and its qualities and which serves as the subject of those qualities can be
proved by reference to the Sacrament of the Altar. For if it were such, the
qualities remaining in the Sacrament of the Altar would be in quantity subjectively. The consequent seems false to many but likewise the antecedent.
I prove the falsity of the consequent as follows: if the supposition were true,
the qualities would not subsist by themselves, which is incompatible with
the view of the Master who, in the fourth Book of the *Sentences* speaking
of color, taste, weight, and other such qualities, says that such accidents
subsist by themselves in the Eucharist. Likewise, if quantity were the subject
of such qualities, the quantity would really be heavy, white, and of this or
that taste; the consequent, however, is incompatible with the gloss "On consecration" in the second distinction in the chapter beginning "If by negli-
gence." The gloss says "Weight remains there with the other accidents;
nevertheless, nothing there has weight."

These arguments prove that a long quantity, a wide quantity, and a deep
quantity are not things distinct from substance and quality.

That the line is not distinct from surface I prove as follows: suppose a
line were the sort of thing that unites surfaces with each other; then let some
surface be divided. Once it has been divided either there is a new line or only
the previous line remains. If there is a new line, there will be an infinite number of new lines, since when a body is divided, there will be an infinite number of surfaces all having new lines. In the same way once a surface is divided,
there will be infinite number of points terminating an infinity of lines. But
if there is no new line, that line which was there before remains; but it is not
more in one part of the surface than in the other. Therefore, either it will
remain per se or it will remain in different places in the two surfaces, but
both of these alternatives are absurd; therefore. . . .

Again, if the line is something different from surface and the point, from
the line, then God could conserve a line and destroy its points. But when this
is done either the line is infinite or finite. Clearly it is not infinite; therefore,

it is finite, but it has nonetheless no points. There is no need then to posit the point for the purposes of terminating the line.

Again, God could conserve a line in existence while destroying all points; but once that has been done the line remains a line, and consequently a quantity. It is not, however, a discrete quantity; therefore, it is a continuous quantity; but although it is a continuous quantity, there is nothing distinct from the line which connects the parts to each other. Thus, there is no need to postulate points as items distinct from lines. For the same reason it is pointless to posit lines as items distinct from surfaces, and for the same reason it is pointless to posit surfaces as objects different from bodies.

I want now to outline a different account of quantity. Whether or not it is an orthodox account, it seems to me to be the account Aristotle holds. I do not want to propound the account as my own. Thus, when I set forth the account in commenting on the Philosopher, I did not write it as my own account, but only as Aristotle's view which I was expounding as I saw fit. In the same way I shall now outline the account without committing myself to it. It is nonetheless a view that many theologians hold now and have held in the past—the view that no quantity is an object distinct from substance and quality; and they hold this view regardless of whether propositions like 'Substance is a quantity' and 'Quality is a quantity' should be construed as true.

They say that a continuous quantity is merely one thing which has parts spatially separated from each other. Thus, the expressions 'continuous quantity' and 'one thing having parts spatially separated from each other' are equivalent in signification; the terms are convertible unless one of them incorporates some syncategorematic expression or equivalent determination which stands in the way of convertibility and mutual predication. Thus, since both substance and quality have parts lying at a distance from each other, some quantity is nothing different from substance and some quantity is nothing different from quality. These theologians do not think it appropriate to say that God could not make the parts of substance be spatially separated from each other without conjoining some additional absolute entity to them. But if He can do this, then substance really will have one part spatially separated from another without any absolute entity added so that substance will be quantified without any other absolute thing. The same argument holds as regards quality. Therefore, since both substance and quality can be quantified without the addition of quantity, in the form of a thing distinct from substance and quality, the notion of an entity standing between a substance and its qualities seems altogether superfluous. Thus they say that no quantity is a thing different from substance and quality, since nothing except substance and quality has parts spatially separated from each other. Speaking of the Sacrament of the Altar, they say that one quantity was there before and

was identical with the substance of the bread; but after the consecration of
the body of Christ, the relevant quantity no longer remains; nonetheless,
there remains a quantity which is identical with a quality. This quantity,
they say, is not the subject of any quality, for all the accidents which remain
after the consecration remain together with the Body of Christ but without
any subject; they subsist, on the contrary, of and by themselves. That is the
account of continuous substance which some theologians present.

As regards discrete quantity, they claim that number is nothing different
from things enumerated. Thus they deny that the unity of a thing is some
accident added to the thing which is one. Likewise, number is not some accident added to things enumerated. That unity is not an accident added to
that which is one can be shown in the following way: if it were an accident,
then according to everyone, it must either be a relative or an absolute thing.
It is not a relative term since it need not have a correlative term associated
with it. Something can be one without being the one of something else or
the one to something else and so on for the other cases in which something
is related to something else. Likewise, it is not an absolute accident because
then it would be a quality which clearly is false, or it would be quantity;
but in that case it would be either continuous or discrete, both of which are
clearly false. The only remaining possibility is that unity is not an accident
which is really distinct from and added to the thing that is one. And for the
same reason number is not an accident added to things enumerated.

Likewise, they claim that place and time are not objects distinct from substance and quality, but this view has already been examined in my book on
the *Physics.*[2] They hold the same view about speech saying that it is simply
uttered words.

Thus, the proponents of the outlined position must hold that the point,
the line, surface, the solid, and number are not objects completely and really
distinct either from each other or from substance and quality. Nevertheless,
while they hold for the identity of the things designated by these terms, they
want to claim that the terms themselves are different predicables constituting different species of quantity. For it sometimes happens that while different predicables signify the same things, it is impossible to predicate one
of the other. Thus, while the terms 'man' and 'men' signify the same thing,
the proposition 'Man is men' is absurd. Although all the terms listed above
signify the same things, they are different predicables and different species
of quantity.

---

[2] *Expositio super Octo Libros Physicorum,* a work extant only in manu-
script form.

45: Responses to Objections

To clarify the view described above we shall set out some objections which seem to show that the view is incompatible with the account of Aristotle and his followers.

(1) First, Aristotle seems to say the opposite in the *Categories,* where he says that a large expanse of white is a quantum only per accidens.[1] However, if quantity were nothing different from quality, then the white would be a quantum per se. Indeed, it would be a quantity per se.

(2) Again, in the fifth book of the *Metaphysics* Aristotle says, "Of things said to be quanta accidentally, some are said to be such in the way in which the musical and the white are said to be quanta—by being in that which is a quantum."[2] But since the white is a quantum only in virtue of the fact that it is in that which is a quantum per se, whiteness is not a quantity.

(3) Again, in the same place Aristotle says, "Some things are said to be quanta essentially and others, only accidentally. Thus, the line is a quantum essentially; whereas the musical is a quantum accidentally."[3]

(4) Again, in the *Categories* Aristotle claims that some quantities are such that their parts are connected at some common boundary.[4] Thus, the parts of the line are connected at the point, the parts of the surface at the line, and the parts of the solid at the surface. Now the parts of a thing are not connected at some different part of the same whole; therefore, the point is to be distinguished from the line, the line from the surface, and the surface from the solid.

(5) Again, in the *Posterior Analytics* he says that the point is indivisible,[5] but that property accrues to neither the line nor the surface.

(6) Again, he wants to claim that unity is indivisible and that consequently it is neither the solid, nor the line, nor the surface; neither is it a point;[6] therefore, it is something over and above these things; but since

[1] 5^a 37-5^b 10.
[2] 1020^a 25-28.
[3] 1020^a 14-16.
[4] 5^a 1-5.
[5] 95^b 5.
[6] 1052^b 15-1053^a 13.

unity is not a number it is something over and above number; but the view outlined above runs counter to these remarks.

(7) In the first book of the *Physics*, he proves, against Parmenides and Melissus, that there are many things by pointing to the fact that both substance and quantity exist.[7] Clearly this proof would fail if substance and quantity were not different things.

But in spite of these objections I think that the position I have outlined, whether true or false, follows from the principles of Aristotle's philosophy.

First it should be noted that the Philosopher uses the terms 'per se' and 'per accidens' equivocally. For the present, it is sufficient to note that in the relevant places, Aristotle does not employ the terms 'per se' and 'per accidens' as generally as he does in the first book of the *Posterior Analytics*.[8] On the contrary, he is using the term 'per se' in such a way that a proposition is per se which is true and has in addition a predicate connoting nothing other than what is connoted in a similar way by the subject. Thus to claim that a proposition per se in this sense is false and that the proposition affirming the existence of the relevant subject is true is to affirm an out-and-out contradiction. Put otherwise, he is claiming that a proposition is per se if part of the definition is predicated of the relevant definition, if the whole definition is predicated of the definition, if a term is predicated of itself, or if a term is predicated of its synonym. He calls all other propositions per accidens.

Response to (1)

This point enables us to handle the first objection; for when he says that a large expanse of white is only a quantum per accidens, the Philosopher means that the following proposition is per accidens: 'The white is a quantum.' It is per accidens since the predicate 'quantum' connotes or signifies that one part of a thing is spatially separated from another part. The subject 'white', however, connotes no such thing. Thus, the predicate 'quantum' is not a part of the definition of 'white' nor vice versa. Nevertheless, it is true that the white really and truly is a quantum and, likewise, that it is a quantity. Thus, the philosopher no more concedes that white is a quantum than that white is a quantity. Just as the white really and truly is a quantum, although only per accidens, so the white is, according to the Philosopher, really and truly a quantity, but again only per accidens. That this is the Philosopher's view is clear from remarks he makes earlier in the same treatise.

Thus, after enumerating the species of quantity and indicating their differences he says "Only the things we have pointed to are properly called quantities; other things are quantities only per accidens. It is in terms of these things that we call other things quantities. We say that a large expanse of white is a quantity since its surface is large."[9] It is clear from this remark

[7] 185a 28-185b 4.
[8] 73a 34-73b 24.
[9] 5a 37-5b 2.

that in Aristotle's view the predicate 'quantity' truly applies to things other than those he enumerates. Thus, the white can be called a quantity, although not properly, but only per accidens. Thus he says "It is in terms of these things that we call other things quantities"; and of these other things the name 'quantity' is predicable, although not per se, only per accidens. Of the things Aristotle enumerates, the term 'quantity' is predicable properly and per se; the reason is that 'quantity' is a part of their definition. 'Quantity', however, is not part of the definition of 'white', 'musical', 'men', or 'stone'.

Thus, it should be noted that as regards their significative power, the Philosopher never distinguishes between the two terms 'quantum' and 'quantity', one which is concrete and the other abstract. Whatever he grants as regards one he grants as regards the other. He treats them the same. For him they are synonyms unless the abstract term incorporates some syncategorematic term or some expression significatively equivalent to a syncategorematic term.

Response to (2)

We can handle the second text in the same way. The white and the musical are said to be quanta per accidens, since the propositions 'The white is a quantum', 'The musical is a quantum', and others like them are not per se. They are not propositions in which a part of a definition is predicated of its definitum. When it is said that they are quanta because they are in something, 'to be in' is not used in the sense of real inherence, but in the sense of predication. Thus, 'The white is a quantum' is true only because the surface which is predicated of 'white', is a quantum; for this is true: 'The surface is a quantum', but 'white' is predicated of 'surface' and vice versa; therefore, 'The white is a quantum' is true.

Response to (3)

We can also handle the third text in this way. Some things are said to be quanta per se—the line, the solid, etc; for the following propositions are per se: 'The line is a quantity', 'The solid is a quantity', etc. Other things, however, are quanta per accidens since propositions like the following are per accidens: 'The white is a quantity' and 'The musical is a quantity'.

Response to (4)

In response to the other passage from the *Categories*, Aristotle does not mean that the parts of quantities exhibiting relative position join at some boundary which is totally distinct from those parts; for in Aristotle's view no subject could be specified for such a boundary. Further, it would have to be in some genus per se, since it could not be construed as a part of something in a genus. The boundary then must be a quantity or a substance or a quality or . . . but each of these is false. On the contrary the Philosopher only means that one part of such quantities is extended to another part, in such a way that nothing lies between those parts. This, indeed, is the reason

such quantities are called continuous quantities; their parts mutually extend
to each other in such a way that did they not reach each other, one continuous quantity would not be formed by them.

The difference between continuous and discrete quantities according to
Aristotle is that with discrete quantity it makes no difference whether the
things which constitute the discrete quantity are in different places and,
similarly, whether something else is between them. Thus, that two men be
two, it is irrelevant whether something is between them; for they are two
when they are one hundred leagues from each other or when they are next
to each other. Nor is the predication of the term 'two' of the two men altered by their moving either closer or farther apart. Indeed, if they were
simultaneously in the same place, they would be two, just as if they were
not in the same place. Things are quite different in the case of continuous
quantity. Quantities can be continuous with each other only if nothing is
between them. They must be in different places, extend to each other, and
constitute something that is numerically one. Otherwise they are not continuous, for if they did not constitute something numerically one, if they
did not mutually extend to each other, or if they were not distinct in location and position, they would not be continuous. But none of these features
are required in the case of discrete quantity. For this reason Aristotle says
that "their parts are connected at some common boundary;"[10] that is, they
are extended to each other and they are not in the same place, so that were
there an indivisible thing, it would limit both of them. But this is not so in
the case of discrete quantity, for its parts do not necessarily extend to each
other. Indeed, they can constitute a quantity when something is between
them as much as when nothing is. And it is for this reason that Aristotle
says that the parts of a continuous quantity have a position relative to each
other. That they be part of a continuous quantity, it is necessary that they
be spatially separated one from another, so that it is possible to say that
one part is here; another, there; a third, there; and so on. No such spatial
separation is required for discrete quantities as was noted earlier. Thus, matter and form are really two things even though they are not spatially separated.

Response to (5)

The response here is that when the Philosopher says that the point is indivisible, he is merely employing the jargon of a renowned position, or he is
speaking conditionally saying that the point would be indivisible if it were
something different from quantity. Or by the proposition 'The point is
indivisible', he means this proposition 'One part of a continuous quantity
extends to another without any divisible thing between them'. Likewise, by
by the proposition 'The parts of a line are connected at some common

[10] 5ᵃ 1-2.

boundary', he means 'The parts of a line are extended to each other without any third thing lying between them'.

Response to (6)

Here the Philosopher does not mean that unity is something lacking parts because for him nothing in this world lacks parts. When he says "Unity is indivisible," he means to say, "That which is one is not many." I have argued that this is his meaning in the second book of my commentary on the *Physics*. In the interests of brevity I will not pursue the point here.

Response to (7)

The reply here is that when the Philosopher claims that since substance and quantity exist there are many things, he is not arguing from the fact that substance is distinct form quantity, but from the fact that it is impossible for something to be a quantum if it does not contain a plurality of parts. Thus, it is necessary that if substance and quantity exist there are many things, for quantity requires a plurality of parts. That is all the Philosopher needs to show the ancients wrong.

Thus, I hold it to be Aristotle's view that nothing existing in this world is indivisible except perhaps the indivisible intellective soul. He also wanted to claim that everything is either a substance or a quality. If he should sometime be found saying that substance is not quantity or that quality is not quantity, he means that the propositions 'Substance is quantity' and 'Quality is quantity' are not per se. The reason they are not per se is that the name 'quantity', if it be taken for 'continuous quantity', connotes that one part of a thing is spatially separated from another. The names 'substance' and 'quality', however, connote no such thing. I claim, therefore, that the view of Aristotle and many other authors was that no quantity is an object distinct from substance and quality and similarly, that the point, the line, the surface, and the solid are not things essentially different from each other.

But those who hold the view that is common among recent writers would say that the point is something different from the line, that it is that which joins the parts of a line; that the line is something different from the surface, that it is that which joins the parts of the surface; and that the surface is something different from the solid, that it is that which joins its parts.. On their view number also is something different from things enumerated. It is an accident existing in those things. Likewise, speech is something different from the uttered word and its quantity. They would make the same point as regards place and time, that they are things different from each other and from all the aforesaid things.

46: On the Items in the Category of Quantity

Now that we have examined the different views on the question of
whether quantity is to be identified with substance and quality, we should
see which items are subsumed on each view under the genus of quantity.
First I shall deal with the account that seems to me to be Aristotle's. For
Aristotle every term by means of which one can answer the question 'How
much?' is to be placed in the genus of quantity; and here I am using the
expression 'how much' in the broad sense, in the sense in which it is neutral as between 'how much' (in the narrow sense) and 'how many'.

Employing this interrogative one can ask how many things there are, so
that the interrogative expresses plurality. Thus, I can ask, "How many are
inside?" or "How many men are there?" The terms by which I can answer
such questions are to be reckoned discrete quantities since they express
plurality. In this way number is a discrete quantity; for if it be asked, "How
many men are they?" and I respond by saying "Three," the term by which
I respond expresses many things. In the same way speech is a discrete quantity; for when some one asks of speech, "How much?" his question should
be understood to bear on the plurality of syllables and their quantity. It is
otherwise of course when we ask about a letter or a syllable, for these can
be only long or short. Thus, that by which we answer the question must
be expressive of many; therefore, it is to be reckoned among discrete quantities.

But when the interrogative of quantity does not express many, it expresses
one thing having parts which are spatially separated. But in that case it expresses distance according to length—and then we have the line; or distance
according to breadth—and then we have the surface; or distance according to
depth—and then we have the solid. Or the interrogative raises a question
about place or time; thus, the two expressions 'place' and 'time' are to be
placed in the genus of quantity.

But in the interests of clarity it should be noted that the expressions
'place' and 'time' do not belong in the genus of quantity per se as the other
expressions do. In the case of 'place' and 'time' a special rationale is required.
Thus 'time' is not to be subsumed under the genus of quantity per se as the
other expressions are, for unlike the other expressions 'time' does not signify a thing existing in nature. Thus, 'line', 'surface', and 'solid' signify objects that really exist; they neither signify nor connote anything but the existing thing. But 'time' as well as 'motion' connotes something which exists
neither actually nor potentially. Thus in the view we are examining, time is
not something really distinct from motion, nor is motion really distinct

from enduring objects. Indeed, 'motion' only designates that a thing has one part after another, that a thing is joined to one thing after another, or that were some body at rest to move towards it, a thing would have something else joined to it. Thus, motion is not something really different from enduring objects. The same point holds in the case of time. Thus 'time' is not placed in the genus of quantity except per accidens or because it is a passion of the permanent things which are in that category. And as Aristotle indicates in the fifth book of the *Metaphysics*, motion is subsumed under the genus of quantity in the same way.

In the case of 'place', a different rationale is required. 'Place' is not said to be in the genus of quantity per se, since place is not something distinct from surface. Furthermore, where a proposition expressing the place of some subject is true, 'place' cannot, in different modes and with different quantity-connoting expressions, be successively affirmed of that subject unless a similar alteration occurs in the predication of that subject of 'surface', 'line', or 'solid'. Thus, suppose the following is now true: '*A* is a place'. Given the proposition '*A* is a place', the propositions '*A* is a greater place', '*A* is a smaller place', '*A* is longer', and '*A* is shorter' cannot successively hold true unless propositions like the following also successively hold true: '*A* is a greater surface', '*A* is a smaller surface', '*A* is a longer line', '*A* is a shorter line', '*A* is a longer solid', and '*A* is a shorter solid'. Speaking generally, no such mutually incompatible qualifications can, by being added to 'place', be successfully affirmed of a place unless they can simultaneously be added to one of the following: 'line', 'surface', and 'solid'.

Thus, although the line, the solid, and the surface are not distinct things (just as place is not distinguished from them), they are more properly construed as per se constituents of the genus of quantity than place. Although the three signify the same thing, the propositions '*A* is longer' and '*A* is shorter', for example, can be successively true while none of the following are true: '*A* is wider', '*A* is more narrow', '*A* has a greater depth', and '*A* has a lesser depth'.

It is clear then that 'place' is not a predicable distinct from 'line', 'surface', and 'body', while these last three are predicables different from each other.

It is also clear that the first and really crucial division and distinction among the things found in the genus of quantity is based on the fact that a term which can be used to answer the question 'How much?' (in the broad sense) expresses either many things (and this gives us number) or one thing composed of many things (and this gives us magnitude which is divided into line, surface, and solid). Thus, neither speech, nor place, nor time finds a place in this division. They are, rather, passions or accidents of these things.

The Philosopher uses this technique for dividing the category in the fifth book of the *Metaphysics*; while enumerating the things that are quanta per se, he mentions only number, line, surface, and solid. Thus, when he first describes quantum he says, "But that is called a quantum which is divisible into constituents which are each of them things capable of being a one-something and a this-something."[1] By the first clause ("divisible into constituents"), 'time', 'speech', and 'motion' are excluded. Each of these terms signifies something that is not; or it signifies, either simply or in relation to something else, something which is negative. (In the *Fall of the Devil*, Anselm employs this form of expression; it is necessary in handling a number of difficulties.) Thus, these things are not called quanta first and foremost. By the second clause all accidents, all forms, and matter as well can be excluded since none can be a this-something. The term 'quantum' then is being used strictly for that which is a per se existent not inhering in another and neither a part nor an accident of something else.

When we take the term 'quantum' strictly, only substances composed of matter and form and, in Aristotle's view, heavenly bodies are quanta. Therefore, after enumerating the things which are quanta the Philosopher says, "A quantum is a plurality if it is enumerable and a magnitude if it is measurable. A plurality is something potentially divisible into non-continuous elements; whereas, a magnitude is divisible into what is continuous. Of magnitude, that which is continuous in one dimension is length; that which is continuous in two dimensions, breadth; and that which is continuous in three dimensions, depth. Of these things, determinate plurality is number; length is the line; breadth is the surface; and depth is the solid."[2] It is clear, then, that Aristotle wants to enumerate these four things—the line, the surface, the solid, and number. Neither time, nor speech, nor place, for the reasons provided above, are enumerated.

But in addition to these remarks it should be noted that some things in the category of quantity are terms by which one can answer the question 'how much?'. Thus, 'two cubits', 'three cubits', 'two', 'three', and similar terms fall under the genus of quantity. But other terms fall under the category of quantity because they are common terms predicable in the first mode of perseity of such expressions. Thus, terms like 'line', 'surface', 'solid', and 'number' are in the genus of quantity.

---

[1] 1020ᵃ 8-9.
[2] 1020ᵃ 9-13.

47: On the Properties of Quantity

Next we should examine the properties of quantity. Aristotle claims that quantity has three properties.[1] The first of these consists in the fact that nothing is contrary to quantity; thus, 'line' is not the contrary of 'surface', nor is 'two cubits' the contrary of 'three cubits'.

But from this property it seems to follow that quantity is neither substance nor quality. For suppose that quantity were quality. Since something is contrary to quality, something would also be contrary to quantity.

It should be said here as earlier that the term 'contrary' has a number of senses. Nevertheless, in denying that anything is contrary to quantity the Philosopher is using the expression 'contrary' for terms designating things that are contrary to other things. The things signified are in turn called contraries since they can be acquired by stages and cannot simultaneously but only successively exist in the same thing. Taking the term 'contrary' in this sense, it is clear that none of the items contained per se in the genus of quantity are contraries of any other predicables; for nothing contained per se in the genus is such that every one of its significata or consignificata is the contrary of and, therefore, naturally opposed to the significata or consignificata of some other term. This is clear from induction. It is something that would be granted even by those who think the following is true: 'Something is the contrary of some quantity' (where 'to be a contrary' means 'to resist simultaneous although not successive inherence in one and the same thing'). Nonetheless, this is true: 'Nothing contained in the genus of quantity per se has a contrary' (where we take 'to have a contrary' in the sense outlined). Thus, although whiteness and blackness are contraries, the terms 'two cubits' and 'three cubits' are not. Neither are the terms 'two' and 'three' nor the terms 'line', 'surface', *etc.* The whiteness that is three cubits is the contrary of the blackness that is two cubits, so that one quantity really is the contrary of another quantity. Nonetheless, the terms 'two cubits' and 'three cubits' are not contraries, because even though whiteness is the contrary of blackness, 'two cubits' signifies whiteness in the same way it signifies blackness.

It should be held then that for Aristotle 'One quantity is the contrary of another' is true, provided that the terms supposit personally for the relevant external objects. Nevertheless, this is true: 'No terms contained per se under the genus of quantity are contraries in the sense that they always signify contrary things'. It is this proposition that Aristotle means when he says that nothing is contrary to quantity.

[1] 5^b 11, 6^a 19, 6^a 26-27.

The second property is that quantity does not admit of more and less; that is, nothing which is contained under the genus of quantity is predicated of something sometimes with the adverb 'more' and sometimes with the adverb 'less'. Thus, it is not said that a thing is sometimes more two cubits and sometimes less two cubits in the way in which we say that a book is sometimes more white and sometimes less. Neither do we say that these things are more three than those, as we *do* say that this is more white than that.

The third property is that quantities can be said to be equal or unequal to each other. Thus, one solid is said to be equal or unequal to another solid. Similarly, in other cases.

From this property it is clear that it is not the Philosopher's intention to deny that quality is quantity nor that substance is quantity. According to the Philosopher this feature is most proper to quantity. Indeed, it is convertible with quantity. Thus, of whatever this property holds true 'quantity' is also predicated. But the following, although possibly not true per se, is nonetheless true: 'One piece of wood is equal to another; and one whiteness is equal to another; and one blackness is equal to another blackness or to a whiteness'. Therefore, 'Substance is quantity' is true, and similarly, 'Quality is quantity', although they are not true per se.

Nor can one deny that everything that is equal or unequal is a quantity by claiming that being equal or unequal is not the property distinctive of quantity, but rather being that according to which something is said to be equal or unequal. The Philosopher does not say that it is according to quantity that something is said to be equal or unequal. He says, rather, that what is proper to quantity is actually being equal or unequal. Thus, he says, "But what is most proper to quantity is that it is said to be equal or unequal. For a singular instance of what is said to be a quantity is said to be equal or unequal. Thus, one solid is said to be equal or unequal to another; a number to be equal or unequal to another. Time too is said to be equal or unequal. Similarly, in the case of other things that are said to be quantities—they are said to be equal or unequal."[2] From this passage it is clear that he holds that quantities themselves are equal or unequal and not that something else is said to be equal or unequal according to quantities; therefore it should be claimed that since both whiteness and substance are equal or unequal to something else (even if only per accidens), both substance and quality are quantities, although only per accidens. Nor does it matter that later the Philosopher says that nothing in the other categories is said to be equal or unequal;[3] for he does not mean to deny that 'equal' and 'unequal' can be predicated of things from the other categories. He only means that nothing

[2] 6[a] 26-30.
[3] 6[a] 31-35.

in the other categories is said to be equal or unequal per se, but only per accidens. He implies this when he says, "But of the things that are not quantities" (supply: per se) " 'equal' and 'unequal' do not seem to be said much," because of these things 'equal' and 'unequal' are not said per se, but only per accidens. But this is perfectly compatible with the claim that 'equal' and 'unequal' are said of other things, and in the same way 'quantity' is predicated of these other things.

48: On Quantity According to the Common Opinion

Things are quite different in the view which construes quantity as an absolute thing distinct from substance and quality, and the point, the line, the surface, and the solid as things different from each other. On that view dimensions are things informing substance and sustaining corporeal qualities. Thus, substance is not dimension, but the subject of dimension, nor is quality dimension, but a thing subjectively existing in dimension. Now quantity either has parts which are joined at some common boundary or it does not. If it does, then those parts are all permanent and they are extended according to length in which case we have the line; or they are extended according to both length and breadth and we have the surface; or they are extended according to length, breadth, and depth and we have the solid. But many who hold this view construe place as something really identical with surface. But if not all the parts of this kind of quantity are permanent, we have time. If on the other hand the parts are not joined at any common boundary, they are either permanent in which case we have number; or they are not permanent in which case we have speech. Thus, the genus of quantity contains the line, the surface, the solid, place, time, number, and speech. But the point, with the instant and unity, does not fall under the genus of quantity per se but only be reduction.

Quantities also are divided into those whose parts have relative position (the species here are the line, the surface, the solid, and place) and those whose parts have no such relative position (the species here are time, number, and speech).

The first property of quantity is that it has no contrary; for although the quality subjectively existing in quantity has a contrary, quantity itself has no contrary. This is clear from induction.

The second property is that quantity does not admit of more or less, for one quantity is not more a quantity than another.

The third property consists in the fact that it is according to quantity that something is said to be equal or unequal. Thus, quantities are said to be equal or unequal primarily and per se; whereas the substances sustaining quantity and the qualities subjectively existing in it are equal and unequal secondarily and per accidens.

These remarks on quantity suffice.

49: On Relation
According to Aristotle's Opinion

The third category Aristotle lists is called ad aliquid or relation. Just as there are opposing views on quantity there are opposing views on ad aliquid or relation. Some hold that relation is not something outside the mind really and completely distinct from one or more absolute things. I think that Aristotle and the philosophers following him held this view. Others, however, claim that while relation is not an absolute thing in the way that a man or a donkey is, it is really distinct from one or more absolute things. Many theologians hold this view. I used to think that Aristotle held it also, but now it seems the opposing view is implied by the principles of his philosophy. First I shall consider the view of relations provided by Aristotle's account and afterward the view which opposes it.

First of all, I shall show that the first view is in fact Aristotle's; next, I shall support the view with arguments; third, I shall present and answer some objections against the view; finally, I shall consider the things that are subsumed under the category.

The view is that nothing except substances and qualities exists either in act or in potency. Nevertheless, different names signify the same objects in different ways. Some names signify their significata in such a way that they can be predicated of something without the addition of another expression in an oblique case. Thus, someone is a man, but he is not the man of something or the man to something (and so on through the remaining oblique cases). Other names, however, so signify their significata that they cannot be truly predicated of anything unless some other expression in one of the oblique cases can be truly and appropriately added to them. Thus, it is impossible that someone be a father unless he be the father of someone else. Likewise it is impossible that something be similar unless it be similar to something else. Thus the names 'father', 'son', 'cause', 'effect', 'similar', and others like them cannot, when taken significatively, be truly affirmed of anything unless it is possible to add truly and correctly some other expression in an oblique case. All such names are called relative names.

According to one view everything for which such a name can supposit in a true proposition is a real relation, so that 'relation' is not a name of second intention or second imposition; it is, on the contrary, a name of first intention. Thus, the term 'relation' can, when it is taken significatively, supposit for a thing which is not a sign. From the fact that Socrates is similar to something or the father of someone, it follows that both 'Man is a relation' and 'Socrates is a relation' are true. Although theologians so use the term that it is necessary to grant that something outside the soul—an object which is not a simple term out of which a proposition can be formed—is a relation; nevertheless, I think that Aristotle held that only a name out of which a proposition—whether mental, vocal, or written—can be formed, is a relative, a relation, or ad aliquid. Therefore, in Aristotle's view 'relation', 'ad aliquid', and 'relative' are names of second imposition or second intention and not names of first intention. In his view it should not be granted that man is a relation or that whiteness is a relation. It is the name 'father' and not the man who is a father that is a relative.

There are good reasons for thinking that this is Aristotle's view. First, in defining relation in the *Categories*, the Philosopher says "Things are said to be relative which are said to be of other things or, in some way to be of or for something else."[1] He gives examples of the different ways in which one thing can be of or for another. In one example it is in the genitive case; in another in the ablative or dative case. On the basis of this I argue: nothing but a name is said to be of or for something in the genitive or some other case; but everything that is said to be related to something else is said to be related under the guise of some case; therefore, every relative is a name. Thus, all the commentators say that the relative is said to be related to something under the guise of one of the cases, but this can only be a property of a name. It follows then that according to the Philosopher a relative is a name so designating its significatum that it cannot supposit for it except when it is possible to add to that name some other expression in one of the oblique cases.

It is beside the point to say the Philosopher takes back this definition of relatives at the end of the chapter; he does not mean to suggest there that the relevant definition does not hold in the case of all relatives. He says, on the contrary, that the definition holds for all relatives, but that since it ap-

[1] 6^a 36-37.

plies in cases where we do not have relatives it is not convertible with 'relative'. This will become clearer later on. For the Philosopher every relation is a name of the relevant sort; that much is clear from the text in question. That text also shows that he calls the names of substances first and second substances, for he says that some are said to be of other things. Substances themselves, however, are not said to be of other things; it is only the names of substances that are said to be of other things.

Again in the *Categories*, the Philosopher says that "all relatives are said with respect to some correlative, provided that the correlative is corectly assigned."[2] He also says that when we lack names we may construct names to stand as the correlatives of existing relatives. But on the basis of this I argue: the only things we can assign are names, just as the only things we can use here are names; but since we can assign relatives it follows that names are relatives. Furthermore, on the Philosopher's view, we can construct relatives to stand as the correlatives of existing relatives; but we can only construct names; therefore, names are relatives.

One might say that according to the Philosopher we do not construct relatives, only the names of relatives. Thus, the Philosopher says, "Sometimes it is necessary to construct names—in the case where there is no name to which the relative can be correctly assigned."[3] Here, it seems that we can construct the relative name, but not the relative itself. But this is not really the Philosopher's intention. He means, rather, that we construct the relative itself; for when there is no relative name in use which corresponds to a given correlative, we can construct such a name. Thus, he says that "it is necessary to construct names—in the case where there is no name to which the relative can be correctly assigned," but then the relative is assigned to the name that has been constructed; but it is assigned only to its relative; therefore, it is the name itself that is the relative. This is clear from the same text; for after giving examples of how some relatives are said with respect to their correlatives, he adds, "The same holds true in other examples, but sometimes the expressions involved differ in case."[4] Here it is clear that, for Aristotle, relatives differ in case; but only names can differ in case; therefore, for Aristotle, only names are relatives.

Again, one can employ the following line of argument to show that relatives are not distinct things for Aristotle: if a relation were a distinct thing, then when it first accrued to an object that object would have some new thing inhering in it; and, consequently, it would actually be changed. But this is contrary to what the Philosopher says in the fifth book of the

[2] 7[a] 22.
[3] 7[a] 5-6.
[4] 6[b] 32-33.

Physics where he claims that a thing can gain a new relation without in the least changing.[5]

Again, according to the Philosopher in the fifth book of the *Metaphysics*, that which is capable of heating exists with respect to that which can be heated. Thus, if the relevant relation were something existing in that which is capable of heating, it would be such a thing as is related to that which can be heated; but that thing is nothing.

Again, there would actually be an infinity of things in one and the same object. Proof: according to Aristotle, one object heats this piece of wood and an infinity of other things as well. This object is the sun; for the sun heats an infinity of bodies. Thus, the sun is now capable of producing heat with respect to each one of them. But if relation is a distinct object, there will be as many things actually existing in the sun as will be heated by the sun. But since the sun heats an infinity of things, there must be an infinite number of objects, each one of which is essentially different from the other, now existing in the sun. But this is opposed to the Philosopher's remark in the sixth book of the *Physics*, where he denies that any such infinity is to be found in nature.[6] Nor will it do to say that there is just one relation for all the things that can be heated and that relations themselves are not altered by altering the terms involved. By the same reasoning one could say that with respect to all these things it is unnecessary to posit even one relation. It is sufficient that there be one thing which can be called by different names or by just one name with different expressions in an oblique case added to it.

Likewise, by the same reasoning employed in showing that one relation suffices, for things of the same sort, I could easily say that with respect to all things, even those which differ in species and genus, one relation is sufficient; but then there is no longer any reason for positing relations as entities outside the soul which differ in species.

Thus, it seems to me to be Aristotle's view that only names are ad aliquid or relatives.

Many grammarians agree with this view. They say that the relative or the ad aliquid is a species of name. Thus, when Priscian enumerates the many species of names in the larger work (book three, the chapter on names) he lists the relative name saying, "A relative is that which cannot be uttered without understanding that with respect to which it is said. Examples are 'son' and 'slave' —for when I say, "Son," I understand 'father'; and when I say, "Slave," I understand 'master'. Thus, if one of these is destroyed, the other in terms of which it is understood is also destroyed."[7] Grammarians who follow the aforesaid writer express the same view.

[5] 225[b] 11-13.
[6] The reference here seems to be to *Physics* VI, 7-10.
[7] *Institutiones*, vol. 1, p. 75.

50: Arguments in
Behalf of Aristotle's View

A number of arguments can be presented in defense of this view. For the present I am not concerned whether they are conclusive.

One can argue as follows: if relation were a thing outside the soul really distinct from absolute things, it would follow that the potentiality of prime matter in virtue of which prime matter can receive form would be something different from matter. The consequent is false; for since matter can successively receive an infinity of forms, there would be an infinity of things in matter.

Again, if there were such a thing, then whenever a donkey would undergo local motion every heavenly body would be changed and would acquire some new thing in itself; for the distance between the donkey and any heavenly body would now be different from what it was before. Consequently, if distance were such a thing, each heavenly body would really lose one thing and gain another.

Again, in any given body there would be an infinity of things. Proof: any body actually lies at a distance from every part of some other body, but the parts of the other body are infinite in number; therefore, there would be an infinity of distances in the first body, each one corresponding to one of the infinite parts in the second body.

Furthermore, a given piece of wood is double its half. If, therefore, doubleness is a thing different from that which is double, then, in the same way there will be a relation by which the wood exceeds half of its half; and that thing will be a distinct entity existing in the wood. For the same reason the wood will have an entity corresponding to each half of each fraction of itself. But since the piece of wood incorporates an infinity of parts fitting this characterization and since the wood is related differently to each of these parts, there will be in that piece of wood an infinity of specifically different relations.

One might claim that since the relevant parts of the wood do not exist in act, but only in potency, the relations are not infinite in actuality. The response is that those parts exist in nature because otherwise an object would be composed of non-beings; therefore, the relations corresponding to the relevant parts exist in nature. Consequently, an infinite number of things distinct in species exist in the wood.

Furthermore, the wood is really double its half; therefore, the relation of being double its own half is really and actually in the piece of wood; but one part is not more in act than another, for all the parts are alike. Therefore, every other part is in act in that there can be a real relation with respect to it. Therefore, to every such part there will be a real and actual relation. Those parts are infinite in number; therefore, there will be an infinite number of relations in the wood.

Besides, if any relation is such a thing, doubleness will be. But *A*'s being double *B* is either a divisible or an indivisible accident. It cannot be an indivisible accident, for no indivisible accident which gives its name to the whole wood is present in that wood. The first subject of that accident would be either divisible or indivisible. Clearly it is not indivisible. Therefore the subject must be divisible. A divisible subject, however, cannot be the first subject of an indivisible accident; therefore, the accident is not indivisible. But neither can one say that the accident is divisible and extended. If it were the parts of that accident would be either similar or dissimilar. If they were similar they would all share the name and the definition of the whole, so that every part of doubleness would itself be doubleness. Every part would be double that to which the whole is double and that is absurd. But if the parts were dissimilar they would be different in species. Consequently, if they were to constitute one thing, one of the things would have to be actuality and the other potentiality. Doubleness would be composed of act and potency. Likewise, if one part were act and the other potency, then since act and potency in making one thing are not spatially separate, the parts could not be spatially separate. But unless new parts are postulated, we would not have one extended object.

Again, one can present the following theological argument for the view in question. Any object that God can make with the mediation of a second efficient cause can be made by Him without any second efficient cause. Since the relation of efficient causality is posited in an efficient cause by the mediation of a second cause, God could by Himself produce that relation without any second cause operating with Him. Suppose it to be the case; I shall prove that it could not possibly happen. If God causes that relation in the relevant object, that object will be an efficient cause. Just as that in which whiteness exists is white, so that in which the relation of efficient causality exists is an efficient cause. But if it is an efficient cause, the only object it can be the efficient cause of is the relation in question. But then it is not by operating alone that God is the cause of that relation. Thus, from the hypothesis we can derive its opposite, so that it is not possible.

Furthermore, anything which God conserves without another thing, He could create, even though the other thing neither is nor ever has been. Therefore, if the paternity by which a father is related to his son is a thing distinct from father and son, God will conserve it without the act of generation; for that is already past. Therefore, God is able or was able to create that paternity even though there had been no act of generation. But then it would be possible for a man to be the father of someone he did not beget.

Again, suppose God creates a man before He creates any other men and that afterwards other men are generated. Employing this supposition I argue: whatever is in any one of the other men, God can by His absolute power produce in the first man; but being-a-son is in one of the other men; therefore, God can produce this relation in the first man. But when this is done, the man will be a son, and he will be the son of some man. Every man, however, will be younger than the man in question. Therefore, the man will be the son of someone who is younger than him, and this seems to involve a contradiction.

Countless additional arguments could be adduced in support of the view. But in the interest of brevity I omit them.

51: Responses to Objections

But someone will object that this is not Aristotle's view.

(1) First, on the basis of what Aristotle says in the *Categories* when he enumerates the categories: "Of simple terms, each one signifies either substance or quantity or quality"[1] and so on for the remaining categories. But here he seems to mean that distinct things are designated by distinct genera. Thus, since relation is one of the ten genera, it will designate something different from the things designated by the other genera.

(2) In addition, he says in the same treatise, "Those things are relatives which are said of other things."[2] Substances, however, are excluded from this class since although they may be of other things, they are not relative to anything else. But the criterion does not seem to fit either terms or external objects which are absolute, so that there must be something different from these things to which being a relative applies.

(3) Besides, how can those things be true which Aristotle teaches about relatives—that they admit contraries, that they admit of more and less, that they are simultaneous by nature? Such features it seems do not hold true of either terms or absolute things.

(4) It seems we can construct an argument derived from the principles of Aristotle's philosophy, for it is impossible for one and the same thing both

[1] 1^{b} 25-26.
[2] 6^{a} 36-37.

to be and not be at one and the same time. Absolute things, however, can continue to exist even when their relations cease to exist. They must then be distinct things.

(5) Also, a passion really differs from its subject; for it is really demonstrated of its subject, and a thing is not demonstrated of itself. 'Equal' and 'unequal' with other relatives are passions; for to be called equal and unequal is the property of quantity; and to be similar and dissimilar is the property of quality as Aristotle teaches in the *Categories*;[3] therefore. . . .

(6) Again, it is necessary that a principle of real operation be itself real. Relation seems to be this sort of thing; for it sometimes happens that things which did not produce pleasure when they were in a certain relation and order, do produce it when their relation and order is otherwise.

(7) Further, how will we be able to preserve the distinction between the ten categories (since relation is one of them); the distinction of created being into absolute and relative; and the distinction of being outside the soul into the ten categories?

(8) What will happen to common locutions like 'The father is a father by paternity', 'The son is a son by fielty', 'The similar is similar by similarity', (for no relation is similar), and 'Relation is an accident'.

(9) If we reject the relation of union it seems impossible to explain how form is united with matter, how one part is united with another to form a continuum, how an accident is united with its subject, and how spirit is united with corporeal nature. The union of spirits with corporeal natures is not merely an element of Christian orthodoxy; every nation, rite, and sect confesses it. It is a piece of common belief even in superstitious religions.

(10) If the view in question were true, then one and the same thing would be in different categories. Aristotle, however, seems to deny this, since for him the negative proposition in which one category is denied of another is an immediate proposition.

These considerations might lead some to think the Philosopher's view is different from the one outlined here. Nonetheless, they should not lead the careful reader to think that Aristotle did perhaps postulate the relevant sorts of entities as things outside the soul.

Response to (1)

In response to the point made in the first objection, Aristotle did not prove that a distinction of things corresponds to the distinction among simple terms. Likewise, a distinction of things in God is not proved by the fact that we say that some of the divine names signify justice; others, wisdom, goodness, power, and so on. Nor can we establish a diversity of things in the horse from the fact that we say that some of the names applied to the horse signify mobility; others, corruptibility, etc. The sense of these lo-

[3] 6^a 26-27; 11^a 15-18.

cutions is rather that some of the terms applied to God designate that God is just; others, that God is wise; others, that God is good; and so on with the rest; and in the case of the horse the sense is that some of the terms signify what the horse is, others that the horse is mobile, corruptible, etc. The same point holds in the present case. Each simple term signifies either substance or quantity. . . . The sense is that some terms signify what a thing is; others, of what quality, how it is quantified, how it is related to other things (e.g. 'similar' and 'equal'), what it does, what is done to it, etc.

Aristotle expresses the nature of the categories more clearly in the fifth book of the *Metaphysics* where he says, "Of the categories, some signify what a thing is; some, how it is qualified; some, how it is quantified; others, how it is related to other things,"[4] etc.

Therefore, Aristotle does not mean that there are as many things as there are significant terms. He means to show, on the contrary, how some terms are absolute; some, connotative; and some, relative, as I have argued in sufficient detail elsewhere.

Response to (2)

The same sort of response applies here. According to Aristotle terms are called ad aliquid or relative which are said to be of other things. Put otherwise, relatives are terms which when signifying something point to something else, so that a proposition in which such a term is predicated of a thing cannot be known to be true unless one knows determinately the other thing that is pointed to. Thus, just from seeing a head, wing, or hand, one can know what it is even if he does not know to what or whom it belongs.

Response to (3)

As regards the contrariety exhibited by relatives, it should be noted that things are sometimes said to be contraries which can be acquired by way of motion and which resist coexistence. In this sense whiteness and blackness are contraries. But sometimes we speak of terms as contraries. We say that terms are contrary when they cannot be truly predicated of the same thing with respect to the same thing. It is in this sense that relative terms can be contraries. Thus, 'similar' and 'dissimilar' and 'equal' and 'unequal' are contraries. They cannot be truly predicated of the same thing with respect to the same thing. Sometimes we confine the term 'to admit more and less' to the real addition of one thing to another. In this sense both whiteness and light admit of more or less. But sometimes we use the term in relation to predication. Here, a name admits a comparison, and in this sense relation admits of more and less. But this does not always happen because of the addition of one thing to another. Commonly this happens because one thing is taken away from another. Thus, what is unequal becomes more equal because one of its parts was taken away. It sometimes happens that a thing

[4] 1017ª 25-28.

comes to bear a relative name solely on the basis of a change in something else. It also happens that things can be called more or less with respect to a relative name because of a change in something else, or this may happen because of a decrease or increase in some other absolute thing inhering in the object itself.

Likewise, relatives are said to be simultaneous by nature. This is not because they are things one of which necessarily requires the other but because if 'to exist' is truly predicated of one of them significatively taken, it is necessarily predicated of the other also significatively taken; for the following is valid: the double exists; therefore, the half exists (and vice versa).

Response to (4)

Here the correct response is simply to grant the conclusion; for absolute things really are distinguished from relations. It is relative terms that are said to be relations, and such things are really different from external objects. Nonetheless, this form of argument frequently deceives the inexperienced. It drives them to admit a plurality of things which one should not in fact postulate. The following inference provides an example: creation is; conservation is not; therefore, creation is distinguished from conservation. It will become clear in remarks that follow when this form of argument works.

One might object that since what is white comes to be similar from being dissimilar, it must now possess something it did not previously possess. My response is that the white comes to be similar from being dissimilar simply by the fact that some other thing has been made white. No new entity need come to the object in question. God becomes a creator from being a non-creator; and a column which was not to the right comes to be on the right; but in neither case need the object in question acquire any new entity. The same holds true in the present case.

Response to (5)

The difficulty about a passion and its subject is easily handled once it is recognized what a demonstrable passion is. It is not an external thing really existing in a subject. It is, on the contrary, a term which is predicable of its subject in the second mode of perseity and which can supposit for the same thing as that subject. In this way 'similar' and 'dissimilar' and 'equal' and 'unequal' are said to be passions of quality and quantity respectively.

Response to (6)

Just because we find that different effects result from the fact that certain things are ordered and arranged in a different way, we should not think that the relation which they signify is the cause of the relevant effect. It is, on the contrary, the absolute things which are ordered in the relevant way that are the cause. One thing can be causative with regard to a thing it could not cause before simply because it has been brought closer to that thing. There is no need for the addition of some new thing. This is the case in music and painting. Things which formerly did not produce pleasure now do merely because they are arranged differently.

Response to (7)

This difficulty about the distinction of the categories forces itself only upon some. Even Avicenna is one who finds it a notorious difficulty. But no one need be bothered by the difficulty. He has the right to examine alternatives. The Peripatetics, faithful to Aristotle, have a different account; they say that the distinction among the categories is not taken from a distinction among the things they designate, but rather from the distinction among questions that can be posed about some individual substance. Averroes makes this point in the seventh book of the *Metaphysics*.[5] But it should not be thought that the ten genera are things outside the soul or that they signify ten things in such a way that each is signified by just one genus. The teaching of the Peripatetics holds that the ten genera are ten terms designating the same things in different ways. Terms representing each of the eight parts of speech can all signify the same thing. 'White', 'being white', 'to be white', 'white-ly', and the remaining forms provide an example of this. The same thing holds in the case of the distinction among the categories; despite their distinction there is an identity among the things they designate.

Likewise, the distinction of being into absolute and relative is not a distinction of being qua being, but a distinction among terms. It is like the distinctions between abstract and concrete terms, proper and apellative terms, and nouns and adjectives. For on what basis could a thing be called absolute? Because it is distinguished from something else? In that case relations, which recent writers construe as external, would be absolute; for they are construed as things really different from everything else. Because it does not require or depend upon something else? In that case no accident would be an absolute thing, nor would substantial form, nor any created thing; for each one of these requires something else and depends on something else for its existence. Perhaps, things are to be called absolute which can be grasped by themselves and do not require any other term to be understood. But, then, matter, all accidents, and even the Godhead turn out to be something less than absolute; for according to many thinkers matter cannot be understood without form; an accident without its subject; nor the Godhead without the notion of finite persons.

The point about the division of being outside the soul is clear to anyone who looks at the text in the sixth book of the *Metaphysics*.[6] The distinction is not a division of things outside the soul, but a distinction among

[5] *Aristotelis Opera*, 164, recto, B.
[6] 1026^a 33-1026^b 4.

terms. This is clear from what is said in the *Categories* and in the fifth book of the *Metaphysics*.[7] In one place he says that composition and division do not belong to the things that the mind combines and divides. In the other he says that being is said in as many senses as there are categories; for one signifies what something is; another how it is qualified; and another how it is quantified. But it is clear that composition, division, and signification cannot be features of things, but only of terms.

Response to (8)

Of the things that are customarily said about relations, many are improper and some are even false. This is clear to one who examines the books of recent writers on relations. Some of the common locutions, however, are in their intended sense true, e.g., 'The father is a father by paternity', 'The son is a son by fielty', 'The similar is similar by similarity', etc. In the case of such locutions there is no need to invent any object by means of which a father is a father; a son, a son; or a similar thing, similar. Neither is there any need to multiply objects in locutions like 'The column is to the right by dexterity', 'God creates by creation, is good by goodness, is just by justice, powerful by power', 'An accident inheres by inherence', 'The subject is subject by subjectivity', 'The suitable is suitable by suitability', 'The chimera is nothing by nothingness', 'The blind is blind by blindness', 'Body is mobile by mobility', and so on with innumerable other propositions.

If we are to make explicit and unambiguous each of these propositions, we must analyze them into two propositions employing a description in place of the name. Thus 'The father is a father by paternity' becomes 'The father is a father because he begot a son', and 'The son is a son by fielty' becomes 'The son is a son because he was begotten'. 'The similar is similar by similarity' becomes 'The similar is similar because it has a quality of the same sort as something else'. The same kind of analysis holds with the other propositions.

But if one finds this technique for handling these propositions unsatisfactory, there is another way of preserving propositions of this type without multiplying entities. One can construe the abstract and relative terms (i.e., 'father' and 'paternity', 'son' and 'fielty', 'similar' and 'similarity') as signifying the same thing. Thus, 'The father is a father by paternity, i.e., by himself' and 'God is creator by His active creation, i.e. by Himself' (for 'active creation' does not signify anything over and above God). 'God is good by His goodness, i.e. by Himself' (for His goodness is not something different from Himself).

Anselm provides us with an account of how relation can be called an accident in chapter 25 of the *Monologion*.[8] Unlike whiteness relation is not said to be an accident because it is a form actually informing the substance

[7] 2ª 4-10; 1017ª 23-30.
[8] P. L., T. 158, 178 D-179A.

of which it is said. It is an accident because it is a term predicable of something contingently; it can be successively affirmed and denied because of a change in that of which it is predicated or, as in the case of terms like 'equality', 'similarity', 'lord', and 'creator', because of a change in something else.

Response to (9)

Nor can one argue from the union of matter and form, subject and accident, parts in a whole, or spirits and bodies to the conclusion that there is something, the relative thing, lying between the things united. For the same question can be asked of these mediating things—how can they, by being added to something else, produce one thing? They do it either by themselves (but, of course, this could be said of the original objects) or by some further union (in which case we would have a regress into infinity). For let the mediating object be separated by some power from the things it unites, then let it be united with them as an accident is united with its subject. How is it in this case that distinct things are united? Is it by way of some further mediating entity? In that case the previous difficulty arises again.

Briefly, one should say, as Aristotle teaches in the eighth book of the *Metaphysics* (where he asks how matter and form make one thing), that one thing is act and the other, potency.[9] Since one is act and the other is potency, each is capable of uniting with the other in its own way. Or the things united are each act and potency, for we do not always have a case of act informing something else. On the contrary sometimes one thing informs another; sometimes one thing moves another; sometimes one thing rules and governs another; and so on.

Response to (10)

From Aristotle's own remarks it is clear that for him there is nothing problematical in one and the same thing being designated by different categories, for he says that knowledge and the knowable as well as sense and the sensible are in the category of relation and in other categories besides.

Nor is there anything problematical in his saying that the proposition in which one category is denied of another is immediate. The point here is not related to the diversity of things they designate. The point is rather that one category is not predicated of another by direct predication in the first mode of perseity. Every such predication is per accidens. Likewise, while the same thing is designated by 'creation' and 'conservation', one is denied of the other. The same point holds in the case at issue.

Therefore, we can conclude that Aristotle construed relations in the way we have claimed.

The contrary view has two sources. First, some lean too much on the peculiarities of speech found in philosophy books. This is a source of error

[9] 1045[a] 22-25.

for many. For one thing, the books have been translated incorrectly. For another, Greek expressions are not perspicuous when translated into Latin; and this makes for difficult reading and sometimes even invites incorrect interpretation. Finally, the remarks of the authors are frequently employed incorrectly for although what the authors say is true, those who incorrectly employ those remarks confound the points being made.

The second source consists in the tendency to multiply entities according to the multiplicity of terms, so that for every term there is a thing. This is a wrong-headed approach, and more than any other it leads one from the truth. For one should not ask in the case of every term what the relevant thing is. In the case of many terms the question is what the term means. Examples include all relative terms and some other terms which are equivalent in signification to longer expressions. Therefore, propositions in which they play a role have to be analyzed and broken down replacing a name sometimes by a description, for words and concepts by themselves can deceive.

52: On the Items in the Category of Relation

Now that we have outlined the view which Aristotle seems to hold, we shall consider the things which are subsumed on that view under the genus of relation.

First, it should be noted that for Aristotle nothing is to be placed in the genus of relation except those mental, vocal and written names to which, when functioning in a proposition, it is possible to add an expression in an oblique case.

There are, however, two different kinds of names to which an expression in an oblique case can be added. When some names are truly predicable of something, the only expression that can be added correctly is the corresponding abstract name. (I am using the term 'abstract' in the first of the senses mentioned earlier.) Expressions like 'white', 'hot', 'sweet', and 'besouled' are examples. Nothing is white except by whiteness, nor is anything hot except by heat, and similarly for the other examples. But while expressions like these are connotative, they are not said to be relatives.

But there are other names which cannot be truly predicated of anything unless it is possible to add to them names which are not their abstract forms;

the added names are in one of the oblique cases, but they are not the relevant abstract forms. Examples are names like 'master' and 'slave' and 'father' and 'son'; for no one is a father unless he is someone's father, nor is anything similar unless it is similar to something. These expressions are called relatives according to being, since they cannot hold true of something unless it is possible to add to them an expression in one of the oblique cases. When relatives according to being are contingently predicated of something and contingently hold true of that of which they are predicated (provided the subject remains the same), then it is impossible for a person to know that the term holds true of something unless he knows determinately that with respect to which the term is predicated. Thus, it is impossible to know that someone is a slave without knowing whose slave he is. Likewise, it is impossible to know that something is similar to something else without knowing that to which it is similar. The Philosopher is referring to relatives of this sort when he says in the *Categories* that "he who knows determinately one of the relatives also knows the other determinately."[1] But if a relative according to being is truly predicated of something in such a way that it cannot fail to hold true of that thing (when the subject remains the same), then he who knows determinately one of the relatives need not necessarily know the other.

There are, on the other hand, names to which it is sometimes possible to add an expression in an oblique case and sometimes not. Thus, sometimes it is possible to say truly that the donkey is Socrates', so that it is the donkey of some one. But sometimes it happens that although 'That donkey is a donkey' is true, 'That donkey is someone's' is false. Expressions like this can be called relatives according to speech. Sometimes they can be said of other things with the addition of some expression in an oblique case, but this addition is not a necessary condition of their being predicated of a thing. Consequently, these expressions do not belong per se in the genus of relation. Names like 'hand' and 'head' are examples. Thus, sometimes that hand is a man's hand; but sometimes it is not any man's hand as when it has been cut off. However, if in that case it were not called a hand, then the term 'hand' would be in the genus of relation. The same holds in other cases. Thus, every name which cannot, when significatively taken, be predicated of anything unless it is possible to add to it the oblique form of some expression other than its abstract counterpart, is in the genus of relation. All such expressions are called relatives according to being. Some expressions, on the other hand, can be called relatives according to speech since sometimes one can and sometimes one cannot add to them an expression in an oblique case.

Nonetheless, the Philosopher does not use the expressions 'relative according to being' and 'relative according to speech', nor does he use another set

[1] 8ª 35-36.

of expressions which teachers of philosophy nowadays employ frequently—
'real relation' and 'relation of reason'. No such distinction is to be found in the
Philosopher's writings. To him names like 'cause' and 'lord' are relatives in the
same way as all the other expressions. He always, or at least frequently, uses
the name 'master' as his example of relatives; for no one can be a master unless
he is the master of some slave. Therefore, for Aristotle there is no distinction
between real relations and relations of the reason. He does distinguish several
forms of relatives in the fifth book of the *Metaphysics,*[2] but I will not deal
with that distinction at this time. It suffices to know that for Aristotle every
name or expression having the force of a name (participles then are included)
which cannot, when significatively taken, be truly predicated of anything
unless it is possible to add to it the oblique form of an expression other than
its abstract counterpart, is really a relative and falls under the category of
relation. It is irrelevant whether the term signifies just substance or quality
or both. It is likewise irrelevant whether it connotes something else, whether
in act or potency, whether affirmatively or negatively, or in some other way.
Thus, all of the following expressions are to be placed in the category of
relation—'master' and 'slave', 'sign' and 'significatum', 'cause' and 'effect',
'producer' and 'product', 'agent' and 'patient', 'what is able to heat', and
'what is able to be heated'.

But it follows that in Aristotle's view, while a verb may be in the category of action or passion or some other category, the participle or verbal
name corresponding to it may be in the category of relation. He implies
this view in the fifth book of the *Metaphysics* in the chapter on Relation
while enumerating the forms of relatives, "Other things are said to be relative—as that which can heat to that which can be heated and that which can
cut to that which can be cut and, in general, the active to the passive."[3] He
says later, "Things are active and passive according to an active and passive
potency and the actualization of such a potency—that which is capable of
heating is related to that which is heatable because it can heat. Again, that
which heats is related to that which it heats and that which cuts to that
which is cut as agent to patient."[4] But note, that which heats is an example
of the second type of relatives. Thus, I think that for Aristotle all names and
participles which cannot truly be predicable of something unless one can add
to them an expression in an oblique case and which correspond in signification to active and passive verbs, being active and passive not only in form but
also in signification (in that they signify that something really acts or is
acted on or that something does something or has something done to it), are
relatives of the second sort. Examples are 'agent' and 'patient', 'cause' and
'effect', 'active' and 'passive', etc.

[2] 1020^b 26-1021^b 11.
[3] 1020^b 28-29.
[4] 1021^a 15-18.

Furthermore, that Aristotle subsumes verbal names or participles under the category of relation and their corresponding verbs in other categories is clear from his remarks in the chapter on Relatives in the *Categories*. He says, "Likewise, lying, standing, and sitting are also positions, but position is a relative. To lie, to stand, and to sit are not themselves positions, but take their names from the positions enumerated."[5] It is clear from this remark that 'to stand' is not in the genus of relation but that 'standing' is; for if there be a standing it is the standing of someone. Nevertheless, in the final analysis it is necessary to resolve a proposition embodying this sort of expression into a proposition of the following form: 'The parts of this body are separated from each other in this or that way'. Here, a name or a participle of the relevant sort (i.e., one that cannot be predicated of something unless it is possible to add some other expression in an oblique case) will make itself explicit.

53: On the Properties of Relatives

Now that we have examined Aristotle's view on relations, we shall consider the properties he attributed to them.

In the case of some relatives there is contrariety. This property, however, does not hold in the case of all relatives. But it is clear that contrariety is exhibited by some relatives; for 'virtue' and 'vice' are relatives, and they are contraries. It should be noted that those relatives are called contraries which cannot simultaneously apply to one and the same thing. Thus, if relatives are contraries, then only one of a pair can apply to a particular individual at a given time; the other can apply only at a different time. In this sense 'father' and 'son' are not contraries, for one and the same person can be simultaneously both father and son. He cannot of course be both with respect to the same person. Likewise, nothing is the contrary of 'triple' because to anything that 'triple' applies some other relative can also apply at the same time. If it cannot apply at the same time, it never can.

The second property of relatives is that they admit of more or less; but this does not apply in the case of all relatives. Some relatives can be predicated of something, first with the adverb 'more' and, later with the adverb 'less'. Thus, something is first more similar and later less similar and vice

[5] 6^b 11-14.

versa. But, this cannot happen with 'triple', 'double', 'equal', or a number of other relatives.

The third property is that all relatives are said with respect to some correlative; that is, to every relative one can add an oblique form of its own correlative. It may happen that we lack the requisite name. In that case we can invent one; and then the oblique case of the existing name can be added to the nominative case of the invented name and, likewise, the oblique case of the invented name to the nominative case of the existing name. Thus, if some one is a master it is necessary that he be the master of a slave, and if something is similar that it be similar to what is similar. Likewise, if 'wing' is a relative, so that it is impossible for something to be a wing without being the wing of something, then we can invent a name to correspond to it, to function as its correlative. Thus, we might say that a wing is the wing of the winged and that the winged is winged by way of a wing. The same holds in all other cases.

But it should be noted that sometimes one and the same name is placed in both the oblique and nominative cases. These are called relatives of similar names or equivalent relations. Thus, 'Every similar thing is similar to the similar' and 'Every equal thing is equal to the equal' and similarly in other cases where the same name is used in both the nominative and an oblique case. But sometimes a different name is placed in the nominative and oblique case. Thus, if someone is a father, he is the father of a son; and it is not necessary that he be the father of someone who is also a father. Likewise, if someone is a slave, he is the slave of a master; and it is not necessary that he be the slave of a slave. These are called relatives of different names or non-equivalent relatives. The general rule, however, is that it is always possible to add an oblique form to the nominative case of a relative, as Damascene indicates in chapter 34 of his *Logic*.[1]

The fourth property of relatives is that they are simultaneous by nature. This should be understood to mean that existence cannot be truly predicated of one relative unless, when the relevant proposition is formed it is also truly predicated of the other. Thus, if 'The double is' is true, then 'The half is' is also true. If 'The father is' is true, then 'The son is' is also true and vice versa. The claim that relatives are destroyed together should be understood in the same way. If the negative proposition in which existence is denied of one relative is true, the corresponding negative proposition in which it is denied of the other is also true. Thus, if 'The father is not' is true, then 'The son is not' is also true and vice versa.

But it should be noted that according to the Philosopher in the *Categories*, these rules are not absolutely general. Thus, he shows that this particular property does not apply in the case of all relatives.[2] He proves this in the

[1] *Dialectica*, chapter 34, 3-18.
[2] 7^b 22-8^a 12.

case of 'knowledge' and 'object of knowledge' and 'sense' and 'sensible'; although he neither establishes the point in any other cases nor provides additional examples, the point does hold in other cases. Thus, 'that which can heat' and 'that which can be heated' are correlatives. Nevertheless, it does not follow that because that which can heat exists, that which can be heated also exists. Likewise, it does not follow that just because that which can be made white does not exist, that which can make white does not either. The same point holds in many other cases.

54: On Relation According to the Opinion of Others

Up to now we have been examining the account of relations which I think Aristotle holds. Now we shall consider relations in the view that is opposed to Aristotle's. On that view every relation is a thing distinct from its foundation, so that the similarity by which white Socrates is like white Plato is a thing really and totally distinct from both Socrates and the white which grounds the similarity. The same sort of account holds in the case of paternity, fielty, and all the other things that are placed in the genus of relation. Thus, although 'foundation of a relation' is not a piece of Aristotle's philosophical jargon, proponents of this view claim that every relation has both a foundation and a term and that it is really distinct from both. They prove that relation is a distinct thing in many ways:

First, each distinct category signifies distinct things; relation is a distinct category; therefore. . .

Again, whiteness is able to remain without similarity; therefore, whiteness is not similarity.

Again, if a relation were the same as its foundation, then since the foundations of relations fall under different categories (i.e., substance, quantity, and quality), some relations would be in the category of substance, others in the category of quality, and still others in the category of quantity; but, then, relation would not be a distinct category.

Again, it is by one and the same foundation that white Socrates is similar to white Plato and distinct from black Socrates; therefore, if a relation were identical with its foundation, similarity and dissimilarity would be identical. But then they would not be different relations.

Again, if relations were identical with their foundations, then since there is motion towards a foundation (e.g., there is motion towards whiteness), there would be motion towards a relation; and that runs counter to the Philosopher's remarks in the fifth book of the *Physics*.[1]

Again, the unity of the universe consists in the order of its parts; if therefore, relation were not a distinct thing, that order would not be a distinct thing, so that the universe would not be one.

Again, when the parts composing some whole are separated the parts remain, but the union does not; therefore, the union is something different from the parts.

Again, in the nature assumed by the Word there is no absolute thing which is not like something in my nature; therefore, since that nature is united with the Word and not mine, that nature has something which mine does not have, but it is not anything absolute; therefore, it is something relative, which is what we set out to prove.

For these and similar reasons, many hold that relation is a thing outside the mind and really distinct from every absolute thing.

Nevertheless, they distinguish between relations, for some are real and others are relations of the reason. Examples of the latter are the relations of God to his creatures and other relations which cannot exist without the operation of this intellect.

The properties previously mentioned are attributed to relations; for while some relatives are contrary to each other (e.g., virtue and vice), others are not, as nothing is the contrary of the triple.

Again, relations admit of more and less, although as I have indicated this is not true of all relations.

Again, every relative is said with respect to a correlative. Nevertheless, it sometimes happens that one real relation corresponds to another real relation. Thus, the similarity of Socrates corresponds to a real relation in the thing to which it is similar. Sometimes, however, a real relation in one thing does not correspond to a real relation in another, but only to a relation of the reason. Thus, to the real relation whereby a creature depends on God, there does not correspond any real relation in God, but only a relation of the reason.

Likewise, relations are said to be simultaneous by nature, so that if one relation is the other must also be. But this property is to be construed as holding only in the case where both objects are real relations. Where one object is a real relation and the other a relation of the reason, the property need not hold. Examples are knowledge and the knowable object and sense and the sensible object.

[1] 225[b] 11-13.

55: On the Category of Quality

The fourth category is the category of quality. As in the case of the first three categories, I shall first deal with the view which, whether true or false, seems compatible with the principles of Aristotle's philosophy. Then I shall outline the contrary position. It seems that according to the principles of Aristotle's philosophy, one should say that the category of quality is a concept or sign containing under it all such terms as do not express a substantial part of a substance and can be used to answer the question posed about substance 'How is it qualified?' For the present, I shall not consider whether concrete or abstract terms more properly belong in the category of quality.

In the genus of quality there are certain terms which designate things that are distinct from substances, things that are not themselves substances. Examples are 'whiteness', 'blackness', 'color', 'knowledge', and 'light'. But the category of quality also embodies terms that do not designate things different from substance and the aforementioned qualities. Examples are 'figure', 'curvature', 'straightness', 'denseness', and 'thinness'.

To determine when a quality should be construed as a thing distinct from substance and when not, one can employ the following test: predicables which, while incapable of being truly applied to one thing at the same time, can successively hold true of an object merely as the result of a local motion, need not be construed as signifying distinct things. 'Curved' and 'straight', for example, can be successively affirmed of one and the same thing merely as the result of a local motion. Thus, take something straight. If as a result of a local motion its extreme parts become closer, then it is said to be curved. No additional entity is required. Therefore, 'curvature' and 'straightness' do not signify things that are distinct from the things that are curved and straight. The same holds true in the case of shape, for merely as a result of a local motion in some of its part an object can take on a new shape. And so it is with 'rare', 'dense', and similar terms. But it is different in the case of terms like 'whiteness', 'blackness', 'heat', and 'cold'. For it is not simply because a thing or its parts undergo local motion that the thing becomes hot or cold. Consequently, these terms designate things distinct from substance.

It should be noted that Aristotle posits four modes or species of quality.[1] The first he calls habit or disposition. Every quality, whether spiritual or corporeal, that is firmly established is called a habit; and every quality, whether spiritual or corporeal, that is easily changed is called a disposition. It follows that a quality in one object can be a habit and a quality of the same species in another object a disposition.

[1] 8^b 26-10^a 17.

And it should be noted that under this mode are included not only those terms which designate something different from substance, but also those which do not designate anything different; for every quality which can, by a change in the thing be taken away from its subject either easily or with difficulty, is included in this mode. As I shall note later, every quality is contained under this mode. Therefore, this is called a species of quality not because there is some quality that is neither a habit nor a disposition, but because some qualities are not habits and some are not dispositions. Or, possibly it is called a species because it connotes something more specific than the name 'quality'.

Another genus of quality includes natural capacities and incapacities. Thus, everything by which something can easily act or resist action is placed in this genus.

The third species is called affection and affective quality; every sensible quality is placed in this third species of quality.

The fourth genus of quality includes the form and determinate shape of a thing. 'Straight', 'curved', and similar terms fall under this genus. It should be noted that a quality on account of which something is said to be beautiful or ugly is called form. The names in this genus do not designate things different from substance and the qualities already mentioned.

It should be noted that, for Aristotle, one and the same thing falls under different species of quality. This is clear, for he says that heat and cold are in the first species of quality and also in the third. Thus, he does not want to say that these species are mutually exclusive, but that they can be predicated of each other at least particularly. The same point holds, for Aristotle, in the case of the categories: they can be predicated of each other particularly.

The Philosopher attributes many properties to quality.[2] The first property is that quality admits of contraries, for one quality can be the contrary of another. Likewise, the concrete names designating these qualities in an oblique way are contrary. Nonetheless, not every quality has a contrary. Some qualities such as light have no contrary.

The second property is that quality admits of more and less, for a concrete form from this category is sometimes predicated of a thing with the adverb 'more' and sometimes with the adverb 'less'. Thus, sometimes this is true: 'A is more white than B'; and sometimes this is true: 'A is less white than B'. But this property does not apply in the case of all qualities; for one thing is not said to be more triangular than another, nor is one thing said to be more square than another.

The third property is that things are said to be similar and dissimilar with respect to quality. Thus, two white things are similar and, likewise, two black things, but the white and the black are dissimilar.

[2] 10^b 12-11^a 19.

Since I have dealt with Aristotle's view on quality at some length in my commentary on the *Categories*, these remarks on his account suffice. Whenever I comment on the Philosopher I express not my view, but Aristotle's as I understand it.

56: On Quality
According to the Opinion of Others

Others however claim that every quality is a thing really distinct from substance, quantity, and relative things. They list four species of quality, and they construe the items contained under each of these species as things distinct from each other. Thus, they say that habit and disposition constitute the first species of quality. These are distinguished in that a habit is something firmly established; whereas, a disposition is something easily changed.

They say that the second species includes natural capacity and incapacity, and they hold that these are things different from habit and disposition.

They say that the third species incorporates affections and affective qualities; that is, all sensible qualities.

They claim that the fourth species includes form and shape, and they hold that these are both really distinct from substance and from qualities of the other species. Thus they say that when a straight body becomes curved, it really loses one absolute entity and acquires a new one.

They attribute to quality the same properties that Aristotle does.

57: On Action

Aristotle discusses the remaining six categories briefly. To benefit those who are less advanced in the study of philosophy I shall discuss these categories in greater detail.

The fifth category is action. When the philosopher enumerates the categories or deals with this category in isolation, he does not refer to it by a name but by the verb, 'to do'. Likewise, Damascene refers to the category by a verb rather than a name. Thus, it seems to me that for Aristotle this category is simply an ordered series of verbs designating that someone acts or does something. The verbs are so ordered that one can be predicated of another with the addition of the pronoun 'whoever'. Thus, 'Whoever heats, acts or does something' and 'Whoever moves, acts or does something'. It is in this sense that this category is a highest genus. And if we always had at our disposal, corresponding to verbs, not only participles but also names suppositing for the same things as participles, there would be few problems with regard to this category. For then it could simply be said that the relevant name (e.g., 'action') is suppositing for the same thing as the relevant participle (e.g. 'acting'), and it would be clear that action was an absolute thing like the thing acting. But since the thing acting is a substance, action itself would be a substance. Nonetheless, substance would only contingently be an action just as substance is only contingently the thing acting; and thus, the verb would be in one category and the noun in another. For as we have already proved, in Aristotle's view 'the thing acting' is in the category of relation (since 'the thing acting' can always admit the addition of an oblique form), but 'to act' is not in that category. Thus, the category of action would not designate anything different from what is in the category of substance and quality. It would simply designate things from those two categories. Thus, in the proposition 'Fire heats the wood', the verb designates the heat, although not nominally but verbally. Consequently, it cannot be predicated of the heat. In the same way 'white' designates whiteness, but it cannot be predicated of whiteness.

In defense of this view and regardless of whether it is true, one can adduce convincing reasons. To take an instance, it can be argued that when one says, "Fire acts or heats", nothing over and above substance and quality is designated.

First, suppose that some other thing is designated. Where is that thing? Either it subsists per se or it inheres in another. If it subsists per se, then it is a substance and the point intended is established. If it inheres in another, it either inheres in the fire that does the heating or in the wood that is heated. If the first be granted, then every agent and every mover would truly receive some new entity into itself whenever it acts or moves. Thus, the heavenly bodies and the intelligences would be continually receiving new entities as they act.

Likewise, in acting and creating things God would receive a new entity in Himself. One might say that things are different with God and creatures. But the response is that if God without receiving any new entity can really and truly act (so that in His case there is simply action without any additional thing), it is pointless to posit such an entity in any agent; for each of them can really and truly be an agent without the addition of any such thing.

One might claim that the relevant entity inheres in the thing heated. The difficulty here is that the heated thing should not be called agent, but would be; and the fire should be called agent, but would not be.

Likewise, the heated thing would receive into itself a number of things— the heat, that entity which is called the action, and another entity entitled the passion. It seems absurd, however, to posit such a plurality of objects without necessity and for no good reason.

Again, one can argue: the object in question is either caused or not caused. If it is not caused it is God. If it is caused I ask "By whom?" It will be caused by some agent; therefore, some agent produced it. But if this is granted I ask the same question about the act of production by which the thing was produced. Thus, we will have a regress into infinity, or it will be held that one thing can be produced without any production. But for the same reason one should have claimed this in the first case above: one should have admitted that the heat is produced in the wood without any new entity in the thing producing the heat.

Again, one can argue theologically as follows: every thing which God produces by the mediation of some second cause He can produce immediately of and by Himself. Therefore, He can produce the thing which is claimed to be the action in the case where the fire acts immediately and without the fire actually acting. Suppose that this is done. Then, either the fire acts or it does not. If it does we must say both that it acts and that only God acts. Against the claim that the fire does not act one can argue: the action is formally present in the fire, but then the fire is actually denominated by that action. Consequently, the fire acts, so that it both acts and does not act which is impossible.

For these and many other reasons one can claim that action is not something distinct from the agent, the thing effected, or the thing produced. And whether correct or incorrect, this is the view I think Aristotle holds. He claims that the name 'action' supposits for the agent so that the following are true: 'Action is an agent' and 'To act is an agent'; or he holds that propositions of this form should be analyzed in terms of propositions in which the verb takes the place of the relevant noun. Thus, 'The action of the agent exists', is equivalent to The agent acts'. Likewise, 'Heating is an act' is equivalent to 'What heats acts', and so on.

It should be noted that in Aristotle's view, 'to act' and 'to do' have a number of uses. Sometimes they are used in cases where something produces, causes, or destroys something else; and sometimes they are used where something destroys something or makes something into something else; finally, they are sometimes used very broadly and generally to cover the two cases listed above and the case of motion as well. It is in this broad use that they mark off a category.

Contrariety belongs to this category, for 'to make cold' and 'to heat'
are contraries. They designate contrary qualities and cannot be applied to
the same thing at the same time, at least not with respect to the same thing.

This category also admits more and less; that is, one can add the adverbs
'more' and 'less' to verbs in this category, although not to all of them.
Thus, one can correctly say, "This heats more than that", "This heats less
than that", and "One man rejoices more and another less". (All these remarks conform to the view which seems to me to follow from Aristotle's
teachings.)

Others say that action is a thing distinct not only from the agent, the thing
effected, and the thing produced, but also from all other absolute things. It is
a respect which some say exists subjectively in the agent and others claim
exists subjectively in the thing effected. Nevertheless, they say that sometimes
action is a real respect of the agent vis-a-vis the thing effected and that sometimes it is a respect of the reason. Thus, when God acts there is only a respect
of the reason. They say that the aforementioned properties (to have a contrary
and to admit more and less) belong to the entity in question.

58: On Passion

The sixth category is the category of suffering (passion). Aristotle always
refers to this category by the verb form. This is clear in the final chapter of
the *Categories* and in the chapter on 'To Do and to Suffer'.[1] Damascene seems
to agree with Aristotle here, for in his *Logic* he also refers to this category
by the verb.[2] In Aristotle's view the preceeding category consists of verbs;
the same is the case here. This category contains all such verbs as signify
that something has been acted upon. Thus, all the remarks made with respect
to that category apply here. For Aristotle, then, to suffer and suffering are
simply the substance which suffers. Damascene makes this point when he
says, "To do and to suffer are simply substance qua acting and suffering in
a certain way."[3] Alternatively, one can always analyze a proposition which
contains the name 'suffering' or the infinitive form of the verb functioning

[1] 11^b 1-14.
[2] *Dialetica.*
[3] *Ibid.*

as a name in terms of a proposition in which the verb takes the place of the relevant noun or infinitive. Thus, 'To be heated is to suffer' is equivalent to 'What is heated suffers'. 'Being heated is a passion' is equivalent to the same proposition.

But it should be noted that 'to suffer' has many uses. In one sense it is used in the case where something receives something from something else. In this sense a subject suffers as does the matter receiving a form. In another sense the term is used more broadly to cover the first case as well as the case where something is moved without receiving something, as in local motion. In a third sense the term is common to the first two cases as well as the case where something is caused or produced. In this third sense the verb marks a category.

To sum up, I think that Aristotle holds that all mental verbs in the active voice belong in the category of To Do and that all mental verbs in the passive voice belong in the category of To Suffer. It is irrelevant whether the verb signifies substance or quality or both substance and quality.

Others, however, say that suffering is a certain respect existing subjectively in the thing acted upon and corresponding to the respect of action.

59: On When

The seventh category is when. According to Aristotle this is an ordered series of adverbs or equivalent expressions by means of which one can appropriately answer a question posed by the interrogative 'When'. He always refers to this category by the interrogative 'when' and not any other expression. We do not have any general term common to all the expressions by which one can respond to that question. For Aristotle, as I understand his view, this category does not designate anything distinct from substance and quality. It designates just those things, although not nominally but adverbially.

Whether this view is true or false, one can argue for it in the following way: suppose when is an entity which inheres in the temporal object. Since it should not be posited with respect to one time rather than another, there will be an entity of the relevant sort corresponding to the future. But the consequent is false; for if in the object which will exist tomorrow, there is an entity without which it cannot be said that the object will exist tomorrow (in the way that something cannot be white without whiteness), the object will have an entity of this sort with respect to every instant included in the time in which it is yet to exist. Those instants, however, are infinite; therefore there will be an infinity of such entities in the object.

In the same way the object has existed through an infinity of times and an infinity of instants; therefore, an infinity of such entities remains in the object from the past.

One might say that the relevant instants did not exist in act. The response is that either some such instant existed in act or none did. If none did, then nothing is an instant; but if some did, then since there is no reason why one instant should be in act rather than another, an infinity of instants existed in act.

Further, of every thing it can be determinately said that it either is or is not. Therefore, in this man there either determinately is such an entity or there is not. Let us focus on the entity associated with tomorrow. If this entity is in the man, then it is determinately true that the man will exist tomorrow. If the entity is not in the man, then the opposite is determinately true. But this seems to be opposed to Aristotle who denies that there is determinate truth in the case of future contingents.

One can also argue theologically: either an entity of the sort in question is in that man or it is not. Suppose it is. Now, the following is formally valid: an entity corresponding to tomorrow is in the man; therefore, the man will exist tomorrow. (This is parallel to the following case: whiteness is in this first subject; therefore, this is white.) But since the antecedent is true it could not happen, even by divine power, that it was afterward false that the thing existed. Therefore, it will always be necessarily true to say, "That man was to exist on that day." Consequently, God could not but bring it to pass that he will exist on that day. But if the entity is not in the man, it will later be necessary that the relevant entity was not in that man. Now, the following is valid: the entity was not in that man; therefore, he was not to exist on that day. Since the antecedent is necessary, the consequent is also. Consequently, God cannot extend the man's life for even one more day.

Again, if when were the sort of entity those holding the contrary view think, just as the hot is hot by heat, the temporal thing would be such by that entity. Consequently, just as it is impossible for something to be hot without heat, it would be impossible for something to be temporal without the relevant entity inhering in it. But the consequent is false, for this is true 'The Antichrist will exist before the day of judgment'. Nonetheless, no such thing is in the Antichrist since he is nothing.

One might say that nothing has such an entity corresponding to a future time, at least not before it reaches that time. Thus, neither that man nor the Antichrist has an entity in him corresponding to the future. The response is that if an object can truly exist tomorrow and at other future times without the relevant entity, then in the same way a thing can truly have existed in the past and in the present as well without entities of the sort in question. It is pointless then to posit such things.

Further, if in the man who existed yesterday there is an entity in terms of which he is said to have existed yesterday (as the wood is hot by heat), then it is impossible that 'The man existed yesterday' be true without the relevant entity (just as it is impossible that the wood be hot without heat). But this seems false. For there is nothing contradictory in the assumption that God conserves the man without the entity, for by His absolute power He can conserve the man and destroy the entity. Suppose that this happens. Either the man existed yesterday or he did not. If he did, he existed yesterday without the relevant entity. But, then, it is not in terms of the postulated entity that he is said to have existed yesterday, and that is what we set out to prove. Against the claim that he did not exist yesterday, one can point out that a proposition referring to the past is necessary in a way that if it is true not even God can make it false.

For these and many other reasons which in the interest of brevity I omit, both believers and non-believers can grant that when is not an entity of the kind described. It seems to me this was Aristotle's view, and it is for this reason that he never refers to this category by a name, but always by an adverb.

Others, however, say that when or whenness is a respect in the temporal thing which derives from the different times and on account of which a thing is said to exist in the past, present, or future.

60: On Where

The eighth category is where, and what I have said in the case of the preceding category applies here. It seems that according to Aristotle's teaching, where is not a thing distinct from place and the other absolute things. On the contrary the Philosopher always refers to this category by the interrogative adverb expressive of place. Thus, all those expressions by which one can appropriately answer the question posed by the adverb 'where' are subsumed under this category. If, for example, an appropriate response to the question 'Where is Socrates?' is that he is in the city or at home, then these prepositions with their objects are in Aristotle's view subsumed under the category of where.

In defense of this view one can argue: suppose that there is such an entity. There seems to be no contradiction in the assumption that God destroys that entity but neither destroys the relevant place nor the thing occupying it nor moves the place or the thing occupying it from one location to another. Lee us suppose that this actually happens. Then, either that body is in the relevant place or it is not. If it is in the relevant place and lacks the entity in question, it is located in a place without that entity; but then it is pointless to postulate such an entity. If it is not in the place where it was before, and if nothing has been corrupted, then something underwent local motion; but this runs counter to the hypothesis.

Others, on the other hand, say that where or whereness is a certain respect which is grounded in the thing occupying place and which derives from the limits of the place in which the thing is. Thus, the thing occupying place grounds the respect in question and the place where the thing is bounds it.

61: On Position

The ninth category is position. In Aristotle's view this category does not signify anything different from absolute things. It signifies, on the contrary, that the parts of a thing are arranged, ordered, and situated in such and such a way. Thus, from the fact that a thing is erect (i.e., that its parts—its legs— are not curved and that its extreme parts lie at a maximum distance from each other), the thing is said to stand, or if the reverse happens, it is said to sit.

Terms like 'to sit', 'to stand', 'to recline', and 'to lie' belong in this category. None of the terms in this category can apply to a thing unless the thing is a quantum, the parts of which can approach each other in different ways. Because of the different ways these parts can approach each other, different or contrary and incompatible predicates can successively apply to one and the same thing.

But because of the poverty of our language, we do not have an interrogative corresponding to this category.

Some, however, say that position is a certain respect inhering in a whole or its parts. Thus, when an object that was sitting rises, it acquires in itself a thing it formerly did not have and loses one it did have.

62: On Habit

The tenth category is habit. As with the preceding categories I claim that for Aristotle this category does not signify a thing distinct from enduring things. It signifies, on the contrary, that one thing is on or around another in such a way that unless there be some hinderance, the first moves when the second does but is, nonetheless, not a part of the second and is distinct from the second in both place and position.

In this category Aristotle places expressions like 'to be armed' and 'to wear shoes'. Nonetheless, for the Philosopher, 'to have' exhibits a number of senses; I indicate this in my commentary on the *Categories*.

Others, however, say that habit is a certain respect in the body which surrounds another or in the body surrounded.

These remarks on the categories are sufficient.

63: On Supposition

Now that we have discussed the significations of terms, we shall discuss supposition. Supposition is a property of a term, but only when it is in a proposition.

First, it should be noted that 'supposition' has two senses, a broad sense and a narrow sense. In the broad sense the term does not stand opposed to 'appellation', on the contrary, 'appellation' is a term under 'supposition'. In the strict sense the two terms stand opposed. But I do not intend to speak of supposition in this sense, only in the first sense. Thus, as I use the term both subject and predicate supposit; and, generally, whatever can be a subject or a predicate of a proposition supposits.

Supposition is said to be a sort of taking the place of another. Thus, when a term stands for something in a proposition in such a way that we use the term for the thing and the term or its nominative case (if it is in an oblique case) is truly predicated of the thing (or the pronoun referring to the thing), the term supposits for that thing; or this, at least, is true when the term is taken significatively. More generally, if the suppositing term is a subject, it supposits for the thing of which (or of the pronoun referring to which) it is asserted by the containing proposition that the predicate is to be predicated. If, however, the suppositing term is a predicate, it supposits for the thing (or the thing named by the name) with respect to which the subject is asserted to be the subject. Thus, by the proposition 'Man is an animal' it is asserted that Socrates is an animal, so that were the proposition 'This is an animal' (referring to Socrates) formed, it would be true. But by the proposition ' "Man" is a name' it is asserted that this word 'man' is a name; therefore, in that proposition 'man' supposits for a name. Likewise, by the proposition 'The white thing is an animal' it is asserted that the thing which is white is an animal. Thus, 'This is an animal' is true, referring to the thing which is white, and on account of this the subject supposits for that thing. The same sort of account holds in the case of the predicate, for by the proposition 'Socrates is white' it is asserted that Socrates is the thing which has whiteness; therefore the predicate supposits for the thing which has whiteness and if nothing besides Socrates were to have whiteness, then the predicate would supposit only for Socrates.

Thus, there is one general rule: a term, at least when it is significatively taken, never supposits in any proposition for a thing unless it can be truly predicated of that thing. But, then, it is false to say, as some do, that a concrete term on the predicate-side supposits for a form, so that in 'Socrates is white', the word 'white' supposits for whiteness. For no matter how the term supposits, 'Whiteness is white' is false. Thus, according to Aristotle's account a concrete name of this sort never supposits for the form that is signified by the corresponding abstract name. But in the case of other concrete names we have considered this is indeed possible. In the same way in 'A man is God', 'man' truly supposits for the Son of God; for the Son of God really is a man.

64: On the Division of Supposition

But it should be noted that supposition is first divided into personal supposition, simple supposition, and material supposition.

Universally, personal supposition occurs when a term supposits for the
thing it signifies, whether that thing be an entity outside the soul, a spoken
word, an intention of the soul, a written word, or any other thing imagin-
able. Thus, whenever the subject or predicate of a proposition supposits for
its significatum so that it is taken significatively, we always have personal
supposition.

As an example of the first kind of case, in 'Every man is an animal' the
word 'man' supposits for its significata; for 'man' is not used to signify anything other than men. It does not signify something common to them. As
Damascene says, it just signifies the men themselves.[1] An example of the
second kind of case is 'Every vocal name is a part of speech'; the word
'name' supposits only for vocal words; but since it is used to signify vocal
words it supposits personally. As an example of the third kind of case,
in 'Every species is a universal' and 'Every intention of the soul
exists in the soul' the subjects supposit personally; for both supposit for the
thing they are appointed to signify. As an example of the fourth, in 'Every
written expression is an expression' the subject supposits for the things it
signifies—written words; therefore, it supposits personally.

It should be clear, then, that those who say that we have personal supposition when a term supposits for a thing do not describe personal supposition adequately. The correct definition, on the contrary, runs as follows:
a term supposits personally when it supposits for the thing it signifies and
does so significatively.

Simple supposition occurs when a term supposits for an intention of the
soul and is not functioning significatively. For example, in 'Man is a species'
the term 'man' supposits for an intention of the soul, for it is that intention
which is a species. Nonetheless, the term 'man' does not, properly speaking,
signify that intention. On the contrary, the word is subordinated to that
intention and signifies the same thing that it does. I have explained this
point earlier. It is clear, then, that those who say that simple supposition
occurs when a term supposits for its significatum are wrong. Simple supposition obtains when a term supposits for an intention of the soul which is
not the proper significatum of that term, for the term exhibiting simple
supposition signifies real things and not intentions of the soul.

[1] Perhaps the reference here is to *Dialectica*, chapter 7, 15-24.

Material supposition occurs when a term does not supposit significatively, but supposits for a spoken word or a written word. A good example is ' "Man" is a name'. The word 'man' here supposits for itself but it does not signify itself. Likewise, in the proposition ' "Man" is written' we have a case of material supposition, for the term supposits for that which is written.

But it should be noted that just as the three forms of supposition accrue to the spoken word, they can accrue to the written word. Thus, suppose that the following four propositions are written down: 'Man is an animal', '*Man* is a species', ' "Man" is monosyllabic', and ' "Man" is a written expression'. Each can be true but only if the subject stands for something different in each case. That which is an animal can in no way be a species, nor can it be monosyllabic or written. Likewise, the *man* which is a species is not an animal, nor is it monosyllabic, and so on. Nevertheless, in both of the last two propositions the term has material supposition.

But we could further subdivide the supposition in which a term supposits for a spoken or written word. We would only need names to distinguish the case where it supposits for a spoken word from the case where it supposits for a written word. The situation would be like that with personal and simple supposition, where we have different terms for the different forms of supposition. We do not, however, have at our disposal terms for dividing material supposition in the relevant way.

And just as these different forms of supposition accrue to both written and spoken terms, they also accrue to the mental term; for an intention of the soul can supposit for that which it signifies, for itself, and for a written or spoken word.

But it should be noted that we do not speak of personal supposition because the term supposits for a person, nor of simple supposition because the term supposits for what is simple, nor of material supposition because the term supposits for matter. It is for the reasons given above that these terms apply. Thus, the terms 'material', 'personal', and 'simple' are used equivocally in logic and in other disciplines. In logic, however, they are seldom used without the addition of the term 'supposition'.

65: On How the Supposition
of Terms Must Be Distinguished

It should also be noted that any term, in any proposition in which it is placed, can have personal supposition unless those who use it limit it to another form of supposition. In the same way an equivocal term can, in any proposition, supposit for any one of its significata, unless those who use it limit it to one particular significatum.

But a term cannot have simple or material supposition in any proposition, but only in propositions where it is coupled with an extreme which refers to an intention of the soul, a spoken word, or a written word. For example, in the proposition 'Man runs', the word 'man' cannot have simple or material supposition; for 'runs' does not refer to an intention of the soul, a spoken word, or a written word. 'Species' signifies an intention of the soul; therefore, in the proposition '*Man* is a species' the term 'man' can have simple supposition. Further, with this proposition we must, in accordance with the third mode of equivocation, distinguish between the case where we have simple supposition and the case where we have personal supposition. In the former case we have a true proposition asserting that a concept or intention of the soul is a species; in the latter we have the false proposition asserting that something signified by 'man' is a species.

The same sort of distinction must be drawn in the case of the following propositions: '*Man* is predicated of many', '*Risible* is a passion of *man*', *Risible* is predicated first and foremost of *man*'. We must distinguish here both on the part of the subject and on the part of the predicate. Likewise, we must distinguish in the case of the proposition '*Rational animal* is the definition of *man*'; for if the proposition exhibits simple supposition it is true; if it exhibits personal supposition, it is false. The same holds true of many other propositions—e.g., '*Wisdom* is an attribute of God', '*Creativity* is a passion of God', '*Goodness* and *Wisdom* are divine attributes', '*Goodness* is predicated of God' and '*Being unborn* is a property of the Father'.

Likewise, when a term is coupled with an extreme that refers to a spoken or written word one must draw a distinction, for the term exhibits either personal or material supposition. Thus, one should distinguish in the case of the following: ' "Socrates" is a name', ' "Man" is monosyllabic', ' "Paternity" signifies a property of the Father'. In the last case a distinction is necessary, for if 'paternity' supposits materially the proposition (' "Paternity" signifies a property of the Father') is true. If it supposits personally it is false, for paternity is a property of the Father or just is the Father. In the same way propositions like the following should be distinguished: ' "Rational animal" signifies man's quiddity', ' "Rational" signifies a part of man', ' "White man" signifies a per accidens aggregate', ' "White man" is a composite term'.

Some rules can be specified here. When a term capable of exhibiting any of the three forms of supposition is coupled with an extreme which is common to either simple or complex terms (whether these be written or spoken terms), the term can have either material or personal supposition; the relevant propositions must be distinguished accordingly. When a term is coupled with an extreme that signifies an intention of the soul, the term can have either simple or personal supposition. But when it is coupled with an extreme which is common to all of these, the term can have simple, material, or personal supposition. Thus, one must distinguish in the case of ' "Man" is predicated of many. If 'man' has personal supposition the proposition is false, for it would be asserted that some entity signified by the term 'man' is predicated of many. If, however, 'man' has simple or material (either as regards vocal or written words) supposition, the proposition is true because both the common intention and the word (whether spoken or written) are predicable of many.

66: Responses to Objections

But one can object against this account in a number of ways:

(1) First, the following is true: 'Man is the most worthy among creatures'. But what form of supposition does 'man' have here? It does not have personal supposition because each of the relevant singular propositions is false. It must then have simple supposition. But if, in simple supposition a term were to stand for an intention of the soul, the proposition would be false; for no intention of the soul is the most worthy among creatures. Conclusion: in simple supposition a term does not stand for an intention of the soul.

(2) Further, this is true: 'Color is the first object of sight'. However, every relevant singular proposition is false; therefore, this must be a case of simple supposition. But if the subject were suppositing for an intention of the soul, the proposition would be false. Conclusion: in simple supposition a term does not stand for an intention of the soul. Likewise, this is true: 'Man is first and foremost risible', but here 'man' is suppositing neither for a particular nor for an intention of the soul. It must then be suppositing for something else. The same point can be argued in each of the following cases: 'Being is first and foremost one' and 'God is first and foremost a person'. Each of these is true; however, the subject is suppositing neither for a particular nor an intention of the soul; therefore, it is suppositing for something else. But in each case the subject has simple supposition; therefore, in simple supposition a term does not supposit for an intention of the soul.

(3) Further, a word is not predicated of a word, nor is an intention predicated of an intention; for then every proposition like 'Man is an animal' would be false.

Response to (1)

In the case of the first objection those are wrong who say that in the proposition 'Man is the most worthy among creatures' the subject has simple supposition. 'Man' has personal supposition in that proposition. Their argument does not succeed and can in fact be turned against them. They argue that if 'man' were to have personal supposition, the proposition would be false since all the relevant singular propositions would be false. But that line of reasoning works against their own account, for if in that proposition 'man' does not stand for any singular thing but for some other sort of thing, that thing would be the most worthy among creatures. But this is false, for then it would be more noble than any man and that clearly is opposed to their own account. They say that a common term or a species is never more noble than the particulars under it. As they put it the less general always includes the more general and something else besides. Thus, the common form, being a part of man, would not be more noble than man. Thus, if the subject in the proposition 'Man is the most worthy among creatures' were to supposit for something other than particular men, the proposition would be false.

Therefore, it should be said that 'man' supposits personally and that the proposition, when construed literally, is false inasmuch as the relevant singular propositions are all false. Nonetheless, what those who assert this proposition mean to say is correct. They do not mean that any man is more noble than every creature universally considered, but only that men are more noble than any creatures who are not men and of themselves to corporeal creatures, excluding the intellectual substances. This same thing frequently happens—propositions taken from classical authors and from teachers are false when construed literally, but when seen in the light in which they were intended, come out true. Thus it is in the case at hand.

Response to (2)

The correct response to the second objection is that all such propositions as 'Color is the first object of sight', 'Man is first and foremost risible', 'Being is first and foremost one', 'Man is first and foremost a rational animal', 'The triangle first and foremost has three angles', and 'Sound is the first and adequate object of hearing' are literally false; nonetheless, the propositions the Philosopher intended by them are true. .

It should be noted that the Philosopher and other writers frequently take the concrete for the abstract (and vice versa) and the singular for the plural (and vice versa). In the same way the effected act is frequently taken for the signified act and vice versa.

An effected act is one designated by 'is' or some other expression which not only signifies that something is predicated of something else but actually effects the predication of one thing of another. Examples are: 'Man *is* an animal', 'Man *disputes*', and 'Man *runs*'.

A signified act, on the other hand, is one which is designated by a verb like 'to be predicated of', 'to have as subject', 'to be affirmed of', and 'to belong to', all of which signify one and the same thing. For example, when one says, " 'Animal' is predicated of 'man'," animal is not actually being predicated of man; for in that proposition 'animal' is functioning as subject and not predicate. The act, then, is signified. It is not the same thing to say ' "Animal" is predicated of man' and 'Man is an animal'. The one is structurally more complex than the other. Likewise, it is not the same thing to say that a genus is predicated of the general term 'man' and to say that the common term 'man' is a genus. Further, saying that a genus is predicated of its species or that the word 'animal' is predicated of the word 'man' is very different from saying, "Species is a genus" or "The word 'man' is the word 'animal'." The first two are true, and the second false. But despite the difference, the Philosopher sometimes takes the effected act for the signified act and sometimes vice versa. Others do the same, with the consequence that many fall into error.

Now, it is precisely this confusion that is at work in the present case. For when one takes 'first and foremost' as the Philosopher does in the first book of the *Posterior Analytics*,[1] the proposition 'Man is first and foremost risible' is false in the same way that 'A species is a genus' is false. Nonetheless, the signified act whose place it takes is true, viz., 'Of *man* the predicate *risible* is first and foremost predicated'. In that signified act both 'man' and 'risible' supposit simply for an intention of the soul. Of this intention of the soul 'risible' is first and foremost predicated, not for itself but for the particulars under it. The effected act should be expressed: 'Every man is risible and nothing other than man is risible'. Thus, in the signified act 'man' supposits simply and for the intention; whereas, in the corresponding effected act 'man' supposits personally for the relevant particulars; for it is only a particular that can laugh. Thus, the term 'first and foremost' is correctly placed in the signified act, but it has no place in the corresponding effected act; for 'first and foremost' means 'predicated of something universally and of nothing else'. Therefore, there should correspond two effected acts to a signified act of this sort. Similarly in the case of a proposition like 'Sound is the first and adequate object of hearing'. Literally construed, that proposition is false for 'sound' supposits either for a singular thing or a universal thing. If it supposits for a singular thing the proposition is false, for all the relevant singular propositions are false. If it supposits for a universal thing the proposition is still false, for according to the objectors nothing universal can be apprehended by the senses. Taken literally then the proposition is false.

Nonetheless, those who use and understand this locution would claim that what is meant by the proposition is the following signified act: '*To be cap-*

[1] 73^b 32-74^a 3.

able of being apprehended by hearing is predicated first and foremost of *sound.*' It is of that common term that the predicate in question is predicated first and foremost, not for itself but for the particulars under it; for in the proposition where 'sound' is the subject and 'is capable of being apprehended by hearing' is the predicate, 'sound' does not supposit simply and for itself, but for the particulars under it. Thus, in the signified act 'sound' supposits simply and for an intention of the soul, but in both affected acts it supposits personally and for the particulars under it, that is, for its significata.

Theology provides a case which clearly exemplifies the foregoing points. This is true: 'A complete intellective substance not depending on any other suppositum is first and foremost a person', and it is true for the same reason that 'man is first and foremost risible' is true. One and the same account holds in the two cases. But suppose the subject of the proposition in question supposits personally for the particulars under it. In that case the proposition is false, for all the relevant singular propositions are false. That is clear from induction. Suppose, then, it supposits simply and for the common form. In that case also it is false since no common form, whether first and foremost or not, is a person. The notion of a person, according to those who object, is incompatible with the notion of a universal. The same holds true of propositions like the following: 'The singular is first and foremost one' and 'The particular is first and foremost distinguished from the universal'. Taken literally they are false; nevertheless, the signified acts corresponding to them are true.

Therefore, it should be said as it was before, that we have simple supposition when a term supposits for an intention of the soul which is either common to many by way of predication or as sometimes happens, proper to just one thing. The reason is that nothing on the part of the thing can be anything other than particular.

Thus, it is the mistaken view of those who think that there is something in things over and above the particular, and that the humanity which is distinct from particulars is something in individuals belonging to their essence which has led them into these and many other mistakes in logic. Nonetheless, it is not the task of the logician, as Porphyry indicates in his prologue, to deal with this mistake. The logician should merely deny that simple supposition occurs when a term supposits for its significatum and should point out that a general term has simple supposition when it supposits for something common to its significata. Whether what is common be in the thing is not for the logician to say.

Response to (3)

The response to the third objection is that a word is predicated of a word and, similarly, an intention is predicated of an intention not, however, for itself but for the thing. Therefore, in the proposition 'Man is an animal', one word is predicated of another or one intention is predicated of another. Nonetheless, it is not asserted that one word is another or that one intention is another. What is asserted is that the thing for which the subject stands or supposits is the thing for which the predicate stands or supposits.

But it might be objected that the proposition 'Pepper is sold both here and at Rome' is true and that, nonetheless, neither of the relevant singular propositions is true. Thus, the proposition cannot be true unless 'pepper' is suppositing simply and for something other than an intention of the soul. But in simple supposition a term does not supposit for an intention. The response here is that this proposition, if it has a conjunctive extreme, is simply false; for both singulars are false. And if the subject is construed as having simple supposition, the proposition is still false; for whether it be a thing outside or a thing in the soul, no one wants to buy the universal, pepper. What people want to buy is the particular thing they do not have. The proposition, however, is true if it is taken as the conjunction, 'Pepper is sold here, and pepper is sold in Rome'; for both parts when standing for different particulars are true. Thus, 'Pepper is sold here and in Rome' is no more true than 'Particular pepper is sold here and in Rome'.

67: On Material Supposition

Next we should consider each of the different forms of supposition in detail. First we shall consider material supposition.

It should be noted that any term which can in any way be a part of a proposition can exhibit material supposition, for every such term can be the extreme of a proposition and supposit for a spoken or written word. This is clear concerning names. Thus, ' "Man" is a name' and ' "Man" is singular in number'. The same point is clear in the case of adverbs, verbs, pronouns, conjunctions, prepositions, and interjections. Thus, ' "Well" is an adverb', ' "Reads" is in the indicative mood', ' "Reading" is a participle', ' "He" is a pronoun', ' "If" is a conjunction', ' "From" is a preposition', and ' "Oh" is an interjection'. Propositions and phrases can also exhibit material supposition. This is clear in the following: ' "Man is an animal" is a true proposition' and ' "That man runs" is a phrase'. This form of supposition can accrue not only to spoken words, but also to written words and elements in mental propositions, whether they be complete propositions or only parts of propositions. In short, any simple or complex term can exhibit material supposition.

One can, however, divide material supposition, for sometimes a spoken or written word supposits for itself. Examples are ' "Man" is a name', ' "Man's" is in the genitive case', ' "Man is an animal" is a true proposition', ' "Well" is an adverb', and ' "Reads" is a verb'. Sometimes, however, a spoken word, a written word, or a concept of the mind does not supposit for itself but for some other spoken or written word which it does not signify. Thus, in the Latin sentence ' "Animal" praedicatur de "homine" ' the word 'homine" does not supposit for the word 'homine', for 'animal' is not predicated of 'homine'. In that sentence the simple term 'homine' supposits for the word 'homo', for it is of 'homo' that 'animal' is predicated in 'Homo est animal'. Likewise, in ' "That man runs" is true', the subject "that man runs" does not supposit for itself but for the proposition 'Man runs', which it does not, nevertheless, signify. Likewise, in the Latin sentence ' "Homo" praedicatur de "asino" in obliquo', the word "homo" supposits for oblique forms, for in the proposition 'Asinus est hominis', it is not the word 'homo', but 'homonis' that is predicated. Likewise, in ' "Quality" is predicated of its subject in the concrete', the term 'quality' supposits for concrete names that are predicable of a subject.

68: On Simple Supposition

Just as any complex or simple term can exhibit material supposition, any complex or simple term that is significative or consignificative can exhibit simple supposition; for every such term, whether mental, vocal, or written, can supposit for a concept of the mind. This is inductively evident. Further, just as a term exhibiting material supposition sometimes supposits for itself and sometimes for something else, so a mental term suppositing simply supposits sometimes for itself (as in *'Man* is a species' and *'Animal* is a genus') and sometimes for some other intention of the soul which it does not, nevertheless, signify (as in a mental proposition like *'That man is an animal* is true'). The same point holds in many other such cases.

69: On Personal Supposition

Next we shall consider personal supposition. It should be noted that only a categorematic term that is being employed significatively as the extreme of a proposition supposits personally.

The first condition excludes syncategorematic terms, not only those that are names but also conjunctions, adverbs, prepositions and any others there may be.

The second condition excludes all verbs because a verb can never be the extreme of a proposition, not when it is functioning significatively. One might object that in 'To read is good', 'to read' functions significatively and, nevertheless, supposits. The response is that 'to read' is not a verb but a noun. It is because of the use to which it is put that an infinitive can function not only as a verb but as a noun. If 'to read' were to remain a verb here and were to be a name no more than 'reads', the proposition 'To read is good' could be no more true than 'Reads is good'. Whence comes the difference? It is from the use to which those who speak the language put the expression.

The expression 'extreme of a proposition' excludes a part of an extreme, even if the part be a categorematic term and a noun. Thus, in 'The white man is an animal', neither 'man' nor 'white' supposits. The whole extreme supposits. Thus, even when the parts of an extreme are ordered according to greater and lesser generality, it is not necessary that the inference from a proposition affirming one to a proposition affirming the other be valid. The rule governing such inferences should be understood to hold only when the extremes which actually do the suppositing are ordered according to greater and lesser universality. Thus, from the Latin sentence 'Tu es vadens ad forum', one cannot validly infer 'Tu es existens ad forum'. 'Existens' and 'vadens' are ordered as more and less general, but the extremes themselves are not so ordered; consequently the inference is not valid. Nonetheless, sometimes the inference is valid, for sometimes the parts cannot be ordered as more and less general unless the wholes of which they are constituents are also so ordered or capable of being ordered. Examples are 'white man'—'white animal' and 'seeing man'—'seeing animal'. Therefore, an inference of this sort is frequently valid, but not always. At any rate, what is a part of an extreme in a proposition does not supposit in that proposition, although it can supposit in some other proposition.

The expression 'taken significatively' excludes all categorematic expressions functioning simply or materially; for since they are not then employed significatively, they cannot supposit personally. Examples are ' "Man" is a name' and '*Man* is a species'.

70: On the Division of Personal Supposition

Personal supposition can be divided into discrete and common supposition. Discrete supposition occurs when the suppositing term is the proper name of some object significatively taken or a demonstrative pronoun significatively taken. Such supposition yields a singular proposition like 'Socrates is a man' and 'That man is a man'. If one should object that 'This herb grows in my garden' is true and that, nonetheless, the subject does not have discrete supposition, the response is that the proposition, taken literally, is false; however, by that proposition one means 'An herb of that sort grows in my garden', where the subject supposits determinately. Thus, when a proposition that is literally false has a true sense, if it is taken in that sense, the subject and predicate should have the same supposition they have in the corresponding true proposition.

We have common personal supposition when a common term supposits, thus 'A man runs' and 'Every man is an animal'. Common personal supposition is divided into confused supposition and determinate supposition. Determinate supposition occurs when it is possible to descend to particulars by way of a disjunctive proposition. Thus, the following is a good inference: a man runs; therefore, this man runs or that man . . . (and so on for all the relevant particulars). The name 'determinate supposition' is employed because where such supposition operates, the assertion is that a proposition of the relevant sort is true in the case of some determinate particular. That particular by itself is sufficient to make the proposition true. Nothing else is required. Thus, for the truth of 'A man runs', it is required that one of the relevant singular propositions be true. Any one will do, and it makes no difference whether the remaining singular propositions are all false. Nonetheless, it frequently happens that many or all of the remaining singular propositions are true. Thus, the following rule can be employed: whenever it is possible to descend to the particulars under a general term by way of a distinctive proposition and whenever it is possible to infer such a proposition from a particular, the term in question has personal determinate supposition. Therefore, in the proposition 'A man is an animal', both extremes have determinate supposition; for the following is a good inference: a man is an animal; therefore, this man is an animal or that man . . . (and so on with all the relevant particulars). Likewise, this is a good inference: this man is an animal (where some particular man is pointed out); therefore, a man is an animal. Likewise, the following is a good inference: a man is an animal; therefore, a man is this animal or a man . . . (and so on with all relevant particulars). It also follows that if a man is this animal, where some particular animal has been singled out, then a man is an animal. Thus, both 'man' and 'animal' have determinate supposition.

Personal confused supposition belongs to every common term exhibiting personal supposition, but not determinate supposition. It is divided into merely confused supposition and confused distributive supposition. Merely confused supposition occurs when a common term supposits personally and it is not possible, without a change in either extreme, to descend to particulars by way of a disjunctive proposition, but it is possible to descend by way of a proposition with a disjunctive predicate and it is possible to infer the original proposition from any particular. For example, in the proposition 'Every man is an animal', the word 'animal' has merely confused supposition; for one cannot descend to the particulars under 'animal' by way of a disjunctive proposition. The following is not a good inference: every man is an animal; therefore, every man is this animal or every man is that animal or every man is . . . (and so on for all the relevant particulars). Nonetheless, it is possible to descend to a proposition with a disjunctive predicate involving particulars; for the following is a good inference: every man is an animal; therefore, every man is this animal or that animal or that . . . (and so on for all the relevant particulars). .The consequent here is a categorical proposition composed of the subject 'man' and the predicate 'this animal or that animal or . . .'. It is clear that this predicate is truly predicated of every man and that, consequently, the universal proposition is true. Likewise, the universal proposition can be inferred from any item contained under 'animal'; for the following inference is valid: every man is this animal (no matter which animal is pointed out); therefore, every man is an animal.

Confused and distributive supposition occurs when, assuming that the relevant term has many items contained under it, it is possible in some way to descend by a conjunctive proposition and impossible to infer the original proposition from any of the elements in the conjunction. Thus, the subject in 'Every man is an animal' supposits confusedly and distributively, for the following inference is good: every man is an animal; therefore this man is an animal, that man . . . (and so on for all of the relevant particulars). The following inference, however, is not valid: that man is an animal (no matter which one is singled out); therefore, every man is an animal.

I said that it is possible to descend *in some way*. I said this because it is not always possible to descend in the same way. Sometimes it is possible to descend without altering the original proposition except by changing the subject or predicate from a common term to a singular term; but sometimes it is possible to descend only with some alteration in the proposition, so that something which is neither a common term nor a term contained under a common term is present in one of the propositions but absent in the other. For example, from 'Every man except Socrates runs', one can descend to a conjunction of singular propositions; for the following inference is good: every man except Socrates runs; therefore Plato runs, Cicero runs, . . . (and so on for all men other than Socrates). But in these singular propositions something is absent that was present in the universal proposition and it is neither a common term nor a sign distributing a common term; it is the exceptive expression with its object. Thus, it is not possible to descend in the same way in the case of 'Every man except Socrates runs' and 'Every man runs', nor is it even possible to descend to the same propositions. The first case of confused and distributive supposition is called confused and distributive mobile supposition; whereas, the second is called confused and distributive immobile supposition.

71: On Rules for Determinate Supposition

Next we shall see when a common term has one kind of personal supposition and when it has another. First we shall consider the case of names and then the case of relative pronouns, for different rules apply in the two cases.

First it should be noted that when in a categorical proposition no universal sign distributing the whole extreme of a proposition is added to a term, either mediately or immediately (i.e., either on the part of the same extreme or on the part of the preceding extreme), and when no negation or any expression equivalent to a negative or a universal sign is added to a common term, that common term supposits determinately. For example, in the proposition 'A man is an animal', no universal sign or any negation or any expression involving a negation or a sign of universality is added to the constituent terms; therefore, both terms supposit determinately. The same should be said in the case of 'Some man runs'; for whether the sign of particularity is added or not does not alter the personal supposition of a term, although it frequently does make the term stand personally. In the same way, although 'An animal is not a man' exhibits a negation, the negation does not precede the term 'animal'; therefore, 'animal' has determinate supposition. Likewise, although the universal sign is present in 'An animal is every man', it does not precede the term 'animal'; therefore, 'animal' supposits determinately. But in 'Every man is an animal', 'man' does not have determinate supposition since it is distributed by the universal sign. Neither does 'animal' have determinate supposition; it mediately follows the universal sign. But because, in the Latin sentence 'Videns omnem hominem est animal', the term 'omnem' does not distribute the whole subject, the predicate supposits determinately. Thus, the following inference is valid: videns omnem hominem est hoc ani-

mal; igitur videns omnem hominem est hoc animal vel videns omnem hominem est illud animal vel . . . (and so for all the relevant particulars). But
in 'Omnem hominem videns est animal', the sign distributes the whole
'hominem videns', so that the predicate does not stand determinately. The
same thing happens in the case of 'Every man's donkey runs', for here the
predicate supposits confusedly only. However, in 'The donkey of every man
runs', the predicate stands determinately. Likewise, in the case of 'A man is
not an animal', 'man' stands or supposits determinately; but because the negation which determines the verb preceeds it, 'animal' does not stand determinately. Likewise, in the case of 'Socrates differs from man' the predicate
does not supposit determinately; for the verb 'differs' includes a negation.

72: Responses to Objections

But there are difficulties with the foregoing account.

(1) First, assuming that Socrates does not exist, how does 'man' supposit
in 'Socrates was a man'? Likewise, how do terms supposit in propositions
concerning the past and future and in propositions concerning the possible
and the other modalities? The source of doubt here is the earlier claim that
a term never supposits for something unless it can be truly predicated of it.
But if Socrates does not exist, 'man' cannot be truly predicated of Socrates;
for 'Socrates is a man' is false. Thus, the term does not supposit for Socrates,
so that it does not supposit determinately.

(2) Second, there is a difficulty in the case of each of the following
propositions: 'The white man is a man', 'The one singing the mass is a man',
and 'The one creating is God'. If we assume that no one is white, that no
one is singing the mass, and that God does not create, for which objects are
we to say that the relevant subjects supposit? It seems that they do not supposit for any of the things they signify because they are not truly predicated
of those things. Nor do they supposit for themselves, for in that case they
would not have personal supposition. But, then, they do not supposit determinately for anything, so that they do not have determinate supposition.

(3) The third difficulty concerns the form of supposition exhibited by the
subjects in 'A horse is promised to you' and 'Twenty pounds are owed you'.
The source of the difficulty lies in the fact that if the terms supposit for the
things contained under them, the propositions seem false, inasmuch as each
of the relevant singular propositions is false. Thus, if the subject-terms supposit determinately, the propositions each come out false.

(4) The fourth difficulty concerns propositions like 'He is deprived of sight' and 'He was born capable of possessing sight'.

(5) The fifth difficulty: what kind of supposition does the predicate have in 'Genera and species are second substances'?

(6) The sixth difficulty concerns propositions like 'Action is a thing outside the soul', 'Relation is a real thing', and 'Creation is really the same thing as God'.

(7) The seventh difficulty concerns the proposition 'He was twice white'; for it does not seem that 'white' supposits determinately here.

(8) The eighth difficulty: how do the subject and predicate supposit in 'Only what is an animal is a man'?

Likewise, there is a difficulty in the case of propositions like 'The Apostle says this', 'England fights', 'Drink the cup', 'The prow is at sea', 'Your goodness acts mercifully', 'The clemency of the king rules the kingdom'.

Response to (1)

The response to the first difficulty is that in all such propositions the terms supposit personally. Thus, it should be understood that a term supposits personally when it supposits for things that are its significata or for things that were, will be, or can be its significata. My earlier claim should be understood in this way. It is for this reason that I earlier said that 'to signify' can in one sense be used in this way. Nevertheless it should be noted that a term cannot supposit with respect to any verb for what is not now its significatum. Although it can supposit for the things it signifies in the strict sense with respect to any verb, it can supposit for things that were its significata only with respect to past tense verbs. Therefore, one must always distinguish in the case of a proposition with a past tense verb, for the relevant term can supposit for things that are its significata or for things that were its significata. Likewise, a term cannot supposit for things that will be its significata except with respect to a future tense verb. Thus, in a proposition with a future tense verb one must draw a distinction: is the term suppositing for things that are or for things that will be its significata? Again, a term cannot supposit for things that are not but can be its significata except with respect to a verb of possibility or contingency, so we must always draw a distinction where propositions incorporate such verbs: is the subject suppositing for things that are or for things that can be or contingently are? Thus, one must distinguish in the case of each of the following: 'Every man was white', 'Every white thing will be a man', 'Every white thing can be a man', and 'It is contingent that every man runs'.

Nonetheless, it should be understood that the relevant distinction does not concern the predicate but only the subject. Thus, there is no need to draw a distinction in the case of the following two propositions: 'Socrates was white' and 'Socrates can be white'. The reason is that the predicate names its form. This should not be understood to mean that the predicate supposits for itself or for the relevant concept. The point is that where the proposition concerns the past, the assertion is that the proposition in which that predicate (under its proper form) is predicated of that for which the subject supposits (or of the pronoun referring to that thing) was once true. If the proposition concerns the future the assertion is that the relevant proposition will be true. If the proposition concerns the possible the assertion is that the relevant proposition is possible, and similarly in the case of propositions that are necessary, impossible, per se, per accidens and so on for the other modalities. For example, for the truth of 'The white was black', it is not required that it was ever true that the white is black. What is required is that 'This is black' was once true, where the reference is to something for which the subject supposits in 'The white was black'. Likewise, for the truth of 'The true will be impossible', it is not necessary that 'The true is impossible' ever be true. It is, rather, necessary that 'This is impossible' will be true where the reference is to something for which the subject in 'The true will be impossible' supposits. The same sort of account holds in other cases. I will consider them in greater detail in the treatise on propositions and consequences.

As regards 'Socrates was a man', I say that the predicate supposits for Socrates. The same point holds in the case of all propositions concerned with the past, the future, and the modalities. Terms suppositing personally in such propositions supposit for those things that are, were, will be, or are capable of being their supposita; and if no sign, negation, or some other such expression stands in the way, they supposit determinately.

But, then, the response to this objection is that it is correct to say that a term never supposits for something unless it is truly predicated of it. But this is not to say that a term never supposits for something unless it is truly predicated of it by means of a present tense verb. Where it supposits for a thing with respect to a past tense verb, it suffices that the term be truly predicated of the thing by means of a past tense verb. If it supposits with respect to a future tense verb, then the requirement is that it be truly predicated by means of a future tense verb and so on for the other cases. Thus, assume that although no man is now white, Socrates formerly was. Then, if it is taken for things that formerly were, 'white thing' in 'The white thing was a man' supposits for Socrates. Therefore, it is truly predicated of Socrates, but not by means of a present tense verb. The predication holds with respect to a past tense verb; for this is true, 'Socrates was white'.

But the difficulty still remains. For what does the predicate in 'Socrates was white' supposit? If it supposits for things that are, the proposition is false. The response here is that the predicate supposits for the things that were, regardless of whether they still are; therefore we have an exception to the rule I stated earlier—that in any proposition in which it occurs, a term

always does or can supposit for things that now are. I meant that rule to
hold only for subjects of propositions. In the case of predicates it does not
hold universally. Thus, suppose that no man is now white but that many men
were formerly white. Then, in the proposition 'The man was white', the
predicate cannot supposit for things that are, but only for things that were.
Thus, generally, a predicate in a proposition concerning the past does not
supposit for anything except for that which was. In propositions concerning
the future the predicate only supposits for things that will be, and in propositions concerning the possible for things that can be. With this however,
it is necessary that the same predicate be predicated of that for which the
subject supposits in the aforementioned way.

Response to (2)

The response to the second difficulty is that if no man is white, and if
no man sings the mass, and if God does not create, the subjects in the preceding propositions supposit for nothing. Nonetheless, they are used significatively, for a term can be used significatively or can supposit personally in
two ways: either the term supposits for one or more of its significata or the
term is asserted to supposit or not to supposit for something. In affirmative
propositions a term is always asserted to supposit for something. Thus, if it
supposits for nothing the proposition is false. However, in negative propositions the assertion is either that the term does not supposit for something
or that it supposits for something of which the predicate is truly denied.
Thus, a negative proposition has two causes of truth. 'A man is not white',
for example, has two causes of truth; for either there are no men, so that
no man can be white; or there is a man but he is not white. But if no man is
white, then the subject of 'The white man is a man' supposits significatively
and personally, not because it supposits for something but because it is asserted to supposit for something. Thus, since the assertion is that the term
supposits for something, the fact that it supposits for nothing has the consequence that the proposition is false. If some of my earlier remarks appear
incompatible with this account, they should be understood to cover true affirmative propositions; for if a term stands personally in a true affirmative
proposition it supposits for some of its significata in the way outlined earlier.

One might contend that the notions of 'to supposit' and 'to supposit
for nothing' are incompatible since the following is a valid inference: the
term supposits; therefore, it supposits for something. The response is that the
inference is not valid. The following, however, is valid: the term supposits;
therefore it is asserted either to supposit for something or to supposit for
nothing.

Response to (3)

The response to the third objection is that the proposition 'A horse is
promised you' and 'Twenty pounds are owed you' are, strictly speaking,

false; for each of the relevant singular propositions is false as is inductively clear. Nevertheless, if we move the problematical terms to the predicate-side of the relevant propositions, there is a way of rendering those propositions so that they pose no difficulty. Once they have been moved it is necessary to say that the terms following the relevant verbs have, in virtue of the force of those verbs, merely confused supposition. Thus, it is not possible to descend disjunctively to particulars, but only by way of a disjunctive predicate enumerating not only present but also future objects. Thus, the inference 'I promise you a horse; therefore I promise you this horse or I promise you that horse or . . .' (and so on for all the relevant particulars) is not valid. The following inference, however, is valid: I promise you a horse; therefore, I promise you this horse or that horse or that horse or . . . (and so on for all the relevant particulars including not only present but also future horses). The reason we must enumerate both present and future horses is that all such verbs in the final analysis incorporate a future tense verb. Thus, 'I promise you a horse' is equivalent to 'You will have a horse as a gift from me', so that in 'I promise you a horse', the word 'horse' supposits for future horses just as it does in 'You will have a horse'.

But does 'horse' in 'I promise you a horse' have what is properly called merely confused supposition? The answer is that strictly speaking 'horse' does not exhibit merely confused supposition. It does not supposit at all since it is merely a part of the extreme. The rule I stated earlier about determinate supposition was stated only apropos of expressions which supposit in the strict sense, i.e., the extremes of propositions and not just the parts of extremes. Nevertheless, extending the usage, it can be said that the word 'horse' has merely confused supposition; for it follows the relevant sort of verb. Universally, a common term which follows a verb of the relevant kind and is only a part of the extreme always has merely confused personal supposition and not determinate supposition.

Thus, it should be noted that propositions of this sort in the present, past or future, sometimes incorporate a verb with a force such that what is asserted is that some proposition in which a common term is placed on the predicate-side will be or ought to be true. The assertion then is not that some singular proposition in which a particular contained under the common term is placed on the side of the predicate will be true. In the case of this sort (if we extend the term 'supposit' in such a way that a part of an extreme can supposit), the common term does not supposit determinately; for it is not possible to descend to particulars by a disjunctive proposition, but only by a proposition with a disjunctive extreme or with an extreme having a disjunctive part. Thus, 'I promise you a horse', given the force of 'I promise', asserts that 'I give you a horse' (or something similar) will be or ought to be true sometime. The assertion is not that a proposition like 'I give you this horse' (where the reference is to some particular horse) will be or ought to be true. Thus, it does not follow that if I promise you a horse, I promise you this horse or I promise you that horse. The same point holds in the case of 'I owe you 20 pounds'.

Thus, while 'I promise you a horse' should be granted, 'A horse is promised you' should not, strictly speaking, be granted. The reason is that in 'A horse is promised you', the word 'horse' is the subject and not a part of the subject. Thus, it is necessary that it supposit determinately; for no sign (of universality), no negation, nor any expression including such precedes the term. Consequently, it is necessary that one be able to make the descent to particulars. But in 'I promise you a horse', the word 'horse' is not an extreme, but a part of an extreme. The whole predicate is 'promising you a horse', for 'I promise you a horse' is equivalent to 'I am promising you a horse' and here 'horse' is only a part of the extreme. The term need not exhibit what is properly called supposition. Thus, it need not supposit determinately; and, consequently, one need not be able to make the descent to a disjunctive proposition of the relevant sort.

But is it not possible to descend with respect to a part of the extreme? The response is that sometimes a descent is possible. Thus, the following is valid: he gives a horse to Socrates; therefore, he gives this horse to Socrates or he gives that horse to Socrates or . . . (and so on for all the relevant particulars). But sometimes for a special reason of the sort involved in the present case, it is not possible to make the descent. Thus, although 'I promise you a horse' should be granted, 'A horse is promised you' should, strictly speaking, not be granted. Nevertheless, it can be granted inasmuch as it is commonly taken to mean 'Someone promises you a horse'. But why the inference 'Someone promises you a horse; therefore a horse is promised you' is not valid will be considered in the treatise on the proposition.

Response to (4)

The response to the fourth difficulty is that in the proposition 'He is deprived of sight', the word 'sight' does not actually supposit. The reason is that it is only a part of an extreme. Nevertheless, to the extent that it can supposit, it supposits confusedly and distributively; for the proposition is equivalent to 'He has no sight' where 'sight' is negatively expressed in a confused and distributive manner. Nevertheless, it does not supposit confusedly and distributively in every proposition involved in the analysis of the original proposition. Thus, in the affirmative proposition 'He was born apt to have sight', it can be said in a way to supposit determinately for those things that were at one time possible. It does not, however, supposit for all such things, but only for those which were capable of belonging to the man in question.

Response to (5)

The response to the fifth difficulty is that strictly speaking while 'Genera and species are substances' is false, one can grant 'Genera and species are second substances'. There the word 'second substances' supposits personally and determinately, for the name 'second substances' is used to signify second intentions designating real substances. Thus, it is wrong to claim that 'substance' can have simple supposition and, nevertheless, supposit for genera and species. But if upon occasion one finds an author saying that genera and species are substances, the claim should be interpreted as follows: either the author understands the signified act by the effected act, so that by 'Genera and species are substances' he means ' "Substance" is predicated of genera and species', where the signified act is effected in propositions like 'Man is a substance', 'Animal is a substance', etc. Or one should explain the author's claim by pointing out that 'substance' is being used equivocally. For sometimes the term signifies real things which are actually distinct from every real accident and every second intention. In that use 'substance' is properly employed. But sometimes it signifies those intentions which designate the things that are called substances in the first sense. Interpreted in this way one should grant the proposition 'Genera and species are substances', and one should grant that under this interpretation 'substances' is suppositing personally; nonetheless, it is not being employed properly, but improperly and in an extended sense.

Response to (6)

The response to the sixth difficulty is that different people use such abstract names in different ways. Sometimes they use them for things and sometimes for names. If they are used in the first way then it should be said that according to Aristotle, they supposit for the same things as their concrete counterparts. Thus, 'Fire is a cause' is equivalent to 'Fire is causality'. Likewise, 'The man is a father' and 'The man is paternity' are equivalent. Indeed, where the abstract names are used to signify the same things, concrete and abstract names are, in the account provided by Aristotle and many other philosophers, synonymous expressions.

Nor should this be surprising, for take the proposition 'Creation is a real thing'. Either 'creation' supposits for something or for nothing. If for nothing, then there will be no genuine proposition or the proposition will be false. If it supposits for something, it supposits for an external object, for a thing in the soul, or for something that is an aggregate of these. If it supposits for an external object, what is that object? It can only be God; therefore, 'creation' supposits for God in the same way that 'creating' does. The same account applies in every other such case. Some hold that this term supposits for a relation of the reason, but it is impossible that it supposit for something in the soul because then 'Creation is a real thing' would be false. Likewise, creation would only exist in the soul, and God would be creative only in virtue of the act of the soul forming the relevant relation of the reason. By the same logic one could maintain that 'heat-induction' supposits for such a being or relation of the reason. Nor is there any good reason why such a relation should be in a created agent and not in an uncreated agent. According to the Philosopher's view, then, there is nothing which could be signified or connoted by a concrete term of this sort that is not in the same say signified or connoted by the relevant abstract name. Therefore, for him, if both are used to signify a thing, they will be synonymous names.

Nor can one say that the mode of signifying stands in the way of synonymy. Diversity in mode of signification does not prevent synonymy unless because of the diversity of mode of signification something is signified or connoted by one name which is not in the same way connoted or signified by the other. This happens in the case of the terms 'man', Man's', and 'men'. It also happens in the case of 'man' and 'risible' and in the case of 'intellect', 'will', and 'soul'. Likewise, in the case of 'creating', 'governing', 'damning', 'living', and other such expressions which, while predicated of the same thing, are not synonymous. If diversity of mode of signification were by itself a hinderance to synonymy, I could claim that 'story' and 'tale' are not synonymous since while 'story' ends in 'y', 'tale' does not. The same point holds in many other cases. Thus, differences in grammatical features such as gender or part of speech do not prevent synonymy.

Nonetheless, where there is what is strictly called a variation in mode of signification, there is no synonymy. But there is no such variation in the present case. That is clear. A concrete name and an abstract name can have exactly the same mode of signification if they are not abstract and concrete names of the first sort. (See the relevant section at the beginning of this treatise.) Thus when the relevant abstract names are used significatively for things, they are in Aristotle's view synonymous with their concrete forms. Theologians, however, may find it necessary to provide a different account in some, but not all, such cases.

Sometimes, on the other hand, abstract names of this sort are used to signify their concrete forms. 'Privation', 'negation', 'contradiction', and other similar words are used in this way. Thus, in 'Man is a relation', the word 'relation' supposits significatively and for relative names. Likewise 'similarity' sometimes supposits for a relative name—the relative name 'similar'. 'Creation' sometimes supposits for the name 'creating' and 'quantity', for 'quantum'. In Aristotle's view this point holds in the many cases where abstract and concrete names do not supposit for distinct things. Therefore, just as we granted that the predicate 'real thing' is predicated of such abstract names, we should grant that their concrete forms are predicated of them and that they supposit for the same thing as the concrete forms. For as has frequently been said, if such abstract names are names of first intention, they will, as I understand Aristotle's view, be names synonymous with their concrete forms. And this is the reason why so few such abstract names are employed by Aristotle, for he construed expressions like the following as synonymous: 'man'–'humanity', 'cow'–'cowness', 'quantum'–'quantity', 'relative'–'relation', 'similar'–'similarity', 'father'–'paternity', 'two'–'duality', 'three –'trinity'. But, sometimes, those who use the terms employ the abstract terms as names of second intention or second imposition; in those cases, there is no synonymy.

Others, however, claim that all such abstract names signify really distinct things or relations of the reason and that they supposit for such things.
Response to (7)

The response to the seventh difficulty is that in 'Socrates was twice white', there is an expression that incorporates a negation, the expression 'twice'. Thus, given the force of that expression, 'Socrates was twice white' has a negative exponent; for the proposition is equivalent to 'Socrates was first white and at a later time he was not white and at a still later time he was white'. Because of the negative expression underlying the proposition, the term does not stand merely determinately. Consequently, it is not possible to descend by means of a disjunctive proposition to pronouns or proper names expressing the things for which the predicate supposits.

The same point holds in the case of propositions like 'Socrates begins to be white', 'Man ceases to be literate', and generally in the case of propositions having a negative exponent.
Response to (8)

In the same way the proposition 'Only what is an animal is a man' incorporates an expression of exclusion and, consequently, has a negative exponent. But neither the subject nor the predicate supposits determinately.

The response to the ninth doubt is that if they are taken strictly, the relevant terms supposit just as they do in other propositions. Nonetheless, those using the expressions so employ them that they supposit for things other than their normal supposita.

73: On Merely Confused Supposition

Now that we have examined determinate supposition we shall examine merely confused supposition. A number of rules hold here.

First, where a common term mediately follows an affirmative sign of universality, it has merely confused supposition. That is, in an affirmative universal proposition the predicate has merely confused supposition. Thus, the predicates in 'Every man is an animal' and 'Every man is white' have merely confused supposition. But where a sign of universality is placed on the subject-side but where the proposition is not a universal affirmative proposition or where the sign of universality does not distribute the whole subject, the predicate does not have merely confused supposition. For example, in 'Seeing every man is an animal', the word 'animal' stands determinately; for the sign of universality does not distribute the whole subject nor does it yield a universal proposition so that the predicate does not stand merely confusedly. Likewise, in 'The Creator of all creatures is a being', the word 'being' has determinate supposition and not merely confused supposition.

Another rule is that when a sign of universality or an expression incorporating such precedes a term on the subject-side of a proposition but does not determine the whole expression preceding the copula, then that which follows on the same side of the copula stands merely confusedly. At least we can say this if we so extend the term that a part of an extreme can stand or supposit. In the relevant case it is not possible to make a descent under the term to a disjunctive proposition. This is clear with 'At every time some created being existed'. Likewise, in 'At every time after Adam some man existed'. Here, the word 'man' has merely confused supposition; for if it were to supposit determinately or confusedly and distributively, the proposition would be false; for each of the relevant singular propositions is false as is clear inductively. The same point is clear in 'Until the end of the world an animal will exist' and in 'Until the end of the world a donkey will exist'. The same thing should be said in the case of 'Until the end of the world men will exist' and in the case of 'The whole day some man was inside' (provided we stipulate that different men were inside at different hours of the day.) Again, the point holds in 'Always a man existed', 'Always a man will exist', and so on with similar examples. I am not concerned whether or not these propositions are, strictly speaking, true. The point is rather to provide an account of their sense.

In stating this rule I stipulated that the relevant syncategorematic term not determine the whole extreme, for if it does, the rule does not hold. This is clear in 'Every donkey of the man runs'. Here the word 'every' determines the whole 'donkey of the man' and neither just 'donkey' nor just 'man'. Likewise, the syncategorematic expression in 'Every man's donkey runs' distributes the whole 'man's donkey'; so that the two are distributed by just one distribution. The same thing happens with terms like 'white man' and 'white animal'. But the situation is different with 'The whole day some man was inside' and 'At every time after Adam some man was'; for the whole expression 'time after Adam some man' cannot be a subject with respect to just any verb, but the whole 'man's donkey' and the whole 'donkey of the man' can be subjects with respect to any verb.

But I am not concerned whether these propositions are actually true. The point I want to make is that in the case where an affirmative sign of universality mediately precedes a common term within one and the same extreme, it is not possible to descend to the items contained under that common term. The descent is not possible either copulatively or disjunctively, no more than if the common term were itself the whole extreme of a proposition having merely confused supposition. This rule should be understood to hold in the case where the term immediately following and the term mediately following the syncategorematic term are not in the same case or where they are not related as adjective and noun. If they are so related it is impossible to make the descent to the items contained under either of the terms. Thus, in 'Every white man is white' it is impossible to descend copulatively to the terms contained under either of the terms. It is otherwise in the first case, for there it is possible to descend to all the items contained under the term immediately following the sign of universality but not to the items contained under the other. Nevertheless, neither term alone has what is properly called supposition; it is the whole composed of the two that supposits. Examples are 'Every man's animal runs' and the Latin sentence 'Omnem hominem videns est animal'.

A third rule runs as follows: the subject of an exclusive affirmative proposition always has merely confused supposition. Thus, in 'Only what is an animal is a man; 'animal' has merely confused supposition just as it does in the universal affirmative proposition convertible with it—'Every man is an animal'.

74: On Confused and Distributive Supposition

A number of rules hold in the case of confused and distributive supposition. First we shall examine the rules governing confused and distributive mobile supposition.

The first rule is that in every universal affirmative and universal negative proposition that is neither exclusive nor exceptive, the subject has confused and distributive mobile supposition. This is clear in 'Every man runs' and 'No man runs'.

The second rule is that in every such universal negative proposition the predicate stands confusedly and distributively.

The third rule is that when a negation determining the principal composition in a proposition precedes the predicate, the predicate stands confusedly and distributively. Thus, the word 'animal' in 'Man is not an animal' stands confusedly and distributively. 'Man' however stands determinately.

The fourth rule is that a term which immediately follows the verbs 'to differ' and 'to be distinguished', the participles corresponding to these verbs, the name 'other than', or an expression equivalent to any of these stands confusedly and distributively. Thus, the following is a valid inference: Socrates is distinguished from man; therefore Socrates is distinguished from this man' (where the reference may be to any man). Likewise, in 'Socrates differs from man', 'Socrates is different from man', and 'Socrates is other than man', 'man' has confused and distributive supposition.

Nevertheless, it should be noted that the aforementioned rules hold only in the case where the term in question would not stand confusedly and distributively if the negation sign or the relevant verb or name were taken away. For if the term were to stand confusedly and distributively when one of these expressions were taken away, then with the addition of such an expression it would stand determinately. This is clear in 'Socrates is every man'. Here, the predicate 'man' stands confusedly and distributively; therefore, if a negation precedes it it will stand determinately, as in 'Socrates is not every man'; for if Socrates is not that man (where any man is referred to), it follows that he is not every man. The same point holds in the case of the other expressions.

Therefore, the following rule is true: whatever makes the immobile mobile also makes immobile the mobile. That is, an expression which, when added to a term standing immobily, makes that term stand mobily also makes a term standing mobily stand immobily when added to it. Thus, in 'Socrates is a man', 'man' stands immobily; but if a negation is added to it ('Socrates is not a man'), the term stands mobily. Therefore, if a term stands mobily without any negation, it later stands immobily when a negation is added to it. Take 'Socrates is every man'; here the word 'man' stands mobily; therefore, in 'Socrates is not every man', 'man' stands immobily. The same thing should be said in the case of 'Socrates differs from every man' and 'Socrates is other than every man'.

A general rule is that if anything makes a term stand confusedly and distributively, it is either a sign of universality, a negation, or an expression equivalent to a negation. Nevertheless, it does not always happen that a term incorporating a negation makes a term stand mobily. This is clear in the case of the expression of inclusion in an affirmative proposition, for there it is not the subject but the predicate that supposits confusedly and distributively. However, in an exclusive negative proposition where the expression of exclusion is added to the subject, both subject and predicate have confused and distributive supposition.

Apropos of confused and distributive immobile supposition it should be noted that the subject of an exceptive proposition always has this form of supposition. This is clear in 'Every man besides Socrates runs'. Here the term 'man' supposits confusedly and distributively but not mobily, for it is not possible to descend to particulars while altering the original proposition only by substituting a singular term for the common term and the sign of universality. The following inference is not valid: every man except Socrates runs; therefore that man except Socrates runs; for the consequent is improper as will become clear later. Nonetheless, it should be noted that it is possible in some way to descend to all the relevant particulars, but not in the same way. One of the relevant propositions will be negative and all of the others, affirmative. Thus, the following inference is valid: every man except Socrates runs; therefore Socrates does not run and therefore, that man runs and that man runs and . . . (and so on for all the relevant particulars other than Socrates). It is the exceptive expression that is responsbile for this.

75: Problems With Expressions Like 'Begin' and 'Twice'

But there is a problem with propositions of the sort we considered earlier: 'Socrates ceases to be white', 'Socrates was twice at Rome', 'Socrates was black three times', and 'Socrates begins to be literate'. The question is, how do the predicates of these propositions supposit?

It is clear that they do not supposit determinately, for it is not possible to descend to a disjunctive proposition. Thus, the following is not valid: Socrates begins to be literate; therefore, Socrates begins to be this or he begins to be that . . .(referring in turn to all the things for which the predicate supposits); for the antecedent can be true while each element in the consequent is false. It does not, then, supposit determinately.

Nor do they supposit confusedly and distributively, for the following is not valid: Socrates begins to be literate; therefore, Socrates begins to be this literate individual (where the reference is to Plato). Thus, we do not have confused and distributive supposition.

Nor do they supposit merely confusedly, for it is not possible to descend to particulars by way of a proposition with a disjunctive predicate. Thus, the following is not valid: Socrates begins to be literate; therefore, he begins to be this literate individual or that literate individual or . . . (and so on for all literate individuals). The reason the inference fails is that the antecedent can be true and the consequent false.

It can be said that the predicate-term in propositions of this sort (as well as that which follows the verb, adjective, or noun) has neither determinate supposition, nor merely confused supposition, nor confused and distributive supposition. It has a different form of supposition for which we have no name.

The relevant form of supposition agrees with merely confused supposition in that in both cases it is possible to ascend from a pronoun referring to any particular contained under a common term to the common term itself. Thus, it follows that if every man is this (where the reference is to some animal), every man is an animal. Likewise, it follows that if Socrates begins to be this (where the reference is to some literate individual), he begins to be literate.

But this form of supposition differs from merely confused supposition in that it is not possible here to descend to the disjunction of the proper names of the things for which the general term supposits. For it does not follow that if Socrates begins to be literate, he begins to be this or that or that or . . . (where the reference is in turn to all literate individuals).

It differs from determinate supposition in that one cannot descend by means of a disjunctive proposition.

The reason why such terms have none of the aforesaid forms of supposition is as follows: the propositions containing such terms are equivalent to conjunctive propositions each composed of two or more propositions. These propositions have the same subject; nevertheless, at least one of them is affirmative and one negative so that one and the same term has different forms of supposition in these propositions. Consequently, these terms do not have any one of the normal forms of supposition in the proposition whose parts are the various exponential propositions. For example, 'Socrates begins to be white' is equivalent to the conjunction 'Socrates was previously not white and now for the first time is white'. In 'Socrates is white' the word 'white' supposits determinately; whereas, in 'Socrates was not white' it has, because of the preceding negation, confused and distributive supposition.

One might claim that a consequence of this analysis is that the subject in 'Only what is an animal is a man' would not have merely confused supposition. The point would be that since the proposition is equivalent to a conjunction of propositions, one of which is affirmative and the other negative, the subject would have a different form of supposition in each of the elements of the conjunction. The response is that in the exclusive affirmative proposition the subject has merely confused supposition, for although the exponents of that proposition have subjects with different forms of supposition, those subjects are not identical with the subject in the original exclusive proposition; and because the subjects of the affirmative and negative exponents differ from the subject of the exclusive proposition, that subject can have one of the three forms of supposition. In 'Socrates begins to be literate', 'Socrates ceases to be white', and 'Socrates was twice black', however, one and the same term is subject in the exponential propositions and in the proposition whose exponents they are.

76: On the Supposition of Relatives

Now that we have examined the supposition of absolute terms we shall examine the supposition of relatives. Here I am using the term 'relative' as it is used by grammarians rather than logicians. In this sense a relative is an expression which refers to an antecedent.

First it should be noted that as grammarians use the term there are relatives of substance and relatives of accident. 'He', 'that', and 'same' are relatives of substance. Those expressions are called relatives of accident which are in some way taken or derived from accidents. Examples are 'such' 'of such a kind' and 'so many'. Among relatives of substance there are relatives of identity and relatives of diversity. Of relatives of identity some are reciprocal and some are not.

Non-reciprocal relatives include expressions like 'he' and 'same'. A number of rules hold as regards these relatives. First, they always supposit for that for which their antecedent supposits, so that if they hold true of anything, they hold true of the same thing as their antecedent. This is clear in 'Socrates runs and he disputes'. For the truth of this conjunction it is required that the second part hold true of the same thing as the first part. Likewise in the case of '*Man* is a species and it is predicated of many'.

It should be noted that a relative of this sort should never be placed in the same categorical proposition as its antecedent. Thus, in 'Socrates is he', the word 'he' is a demonstrative and not a relative pronoun.

Likewise, it should be noted that when the antecedent of a relative is a common term with personal supposition, one can never, by substituting the antecedent for the relative, generate a proposition which is convertible with and equivalent to the original proposition. Thus, 'A man runs and he disputes' and 'A man runs and a man disputes' are not equivalent. But in other cases one can do this for 'Socrates runs and he disputes' and 'Socrates runs and Socrates disputes' are equivalent.

Likewise, it should be noted that a negation never makes a relative stand confusedly and distributively. On the contrary a relative always supposits for just that thing of which its antecedent holds true or is asserted to hold true. Thus, while 'Some man is Plato and Socrates is not he' is true, one cannot infer from this that Socrates is not a man. All that is required is that 'Socrates is not Plato' be true. Thus, the following two propositions can, strictly speaking, hold true simultaneously: 'Some man runs and Socrates is not he' and 'Some man runs and Socrates is he', for if Socrates and Plato are both running both conjunctions are true.

Concerning reciprocal relatives of identity it should be noted that they differ from other relatives in that they can be placed indifferently in either different or the same categorical propositions as their antecedents. This is clear in the case of 'himself' and 'his', for 'Socrates disputes and sees himself' and 'Socrates sees himself' are both well formed. So are the following: 'Socrates sees his donkey' and 'Socrates runs and his donkey walks'.

It should be noted that sometimes a relative is a part of an extreme and sometimes it is an extreme. When it is an extreme, so that it immediately precedes or follows the verb, it supposits for that for which its antecedent supposits. Thus, 'Socrates sees himself' and 'Every man sees himself'. But when it is a part of an extreme, it does not supposit for that for which its antecedent supposits. It supposits, on the contrary, for something that is designated by that to which it is added. This is clear in 'Socrates disputes and his donkey runs'. Here the word 'his' does not supposit for Socrates; it supposits for Socrates' donkey rather than for some other donkey.

It should also be noted that a relative of this sort has the same kind of supposition and supposits for the same things as its antecedent. However, when its antecedent supposits either confusedly and distributively or determinately, it has a similar form of supposition but exhibits this singularly—by referring particulars to particulars. Therefore, it is not possible to descend either conjunctively or disjunctively or in any way other than with respect to something contained under the antecedent. For example, in 'Every man sees himself', the word 'himself' supposits for every man by means of confused and distributive mobile supposition; but it does this singularly since it is not possible to descend without altering the other extreme. It does not follow that if every man sees himself every man sees Socrates. Nonetheless, it is possible here to descend to Socrates with respect to Socrates. Thus, 'Every man sees himself; therefore, Socrates sees Socrates'. This is not, however, the case with a proposition like 'Man is an animal'. Likewise, in 'A man sees himself' the word 'himself' supposits determinately yet singularly, for it is possible to make the descent only in the following way: a man sees himself; therefore, Socrates sees Socrates or Plato sees Plato or . . .' (and so on for all the relevant particulars). It is also possible to ascend, but not in the following way: a man sees Plato; therefore a man sees himself. The ascent operates as follows: Socrates sees Socrates; therefore, a man sees himself.

It is clear then that when a relative of this sort mediately follows the sign of universality it has confused and distributive supposition, yet only singularly. Likewise, a relative in a categorical proposition (whether reciprocal or not) has confused and distributive supposition as a result of the addition of the sign of universality to its antecedent. In the same way a term of this sort has merely confused supposition, even if there is no sign of universality in the relevant categorical proposition, and provided that in the preceding categorical the sign of universality mediately precedes its antecedent. This is clear in 'Every man is an animal and every donkey sees him'.

Concerning relatives of diversity it should be noted that an expression is called a relative of diversity because it is not truly predicated of the same thing as its antecedent. This is clear in the following example where the reference is to two contradictory propositions: 'One of them is true and the other false'. Here 'other' is truly predicated of something of which its antecedent in 'One of them is true' is not truly predicable.

Relatives like 'so much', 'such', and 'how much' are not, in Aristotle's view, called relatives of accident because they supposit for accidents, but because they supposit for something while connoting something predicable in a way other than *in quid*. It should be noted that a relative of this sort neither supposits for nor holds true of that for which its antecedent holds true. It supposits for something other than but similar to or equal to that for which its antecedent supposits. This is clear in 'Socrates is white and Plato is such'. Here the word 'such' does not supposit for Socrates but for something similar to Socrates: likewise, in 'Socrates and Plato run and they dispute as much'. The word 'as much' does not supposit necessarily for Socrates and Plato nor does it supposit necessarily for the things for which 'run' supposits. It can supposit for other things. The same is true in the case of 'Socrates is six feet tall and Plato is as much.' Thus, it should be noted that while a relative of this sort can supposit for the same thing, this is not necessary. Likewise it should be noted that the antecedent of this sort of relative is frequently or always a name in the genus of quantity or quality or in some other accidental category.

77: On Improper Supposition

Just as proper supposition occurs when a term supposits for that which it properly signifies, improper supposition occurs when a term is employed improperly.

There are many forms of improper supposition. There is antonomasia, in which a term supposits for that to which it most especially belongs. Thus, 'The Apostle says this', 'The Philosopher denies this', and so on. There is synechdoche in which a part supposits for the whole. Another form of improper supposition is metonymy where that which contains supposits for that which is contained or where the abstract form of an accident supposits for the subject and so on.

Thus, it is necessary to determine when a term and a proposition are being taken literally and when those uttering or writing them are using them in a different way. The reason is that there is scarcely a term which is not in some way employed equivocally in different places in the writings of the philosophers, saints, and authors. Those who always want to take a term univocally and in just one sense frequently make mistakes about the intentions of authors and go wrong in the inquiry after truth, for almost all words are employed equivocally.

In terms of the foregoing one can make explicit how the relevant terms supposit in propositions like 'The intelligible being of a creature was from all eternity' and 'To be white belongs to Socrates'. They supposit either for a thing, a word, an aggregate of these, or an intention of the soul. But when the terms are taken in their proper signification, we can determine in the case of each of these whether the proposition is true or false. Thus, if the subject in 'The intelligible being of a creature was from all eternity' supposits for a thing, that thing is either a created or an uncreated thing. If it supposits for a created thing the proposition is clearly false, but if it supposits for an uncreated thing the proposition is clearly true. If it supposits for something that is an aggregate of both it is clearly false, and if it supposits for an intention of the soul, a word, or something else the proposition should be denied. But if propositions like these are not employed literally, one must focus on the propositions whose place they are taking; and as these are true or false, the original propositions should be judged accordingly. Thus, since by 'The intelligible being of a creature was from all eternity', one means 'God from all eternity understood a creature'; and since this is true one should also grant the original proposition which conveys this second proposition.

These remarks about terms and their supposition are sufficient. Here ends the first part of this *Summa.*